THE CIVIL SERVICE IN BRITAIN

G. A. CAMPBELL

G. A. CAMPBELL

THE CIVIL SERVICE
IN BRITAIN

GERALD DUCKWORTH & CO. LTD.
3 HENRIETTA ST. LONDON, W.C.2

First published by Penguin Books 1955
Second Edition 1965
First Paperback edition 1971

ISBN 0 7156 0599 2

Printed in Great Britain by Richard Clay (The Chaucer Press) Ltd.,
Bungay, Suffolk.

Contents

APPENDICES

ACKNOWLEDGEMENTS

A SERVING or retired Civil Servant must obtain permission before, as the warning runs, "publishing a book the subject matter of which is concerned with the official duties of himself or other public servants". The manuscript of this book was therefore submitted to H.M. Treasury. The responsibility, however, rests with the author.

Friends in Government service have supplied me with much information, but in a book of this kind, ranging over a wide field, it has unfortunately been necessary to omit a great deal of interesting material. I have benefited greatly from the guidance of experts, especially on the working of the departments with which they are, or have been, connected. The rule of anonymity precludes me from making acknowledgements by name to such officials.

The Controller, H.M. Stationery Office, has kindly granted permission to quote from documents which are Crown Copyright and to reproduce the documents in Appendices VI and VIII; and the Foreign Office, in addition to giving other assistance, has agreed to the reproduction of the Commission in Appendix IV.

November 1954

Revised Edition.

Many changes have taken place in Civil Service organization since this book was first written ten years ago. In making the revision I have again received generous assistance from friends within the Service, and I am also grateful for the co-operation of Government departments, in particular the Treasury, the Home, and Foreign Offices, the Ministries of Defence, Education, and Housing, the Civil Service Commission, and the General Post Office. The Controller, H.M.S.O., has kindly granted permission for extracts from further official publications.

January 1965   G. A. C.

Chapter One

THE INFLUENCE OF THE CIVIL SERVICE

WITHIN the last hundred years the British Civil Service has grown from a small, ill-constructed series of more or less independent Government offices into a vast, highly organized and unified machine. The growth in the power of officials is not a new development, but it has been particularly marked in recent years, and Civil Servants now exercise an authority which would have seemed incredible even a generation ago. The tentacles of officialdom stretch into almost every part of our daily lives, and none of us is unaffected by the triumphs and failures of Government departments. The State employs[1] a non-industrial staff of 692,158 at a cost of over £661,000,000 a year in salaries. In addition, the industrial staff numbers 350,000. One out of about every twenty-two of the insured population of the country is on the Government's payroll.

No Civil Service can escape a large measure of power if it is to perform its duties effectively under modern conditions. The British Civil Service is often accused of seeking to acquire dominion; almost as frequently, many people protest that officials use their authority irresponsibly, while others complain that all officials are ditherers and are much too timid in tackling their jobs. Officials do not make statutes; the departments have only such power as the Legislature has conferred on them. But the Civil Service is consulted at almost every stage, and inevitably it exerts far-reaching influence in the shaping of new measures. Ministers of the Crown decide the policy to be followed within a department, but the province of the official can never be strictly confined to the carrying out of schemes. Execution and policy must often go hand in hand, and so Civil Servants are unavoidably involved in the formulation at all levels of nearly every Government project.

Where a question is of sufficient weight to require submission to a Minister, he necessarily relies to a considerable extent on the recommendations of his permanent officials. A politician in charge of a department is rarely an expert in its work, and he need not even be interested in it, or show himself possessed of any administrative ability. A few years ago, on the death of a prominent statesman who had held one of the principal financial posts and had also been at one

---

[1] The figures of staff are as at 1 April, 1964, unless otherwise stated.

9

time in charge of a Government office faced with the most perplexing problems, a newspaper wrote of him that "he took little interest in administration, and even less in public finance". Neither department was noticeably more or less efficient under his predecessors or successors. On the other hand, it was a doubtful compliment when a Minister was more recently described as having "the habit of mind of a first-class administrative Civil Servant" and to be "a great intervener in the affairs of his department at all levels". The political head of an office should possess other qualities. The officials have their own field of activity.

No proposal is likely to be considered by the Cabinet until the senior officials of the interested departments have had the opportunity to examine it thoroughly and express their opinion. No Government, whatever its political complexion, will lightly brush aside the recommendations of the officials, though some administrations are more inclined than others to follow the lines favoured by the departments.

Obviously, Civil Servants would not submit to a Labour Government a scheme for the imposition of fees from every trades union procession as it meandered into Hyde Park on May Day; nor suggest to a Conservative Chancellor of the Exchequer that levies should be imposed on the meetings of the Primrose League. But the most experienced Civil Servants must sometimes make proposals which they regard as quite innocuous and unrelated to party only to find that their recommendations are tossed back as political dynamite. Most Ministers quickly develop an instinct for recognizing proposals which would have unfortunate repercussions, and they possess a sure eye for what their Cabinet colleagues will find unpalatable. It is still true that the politicians must tell the Civil Servants what the public will not swallow, though to a lesser extent than formerly: the public does not choke so easily as it once did. Even where execution may seem to be the predominant factor, the ideas of the Civil Servants may be rejected. The Government has many interests to keep in mind, and what is admitted to be highly desirable is sometimes agreed also to be quite impracticable, judged by standards other than those of the administrator.

All Government expenditure, other than on the defence services, is in general civil expenditure. As late as the end of the seventeenth century much of the country's expenditure was met by the Sovereign from personal revenues and from the product of taxes which Parliament had agreed should be assigned to the Crown. Parliament did not control the disbursements and could not ascertain how much revenue accrued from taxes and duties and how the money was spent, nor could it separate the costs of the Court from the expenditure on the running of the country. The Crown surrendered the income from its hereditary estates to the Exchequer in exchange for an annual grant—the Civil List. This grant at first covered all expenditure other than that on the fighting services; but Parliament bit by bit pruned the Civil List of the costs of public administration. Only in the reign of Queen Victoria, however, was the Civil List strictly confined to the cost of the royal household. All other expenditure, with the exception of some payments authorized by statute, such as the interest on the National Debt, is now provided for in the Estimates. Many of the features of our present system of Government finance which are most severely criticized are the outcome of the long struggle between Crown and Parliament for the control of the nation's money. Some anomalies perhaps survive for no better reason than that officials have learned to take a pride in manipulating a complicated system.

The Civil List is agreed at the beginning of every reign, but the estimates of departmental expenditure are presented each year in detail to Parliament, and, apart from a number of officials in a special category, contain provision for the remuneration of all Civil Servants.[1] Broadly, no Civil Servant may be paid from public funds without legislative authority given annually by both Houses. The House of Commons could withhold supplies and so there would be no money to pay the salaries of officials, but, of course, this would mean the resignation of the Government. Parliament controls the Civil Service by means of checks which it imposes at regular intervals. These restraints closely affect the working of the departments and every other agency of the central Government.

We take it for granted that there should be a fair field for anyone of British nationality who wishes to enter State Service and who complies with prescribed conditions. Open competition is the rule[2]

---

[1] The following working definition is generally adopted: Civil Servants are "those servants of the Crown, other than the holders of political or judicial offices, who are employed in a civil capacity, and whose remuneration is paid wholly and directly out of monies voted by Parliament".

[2] The examinations are almost entirely suspended during wartime, when it would be unfair to hold competitions in which the members of the armed forces could not take part on equal terms. Nor can the examinations be resumed immediately after the end of hostilities, since the claims of temporary staff must be considered and special arrangements made to recruit from among men and women who have lost their chance to compete for posts because of the emergency.

and the candidates considered to be the most suitable are automatically appointed to fill the vacancies, if their health and character are satisfactory. Only exceptionally is this procedure waived for the general classes of the Civil Service.

The suggestion of open competition for posts in the public service met with fierce resistance when pressed in the middle of the nineteenth century by enthusiastic reformist groups. Patronage had become traditional, and a politician entrusted with authority over a department considered himself entitled to dispose of official appointments at his discretion. The gift of posts was indeed looked upon as essential for the management of the House of Commons in a period prior to the introduction of stringent party discipline. A lucrative appointment might ensure an opponent's silence or win a wavering member's support, and such useful weapons were not readily surrendered. Nepotism has always existed and will never entirely disappear. In some countries today it would be regarded as perfectly right and proper for a man in power to use his authority to allot posts in the public service to his favourites. He would be despised as lacking in human feelings if he did not acknowledge it as his duty to see that his needy friends and relations were placed on the public payroll at the earliest possible opportunity and with no nonsense about choosing the most competent man. Nor, of course, in some fields has patronage died out in Britain.

A number of officials in this country had the privilege of making appointments to Civil Service posts on their own responsibility a hundred years ago, and the sale of jobs earned them useful additions to their income. Most nominations, however, remained in the hands of Ministers, who exercised their prerogative in favour of anyone in whom they had an interest. Among the papers of the Prime Minister in office in 1849 is a letter from a correspondent who thanks him for giving her an interview in which he had indicated that he might find a clerkship in the Audit Office for her son, and who goes on: "I am reluctant to accept an offer of so low a grade because experience teaches that when a Petitioner is given the smallest mite he is dismissed from the mind of his Benefactor as being off his hands. . . I am more inclined to join my faith to your kind and repeated assurances of 'I will not forget him'. You may ask now, as you might have asked when I had the pleasure of seeing you, what right have I to expect anything at all at yr hands? None except that of distant relationship. A Drowning Man catches at a Straw, but I look upon it as a very substantial straw, you being not only the greatest Man in the World (for I look upon One who wields the destinies of this vast Empire as such), and when I reflect that your Mother and my Father were first Cousins," etc. The correspondent decided not to accept the clerk-ship for her son but to send him to Cambridge, and "in the meantime I still live on the hope that he may at some time, if not immediately, be placed by you in some suitable condition". Nor was it necessary to be related to a Minister to be able to press a claim. Members of the Lords and Commons or those connected with ruling families demanded posts for their dependants, and an influential member of the community could usually secure a situation in a public office for a nominee. "You have caused the happiness of an old servant by placing his son Meynell at the Custom House in the Long Room, where he is no discredit," wrote the head of a political family to the Prime Minister in the following year; and, after expressing his views on a Bill before Parliament, he makes his appeal for patronage in favour of a poor barrister. "I have in vain tried to employ him as a private secretary, but I have nothing to give him to do. He is unwilling to be idle, as I am to encourage idleness. It may fall in your power to give him a clerkship or anything—*bread* in short. He is excellent and deserving, about 27 years old—and I think you will do this for me if you can, and when you can." But the place-seekers always outnumbered the vacancies.

Not only clerkships but the highest official posts were in the gift of members of the Government, though by usage a number was filled by serving staff who had started in lower ranks. Many of the better places went to politicians who had lost their seats in the Commons and who accepted salaried official posts until they could find a constituency. This created a flow between the House and the depart-ments, and the political and official world were associated in a manner quite different from that of today. Sometimes the top post in an office would be filled by a man who had withdrawn from active politics and wanted a quieter life; and other recipients were those who had outlived their usefulness to their party. Although posts in the Civil Service which fell vacant were in the gift of the Govern-ment of the day, an official once appointed had as a rule security of tenure. A different Government might affect his prospects of higher rank but did not deprive him of his job.

Governments of the first half of the nineteenth century attached importance to the selection for the superior posts in the Civil Service of men who had experience in Parliament and retained their connec-tion with members. It facilitated the conduct of business, and,

THE CIVIL SERVICE IN BRITAIN

moreover, such appointments were regarded as introducing new ideas and new vigour into the departments. The good of the Service was not the main consideration, however, and the system of nomination was retained chiefly because patrons found it very pleasant as well as very useful to be able to bestow places. A pamphleteer of the time commented:

> The most important, the most seductive, and the most tempting adjuncts to public offices of the higher grade are the vast patronage, the power and personal consideration they confer on the possessors . . . observe the good things they have at their disposal—the benefices, bishoprics, commissionerships of customs and excise; the clerkships, registrarships and secretaryships . . . and think of the opportunities afforded by these splendid gifts for enriching their families and friends—and think, too, of the delightful incense of adulation and obsequiousness the dispensers of such favours must enhale, and of the host of fawning sycophants, expectants and dependants they must everywhere raise up around them. Here are the real *sweets of office*.[1]

In the later years of the eighteenth and the early years of the following century a series of inquiries into public offices revealed a number of glaring abuses. Nowadays, if anything goes wrong in one department the clamour is likely to arise for the reform of the Civil Service as a whole. A hundred years ago the public were not accustomed to think of the departments as forming part of a single service, and when they complained it was against individual offices—the Hackney Carriage Office and the Woods and Forests were the subject of stern rebukes. But the critics did not demand a revision of the Civil Service organization. The Government of the time concerned itself mainly with the defence of the realm, the maintenance of good order within the country, the collection of revenue and, to a limited extent, the control of trade; it was only beginning to make the first tentative steps towards intervention in matters of health and employment and to interest itself in matters previously entirely left for settlement locally. In these circumstances, relatively few people came into direct contact with the central departments. When they did so, they took it for granted that there would be some inefficiency and that the official would have an itching palm. The country had never known a high standard of conduct among the public employees, and did not demand that the disparate agencies should be overhauled and organized into a united service. Parliament's inquiries into the work of the departments had been instituted not primarily with the intention of bringing

[1] *Black Book of Corruption*, 1831.

about an improvement in the conduct of business, but of reducing the expenditure and setting up a better means of controlling the nation's finances. Any other reforms were regarded to some extent as incidental.

The number of sinecures in the public service had long been a cause of complaint, but Parliament was reluctant to interfere, perhaps because so many members had a family interest. Many posts were filled by deputies; they performed the duties of an office on behalf of the titular head, who took for himself a large part of the income. This deputy system was also much resented in the colonies; the holder of a post sent a substitute to undertake the duties while he himself lived comfortably in England on a share of the total revenue accruing from the office. Some holders had purchased their posts; others had received them from one Government or another for political services; and still others had obtained the positions by the favour of the court. However they had acquired the places, the holders all agreed that it would be unjust to penalize the occupants because Parliament tended to develop an inconvenient conscience. Pluralities were also a source of abuse. A Commissioner of the Salt Office, for example, received £500 per annum in that post, and as Receiver-General of the Post Office earned a further £800. A return of the Treasury staff at the end of the eighteenth century showed that one clerk received £300 per annum from the Customs revenue for his work in the Treasury, £77 as Sluice Master at Purfleet, and £148 as a Commissioner of the Lottery; while another had a salary of £220 plus £150 as Agent for the Civil Establishment of New South Wales, the same amount in respect of the Bahama Islands, and £50 as Receiver of Fees of Suppressed Offices.

The investigators proceeded very slowly and cautiously—a bitter critic wrote that the inquiries "end in nothing but bills of charges for commissioners, secretaries, office-keepers, and so forth". Vested interests were strong, and only in 1810 did the Government begin to put an end to the abuses. About the same time the fees and perquisites of Government offices came under review. Many of the fees were abolished in the early years of the century, but in 1836 a number still survived and the proceeds went into the pockets of officials. A committee appointed in that year to "inquire into the Fees and Emoluments of Public Offices" recommended that practically the whole of the remaining impositions of this kind should be abolished. Most of of the exceptions were in respect of trifling amounts, such as 13s. 6d. per annum, which the Committee decided should continue to be paid to the official who had custody of horseshoes, charged with "producing the same in the Court of Exchequer, on swearing the Sheriffs of London into office".

The Government gave little thought to the cure of the ineptitude in the public offices, and to the creation of a body of Civil Servants capable of conducting business efficiently and prepared to work diligently in public administration. Some of the difficulties arose because of the misuse of patronage, but when in later years proposals were made to award clerkships other than by this means, an administrator of long experience, Sir James Stephen, produced an unexpected argument:

> The patrons of these clerkships—that is, the principal Ministers of the Crown—are themselves so ill remunerated that these high trusts are practically confined to persons of ample fortune. . . . The consequent narrowness of the range is, I apprehend, a serious evil. But the range of choice will become more narrow, and the evil yet more serious, if the remuneration of these great offices be further reduced by depriving the holders of them of all the most valuable patronage.[1]

The staff of the whole of the public service at the beginning of the nineteenth century numbered less than half the complement of a large present-day department, such as the Inland Revenue or the Ministry of Pensions and National Insurance. Nor did the numbers swell rapidly, though the cost of the Service rose steeply, as the following figures show:[2]

Year	Number	£ Per Annum
1797	16,267	1,374,561
1805	20,221	1,939,641
1810	22,931	2,822,727
1815	24,598	3,203,439
1819	24,414	3,167,441
1821	26,880	3,722,805
1827	22,921	2,788,907
1832	21,305	2,819,622

By the middle of the century, however, the staff had nearly doubled in number, and in the opinion of those well able to judge, the Service had become overstaffed. The work was unevenly spread. Offices to which extra duties had been allocated could not obtain additional

---

[1] Papers relating to the Reorganization of the Civil Service, P.P. 1854-5, V. 20.
[2] The figures for 1797–1819 and for 1827 are from "Number of persons employed . . . in the year 1797, and in the years 1805, 1810", etc., and for 1821 and 1832 from the "Return of Establishments" for those years.

staff, and new agencies set up to carry out heavy administrative programmes were also allowed only an inadequate complement. Yet at
the same time a number of other departments had been relieved of
work and retained more men than could be usefully employed. No
unification had been attempted, and no real co-ordination existed.
Except in the highest ranks, transfers between one office and another
were almost unknown, and no machinery had been set up so that
offices with redundancy could give assistance to those departments
which threatened to break under the load. Parliament tried to put
a stop to expansion, but it gave no thought to a thorough-paced
reorganization of officialdom.

Some of the employees were dishonest, many were indolent, and
most were discontented. Men could not be expected to work con-
scientiously when they saw the plums of the departments presented
to place-seekers who had no qualification except the support of a
powerful Minister or a connection with an aristocratic house. No
office was safe from jobbery, and a man who waited for years to succeed to a higher post might have his hopes dashed at the last minute.
The following appeal by the Chief Clerk of the Ordnance Office is
among the Prime Minister's papers for 1849: "In about two months
from this Date, I shall have completed a service in this office of 46
years, including 23 years as 'Chief Clerk', during which latter period
I have, as it were, stood on the very threshold of the Secretaryship
and *every year* in the course of that time have acted in the Absence,
through illness or otherwise, of the Secretary, looking naturally in
the event of the retirement or Decease of Mr Byham, to be appointed
at once to succeed. This expectation was justified by what I believe
to have been the immemorial Practice of the Ordnance Department. . . ."

As in all times, able men made their way to the top despite lack of
influence, provided they had the good fortune associated with success
in any career. The Accountant-General of the Navy stated proudly
five years later: "I have been bred in the Civil Service, having passed
through the various gradations of a clerk's career, and risen, without
interest or in any way seeking it, to the highest appointment in the
office in which I commenced that career." He was among the exceptions: usually the most senior posts could be attained only with the
backing of a powerful patron. But apart from the chief posts,
permanent officials normally had the right of succession to the positions above the basic grade. Almost all Civil Servants entered on the
same rank and started their official career as clerks. Seniority governed

promotion thereafter to most posts and the staff as a whole preferred that advancement should be the reward of length of service. Any divergence from this practice brought forth protests from the officials, who feared that, if the departments adopted the principle of promotion other than by seniority, the way would be open to favouritism and that preferential treatment would go to the man with the most influential patron.

Most departments applied no age limit for recruits to the Service, and candidates might be as young as fifteen or as old as forty or more. With promotion ruled by seniority, the earlier one entered the public service the better the ultimate prospect. The keen and eager official quickly lost his enthusiasm when he realized that no efforts he could make, and no qualities he could demonstrate, would affect his career, and that he must wait until death or retirement created vacancies in the next grade. The superior clerks—senior clerks, principal clerks, or chief clerks—might be men of little education and less native ability, but, once nominated to a clerkship, promotion came by sheer weight of years of public service. And promotion meant remuneration on a much higher scale. The salaries varied from department to department, but the lowest grade of clerk might enter at £90 per annum, and the highest clerkships carried salaries ten times as much. The top posts in the departments, often political appointments, were worth £2,000 or more.

Complaints about the low calibre of the clerks led to the introduction in some offices of a probationary period for new entrants. In practice the system proved derisory. To obtain a nomination a candidate had to have access, directly or indirectly, to a patron, and it might be dangerous to fail such a recruit. While some nominees might be discharged as unsuitable during the period of probation, nearly all of them passed it triumphantly. The Treasury had tried to encourage departments to select suitable staff, and in a minute of 16 August, 1833, pointed out: "My Lords deem it important that all offices under the Crown should be filled by persons competent to perform the duties of these situations; and that strict regulations should be established for the purpose of securing that object, so far as may be practicable." Most departments did not find it practicable to do anything of the kind. A few of them made the gesture of imposing written tests on candidates, but such tests were designed to do no more than establish that the nominees did not fall below a certain educational standard. Out of 300 marks, a man would be accepted for a vacancy if he scored 100 in a simple qualifying examination. If the nominee could not gain a third of the marks, and if he had a sponsor of sufficient importance, he could always be given another test, even less exacting.

A new Minister might set out with the intention of staffing his department with efficient men, but he could not readily dislodge Civil Servants from their posts. Once appointed, an official had security for life unless grossly inefficient or guilty of some heinous offence. No compulsory retiring age had been fixed, and men clung to office long after the time when they could make any effective contribution. Officials in some departments were entitled to a pension on retirement, but men who had worked for some forty years before reaching a relatively remunerative position did not willingly surrender a salary which could be earned merely by turning up at the office and sitting at a desk for a few hours a day.

The most forthright critic of the Civil Service recruitment was Sir Charles Trevelyan, Assistant Secretary to the Treasury—at that time the principal permanent post in the department. No one has made a more notable contribution to the Civil Service of this country. It would be impossible now, with the growth in the number and size of Government offices and the complexity of their work, for any single person to have the detailed acquaintance with all parts of the administration which Trevelyan possessed. From his place in the Treasury he saw much of the working of the departments, but his intimate knowledge of the organization of the public service came to him through his membership of a number of small committees[1] set up to inquire into individual departments. The composition of the committees often changed, but Trevelyan always served on those which examined the English, though not the Irish, offices.

While still insisting on nomination, the East India Company had prescribed educational requirements for those who wished to join its staff, and at the beginning of the century had founded Haileybury College for the training of young men who intended to make a career with the Company. Trevelyan had been a pupil at Haileybury, and at the age of nineteen received appointment as a clerk in the Company's service in India. He did not regard the system of recruitment for that service as by any means perfect, but the choice of candidates was much stricter than in the Civil Service at home.

Trevelyan returned to England at the age of thirty-one, after winning a reputation as a skilled and incorruptible administrator.

[1] The Committees sometimes consisted of Trevelyan and one other, and rarely had more than four members.

Two years later, in 1840, he received his appointment to the Treasury, and shortly afterwards he began a campaign for reform in official administration. An earnest man, prominent in a number of good causes, Trevelyan had an unswerving will, and he pursued his aims with great energy and without much regard for the feelings or interests of others. He had married Macaulay's sister, and through his brother-in-law's connections and by his own persistence he obtained access to the highest quarters. The most bitter criticism did not deflect him in the slightest degree from what he considered to be a clear duty —the establishment of a Civil Service which would have the choice of the most able men in the country and would open to them an inter-esting and useful career for life. Trevelyan was convinced that public business could not be properly organized and efficiently performed without radical changes which would interfere with many long-estab-lished practices.

One of the committees appointed by the Commons in 1848 had the duty to "Inquire into the Expenditure for Miscellaneous Services, and to report to The House whether any reduction can in their Opinion be effected. . . ."[1] Trevelyan gave evidence at great length. As the Committee's primary object was to reduce expenditure, some members naturally put forward the suggestion that this should in part be achieved by cutting the salaries of Civil Servants. Trevelyan refused to agree that much over-payment could be found in depart-ments. He defended the remuneration paid to officials generally, but he claimed that the Service failed to make the best use of its man-power and hinted that the work of his own department could be better handled by a smaller number of people if highly competent. Trevel-yan insisted that clerks ought not to be appointed until they had undergone an exacting test of their capacity, and he suggested that the Service should be recruited in two classes—one for the superior work and another, kept quite separate after recruitment, for the inferior work. Other witnesses contested these views vigorously and praised the achievements under the existing arrangements.

The Committee sought anxiously to find means of reducing the Miscellaneous Services Vote, which comprised the cost of Works and Buildings, some Salaries, Law and Justice, Science and Art, Colonial and Consular Services, Superannuation and Charities, as well as "Special and Temporary Objects". The Vote had risen as follows—1834-5: £2,236,717; 1837-8: £2,646,699; 1839-40: £2,651,674; 1844-5: £3,005,748; 1847-8: £3,782,613.

[1] P.P. 1847-8, V. 37.

In its report, the Committee said: "... when the proposed Votes of this year[1] were laid upon the Table, they amounted to 3,770,427*l.*, instead of 4,006,000*l.*, as originally estimated, being a diminution of 235,573*l.* ...." Such a cut had been the aim of the Committee, and Trevelyan's proposals, which could not affect the immediate expenditure to any appreciable degree, if at all, failed to attract the interest of the investigators. His scheme contained the germs of a revolution which would stretch far beyond the field which the Committee had under discussion, and the members were "not prepared to express an opinion favourable to the suggestions submitted by Sir Charles Trevelyan for an alteration in the Establishment of the Treasury, which must, if advantageous, be extended to all other Departments of the public service, to which the objections, made by gentlemen of high standing in the department, will be found in the Evidence". Such gentlemen felt that the system came close to perfection.

This was the first occasion on which Trevelyan had presented his reforms to an influential body in public. The opposition they aroused would have discouraged anyone less resolute and forceful. Trevelyan never doubted that his views were right, and he had a fixed determination that they would prevail. In the following year he discussed his proposals with the Prime Minister, Lord John Russell, who expressed his interest. On 13 August, 1849, Trevelyan wrote to him:[2]

My dear Lord,

    I am much gratified and encouraged by your letter to me on the arrangements for securing more efficient service in the public offices. The reference of the subject to a Committee of the kind your Lordship proposes, will furnish such a decisive proof of your readiness to allow the exercise of your patronage to be subjected to any regulations which the public interest requires, as must have an important moral and political effect, beside attaining the immediate object of securing for the future a superior class of public servants.

    At the same time I am sensible that the measures I have recommended are of a negative and preventive character, and that the public will not be served as it ought to be, until as your Lordship remarks, the present Civil Servants are brought under the stimulating influence of adequate rewards. This might, I think, be accomplished without difficulty and without any additional expence, but it will be by a further interference with patronage. The Revenue Boards, the Audit Board and the permanent situations of that class would afford ample measure of rewarding those who distinguish themselves by zeal and ability if, instead of being almost systematically bestowed for personal or political motives, these offices be conferred on the most highly qualified persons selected for the purpose from the whole

[1] i.e. 1848–9.
[2] Russell Papers, Public Record Office.

of the public service. The work would be better done, and new life would be given to the whole body of public servants. The remarkable reform which has been accomplished at the Audit Office owing to the appointment made by your Lordship of the Secretary solely on the grounds of his merits, shows what might be expected if this course were habitually pursued on a large scale. . . . The Chairmen of the two great Revenue Boards ought, however, to be men of John Wood's stamp who have acquired a high character in Parliament (if these appointments are not made Parliamentary offices like the Chairmanship of the Poor Law Board, which I think is the true system) and even the less prominent situations should not be filled up from the Civil Service when more highly qualified persons are to be found out of it. All I contend is that superior qualities and merit on the part of the Junior Civil Servants should be habitually recognized and rewarded, as opportunities offer, *where those qualities are to be found to exist*, which is not the case at present.[1]

It will be my duty—and a very satisfying one it will be—to give all the assistance in my power to carrying out any course of proceeding your Lordship may determine for these objects. . . .

I will reserve any suggestions I may have to offer in regard to the persons to be appointed to the Committee until I have an opportunity to see your Lordship, but I may mention in the meantime that I think that the experience of the Bank and of East India House should be represented in the Committee.

But Lord John Russell had more urgent problems to occupy him during the remainder of his Premiership, and perhaps also he could not, on reconsideration, contemplate the surrender of the patronage so valuable to any man in his position. Trevelyan's chance did not come until more than three years had passed. In April 1853 the Treasury asked Sir Stafford Northcote and Sir Charles Trevelyan to report on the Civil Service as a whole. The investigators who had inquired into the work of individual departments recognized that a number of the problems were the same in all. Northcote and Trevelyan were therefore invited to consider "the conditions which are common to all the public establishments . . . so as to obtain full security for the public that none but qualified persons will be appointed, and that they will afterwards have every practicable inducement to the active discharge of their duties". The committee of which Lord John Russell had spoken, and on which Trevelyan had felt that the Bank of England and the East India Company should be represented, had not met with approval. The inquiry was to be by Civil Servants into the Civil Service, without the intervention of outsiders.

[1] Wood, Chairman of the Board of Inland Revenue, supported Trevelyan's scheme of reform when it appeared five years later.

Sir Stafford Northcote, some ten years younger than Trevelyan, was then a man of thirty-five, already beginning to make something of a name for himself. He had served as Gladstone's full-time private secretary, and on Gladstone's resignation he had been able to obtain a legal post in the Board of Trade. Although drawing a salary from the new Government, he continued to serve Gladstone while the latter was out of office, an arrangement of a kind which would be wholly unacceptable now. Northcote soon afterwards became a commissioner for the Great Exhibition of 1851, and later he turned to a political career. He appears to have been easily swayed by others, and it is doubtful whether he could have stood out against so strong a personality as Trevelyan, however much he might have wished to do so. In fact, no evidence exists of any disagreement between them at the time, and only Northcote's later vacillation suggests that he may have been carried away by Trevelyan's burning enthusiasm for widespread reform.

Their report was completed by November 1853 and bears the title "The Organization of the Permanent Civil Service; together with a Letter from the Rev. B. Jowett".[1] It expresses succinctly the views long pondered by Trevelyan and, judged by any standards, it is a remarkable piece of work. It envisaged a public service recruited and organized on principles so novel that they were hotly debated inside Parliament and out for a generation before they won acceptance.

Before referring to the report, reference may be made to the further careers of its authors. After nineteen years as permanent head of the Treasury (which did not mean then, as it means now, the permanent head of the Civil Service also) Trevelyan returned to India, this time as Governor of Madras. Certain financial proposals made by the central Indian Government which were referred to Madras met with Trevelyan's strong censure, and when a leakage of the confidential information took place to the Press Trevelyan was held responsible. In 1860 the Government recalled him in disgrace; but two years later he was restored to favour and appointed Finance Minister in India, a post he occupied with much distinction. Trevelyan came back to England in 1865 and devoted himself to the cause of Civil Service reform and the support of a variety of social measures.

Far higher public honours fell to Sir Stafford Northcote. Two years after the completion of the report he entered Parliament and held several of the chief ministerial positions, acting as Chancellor of the Exchequer, Foreign Secretary, and Conservative Leader in the

[1] P.P. 1854, V. 27.

Commons in later years; in 1885 he was created a peer as Earl of Iddesleigh. On Northcote's death in 1887, Gladstone paid tribute to the sacrifices which Northcote had made for the good of great public objects, and others also praised the pure-mindedness which he brought to politics.

One would always expect to find Sir Charles Trevelyan pressing ahead relentlessly with his plans, however much they shocked authority and public opinion, but Northcote was a man who seemed to have little real tenacity of purpose and who went to great lengths to avoid personal unpopularity. It was a strange turn of the wheel that brought two men of such violently contrasting character into collaboration in an inflammatory report now recognized to be among the most important of its time.

Chapter Two

NINETEENTH-CENTURY REFORM

NORTHCOTE and Trevelyan presented their report, "The Organization of the Permanent Civil Service", on 23 November, 1853.

It may safely be asserted [they wrote] that, as matters now stand, the Government of the country could not be carried on without the aid of an efficient body of permanent officers, occupying a position duly subordinate to that of the Ministers who are directly responsible to the Crown and to Parliament, yet possessing sufficient independence, character, ability, and experience to be able to advise, assist, and, to some extent, influence those who are from time to time set over them.

The existing system of patronage had failed to produce the right candidates, and incompetent men encumbered many of the public offices.

It would be natural to expect that so important a profession would attract into its ranks the ablest and the most ambitious youth of the country; that the keenest emulation would prevail among those who had entered it; and that such as were endowed with superior qualifications would rapidly rise to distinction and public eminence [said the investigators]. Such, however, is by no means the case. Admission into the Civil Service is indeed eagerly sought after, but it is for the unambitious, and the indolent or incapable, that it is chiefly desired. Those whose abilities do not warrant an expectation that they will succeed in the open professions, where they must encounter the competition of their contemporaries, and those whom indolence of temperament or physical infirmities unfit for active exertions, are placed in the Civil Service, where they may obtain an honourable livelihood with little labour and with no risk; where their success depends upon their simply avoiding any flagrant misconduct, and attending with moderate regularity to routine duties; and in which they are secured against the ordinary consequences of old age, or failing health, by an arrangement which provides them with the means of supporting themselves after they have become incapacitated.

The report recommended that the Service should be reorganized:

1. To provide, by a proper system of examination, for the supply of the public service with a thoroughly efficient class of men.

2. To encourage industry and foster merit, by teaching all public servants to look forward to promotion according to their deserts, and to expect the highest prizes in the services if they can qualify themselves for them.

3. To mitigate the evils which result from the fragmentary character of the service, and to introduce into it some elements of unity, by placing

25

first appointments upon an uniform footing, opening the way to staff appointments in departments other than their own, and introducing into the lower ranks a body of men (the supplementary clerks) whose services may be made available at any time in any office.

Apart from the minor staff engaged in copying—such work required a large number of employees before the days of mechanical aids—two main classes of clerks should be attracted to the public service: a superior, or higher, class, recruited between the ages of twenty-one and twenty-five from men of university education; and an inferior, or secondary, class, recruited between the ages of seventeen and twenty-one from among those who had received a good general education.

Northcote and Trevelyan felt that candidates should be selected by means of literary examination and that no technical qualifications should be required before appointment. The best experience for new entrants was that acquired within the departments, and the public service should train its own staff for a lifelong career. The existing arrangements were totally unsuitable: "The character of the young men admitted to the public service depends chiefly upon the discretion with which the heads of departments and others who are entrusted with the distribution of patronage exercise that privilege. The young man thus admitted is commonly employed upon duties of the merest routine. Many of the first years of his service are spent in copying papers and other work of an almost mechanical character. In two or three years he is as good as he can be at such an employment. The remainder of his official life can only exercise a depressing influence on him, and renders the work of the office distasteful to him. Unlike the pupil in a conveyancer's or special pleader's office, he not only begins with mechanical labour as an introduction to labour of a higher kind, but also often ends with it. In the meantime his salary is gradually advancing till he reaches, by seniority, the top of his class, and on the occurrence of a vacancy in the class above him he is promoted to fill it, as a matter of course, and without any regard to his previous services or his qualifications."

Four years earlier a committee of three, including Trevelyan, had reported on the Colonial Office: "The first years of official employment are those in which the knowledge, the self-confidence and the aptitude for business required for the proper discharge of difficult and responsible duties should be obtained; and it is much to be regretted that persons likely to succeed to important situations in the public service should have occupations assigned to them at this critical period of their life which are unimproving and unsuited to their education and prospects, and as such likely to give them a distaste for their profession. If, after ten or fifteen years spent in incessant copying and other routine work, the spirit, the mental activity, and the wide extent of acquired knowledge necessary for vigorous intellectual execution of the transaction of business like that of the Colonial Office, are wanting it is the fault of the system. . . ." The Northcote–Trevelyan report stressed the need for employing the superior grade of clerk on good-class work from the early years of service, since routine duties would lead to mental deterioration in men of this calibre and tend to unfit them for promotion to senior rank in the latter part of their career. Northcote and Trevelyan recognized that most of the work in the public offices would be of a routine kind, and they urged that only a small part of the total staff should belong to the superior class.

The system of nomination to official posts was condemned. No tinkering with that system would overcome its inherent defects, and Northcote and Trevelyan recommended that the vacancies in departments should be filled by means of open competitive examinations to be held at regular intervals. The arrangements by which Government departments conducted their own examinations should be discontinued, and the investigators recommended "that a central Board should be constituted for conducting the examination of all candidates for the public service whom it may be thought right to subject to such a test". The examinations should "test the intelligence, as well as the mere attainments of the candidates. We see no other mode by which (in the case of inferior no less than of superior offices) the double object can be attained of selecting the fittest person, and of avoiding the evils of patronage."

Candidates should provide references as to character and submit a doctor's certificate of their physical fitness. The Civil Service had attracted those in delicate health.

> It may be noticed in particular [the Report pointed out] that the comparative lightness of the work, and the certainty of provision in case of retirement owing to bodily incapacity, furnish strong inducements to the parents and friends of sickly youths to endeavour to obtain for them employment in the service of the Government; and the extent to which the public are consequently burdened, first with the salaries of officers who are obliged to absent themselves from their duties on account of ill health, and afterwards with their pensions when they retire on the same plea, would hardly be credited by those who have not had opportunities of observing the operation of the system.

Recruits should appreciate that their advancement depended on merit. "In the public establishments," the investigators commented, "... the general rule is that all rise together." They recognized the difficulties of promotion by merit.

> If the opinions of the gentlemen engaged in the Civil Service could be taken on the subject of promotion [they wrote], it would probably be found that a very large majority of them would object strongly to what is called promotion by merit. The reason they would assign would be, that promotion by (so called) merit would usually become promotion by favouritism. The effect of the system of departmental patronage has been to inspire the clerks in each office with a feeling of jealousy towards any one who is supposed to enjoy the especial favour of the chief of the department, or, still more, of the principal permanent officer in it. Constituted as our official system now is, men feel, and not unreasonably, that the recognition of their merits, even within their own departments, is extremely uncertain, and that there is no appeal to any public tribunal if injustice is done them there. Even in an open profession a consciousness of unrecognized merit will sometimes weigh a man down, though he has always the hope that the justice which is denied to him in one quarter will be done to him in another. In an office, if a clerk fails to please his immediate superior, he is probably condemned to obscurity for his whole life. ...

In February 1854 the Government published the Northcote–Trevelyan Report, accompanied by the letter to Trevelyan from Benjamin Jowett of Balliol discussing the type of examinations which might be adopted for entry into the Civil Service. Jowett felt that, in respect of the moral character of the candidates, the examination itself should be trusted, since "the perseverance and self-discipline necessary for the acquirement of any considerable amount of knowledge are a great security that a young man has not led a dissolute life". He went on to say:

> A smile may be raised at the idea of subjecting excisemen and tide-waiters[1] to a competing literary examination, as there might have been thirty years ago at subjecting village schoolmasters to a similar test—but it must be remembered on the other hand ... that such a measure will exercise the happiest influence on the education of the lower classes throughout England, acting by the surest of all motives—the desire that a man has of bettering himself in life.

Moreover, Jowett remarked, the effect of the scheme "in giving a stimulus to the education of the lower classes can hardly be over-estimated".

Lord Aberdeen's administration hesitated to embark on a series

---

[1] The tide-waiters were in charge of the vessels and their cargoes until such time as the land-waiters took over, the latter being responsible for the safe custody of the goods until Customs clearance was given.

of proposals so far-reaching and so contrary to long-established usage on the advice only of Northcote and Trevelyan. The report was circulated to a number of divines, teachers, officials, and others who were, or had been, prominent in public work, and they were asked for their observations. Thirty-eight replied to the request, some of them at considerable length and a number with great acumen. Their views on the proposals were published in 1855 as "Papers relating to the Re-organization of the Civil Service".[1]

The schools and universities welcomed the suggestion in the report that recruitment should be by means of open competitive examination, though several put forward criticisms of the subjects which Jowett proposed. The principle of promotion by merit received support from the heads of a number of Government departments in which work had suffered by the insistence of the staff that advancement should be by seniority. Some commentators gave firm approval to the idea of examination by an independent central body, for tests conducted by the individual departments had proved useless. "If a clerk is rejected," said an administrator of experience, "the chances are he will be returned to the examiner (who is usually another clerk in the office) having been crammed for a few weeks to prepare him for another jump at the leaping-bar test, which on this occasion is not unlikely to be lower, the examiner not feeling disposed perhaps to run the risk of further rebuke or of making an enemy of some person of consideration."

Complaints had been made that open competitive examination would lead to the success of men who underwent intensive preparation, but one correspondent expressed full confidence that "the subjects and course of examinations may be so arranged as to test not merely the amount of knowledge possessed by candidates in such subjects, but to distinguish between the results of cramming and those of industry and talent". Some feared that "there may be important defects in the character of a candidate for public office, not ascertainable by an examination into his intellectual attainments", and that the tests would fail to "secure the appointment into public service of gentlemen having the high standard of honour for the satisfactory discharge of their confidential duties".

Sir James Stephen referred to the staff who had been in the Colonial Office while he served as Under-Secretary, and commented that "with an occasional exception, they all had the education, the manners, the feelings and the characteristics of gentlemen", but that

[1] P.P. 1854–5, V. 20.

the largest number of them "possessed only in a low degree, and some of them to a degree almost incredibly low, cither the talents or the habits of men of business, or the industry, the zeal, or the knowledge required for the efficient performance of their appropriate functions". But he poured scorn on the suggestion that the Service could ever attract the best men by competitive examination. "The money to be earned is the solitary attraction," he wrote. "A clerk in a Public Office may not even dream of fame to be acquired in that capacity. He labours in an obscurity as profound as it is unavoidable. His official character is absorbed in that of his superior. He must devote all his talents, and all his learning, to measures, some of which he will assuredly disapprove, without having the slightest power to prevent them; and to some of them he will most essentially contribute, without having any share whatever in the credit of them. He must listen silently to praises bestowed on others which his pen has earned for them; and if any accident should make him notorious enough to become the suspected author of any unpopular act, he must silently submit to the reproach, even though it be totally unmerited by him. These are indeed the indispensable disadvantages of the position of a clerk in a Public Office, and no man of sense and temper will complain of them. But neither will any man of real mental power, to whom the truth is known beforehand, subject himself to an arduous examination in order to win a post so ill-paid, so obscure and so subordinate. Or should he win, no such man will long retain it."

Stephen's views were, however, often highly biased. University teachers in particular disagreed with his opinion about competition, and felt there would be no difficulty in tempting first-class men to compete for posts in the superior class. Though admittedly the rewards could never be so great in the public service as in the open professions, "in comparing the emoluments and prizes of the Civil Service . . . ample allowance must be made for the absence of risk, the early acquisition of income, the prospect of retiring allowances, and the less harassing nature of the Civil Service". A correspondent referred to the criticism, with which he disagreed, "that many lads of spirit and energy and practical ability may be set aside in favour of studious youths, whose very habits of study may have impaired the prompt intelligence, clear head, and natural sagacity". An inspector of schools condemned the suggestion that young men, at the close of their university career, should be able at once to enter into a superior grade and thus obtain an advantage over others which would place them in a specially privileged position for the rest of their working lives. "It is not *fair*," he wrote, "to distribute the prizes of life among men *too early*." The Dean of Carlisle, who had been Headmaster of Rugby, referred to the objection that the introduction of promotion by merit would have unhappy consequences. "Appointments now conferred on young men of aristocratic connection will fall into the hands of persons in a much lower grade of society; and the tone of honourable feeling and the like, which at present exists among those holding such appointments will be endangered." None was more impressed by the aims of the report than John Stuart Mill, who was familiar with the working of the East India Company's scheme. "The proposal to select candidates for the Civil Service of Government by competitive examination appears to me to be one of those great public improvements the adoption of which would form an era in history. . . . It is difficult to express in any language which would not appear exaggerated, the benefits which, as it appears to me, would ultimately be the consequence of the successful execution of the scheme."

It was widely believed that examinations would be won by men of the lower social orders, with whom Ministers would find it repugnant, if not quite impossible, to work, and that the result of competition would be a serious debasement in the standard of public service. The attacks on patronage made in the report aroused much resentment. While some politicians and others admitted that the reforms might improve the quality of the staff, they insisted that patronage represented an essential part of the political system and could not be surrendered without great loss. The proposals in the report might be appropriate in an ideal world, they conceded, but practical considerations must render them unacceptable in existing conditions, and it would be folly to upset the established procedure.

The reforms were clearly in advance of public opinion, and many senior Government officials criticized them violently because they struck at departmental autonomy. Nevertheless, Lord Aberdeen's Government, in which Gladstone served as Chancellor of the Exchequer, was willing to revise the method of recruitment at least, and, on the opening of Parliament in 1854, the Queen referred in her Speech to the forthcoming reform in the Civil Service. "The establishment required for the conduct of the Civil Service," she announced, "and the arrangements bearing upon its condition, have recently been under review; and I will direct a plan to be laid before you which will have for its object to improve the system of admission, and thereby to increase the efficiency of the service."

The Aberdeen Government resigned without taking any action on the Northcote–Trevelyan Report, and Palmerston, who led the new administration appointed at the beginning of 1855, saw little need to interfere with the organization of the departments. He had never had much difficulty with his officials; when in charge of Army finance and later as Foreign Secretary, he had the reputation of making his Civil Servants work hard and of laying down strict rules. Any Minister ought to be able to control the men under him, Palmerston thought, and would probably have done nothing towards a reform in the Service had it not been for the scandals of the Crimean War. During the preceding fifty years, parliamentary investigations had revealed inefficiency in nearly every Government department examined, but relatively few people read the reports of such inquiries or took the slightest interest in the findings. The public, however, paid close attention to anything relating to the war, and the maladministration in the offices concerned with military supplies received wide publicity.

Something had to be done, and Palmerston decided to accept a few of the less contentious of the recommendations in the Northcote–Trevelyan Report. By Order in Council of 21 May, 1855, he established the Civil Service Commission under three commissioners, who were charged with the duty of satisfying themselves on the suitability of "such young men as may be proposed to be appointed to any junior situation in any department of the Civil Service". The candidates, before being admitted to probation, were to "be examined by, or under the directions of, the said Commissioners; and shall receive from them a certificate of qualifications for such examination". The Commissioners must ascertain that an entrant fell within the limits of age prescribed by the department and was "free from any physical defect or disease which would be likely to interfere with the proper discharge of his duty"; and that "the character of the candidate was such as to qualify him for public employment". Finally, the Commissioners should ensure that the candidate had the "requisite knowledge and ability for the proper discharge of his duties".

But there was no suggestion of recruiting separately for superior and inferior work, or for forming a class of copyists who would be interchangeable between departments. All the Government had done was to require examination by an independent body; and candidates must still find a sponsor before they could present themselves to the Commissioners. The new arrangements did not necessarily do more than deny admission to the obviously incapable and to the sick.

Departments still retained much latitude. Not all candidates needed to be submitted to the Commission for test: the Order in Council provided a loophole, stating:

> In case the Chief of any department considers it desirable to appoint to any situation for which there are no prescribed limits of age, a person of mature age having acquired special qualifications for the appointment in other pursuits, such persons shall not in virtue of this Order be required to obtain any certificate from the said Commissioners in order to obtain such appointment; but the Chief of the department shall cause the appointment of any person not previously examined to be formally recorded as having been made on account of such special qualifications.

These regulations did not go very far to check abuses or to provide for a real reform of the Service, and they must have been a disappointment to Trevelyan, who had described his ambition as "to knock the brains out of patronage" but who now saw the system of nomination in danger of becoming more firmly installed. He had reason to complain of Northcote, for his collaborator in the report, now becoming a prominent figure in politics, had not pressed for the introduction of the full reforms and had made a feeble contribution to the Commons debate on the subject. The Order in Council nevertheless pointed the way to important developments. Ministers could still appoint older men to positions in the public service without any test of fitness, but, for the first time, an impartial body had the right to satisfy itself that young men put forward for clerkships had a certain measure of education and ability. The knowledge to be required of the candidates and the ages of recruitment had to be agreed between the Commission and the employing departments; otherwise, the departments were precluded from intervening. The Commission conducted the examinations strictly, and the rejection of favoured candidates inevitably gave rise to much criticism. Patrons protested that the tests had been set at an unreasonably high standard. The Commissioners, however, refused to be deflected from their course, and to a large extent they brought to an end the recruitment of candidates of low calibre into the junior ranks. Their authority did not extend further, and they were unable to attract into the Service by open competition "the best men the country can afford", as Trevelyan had hoped, "the ablest and most ambitious youth".

The Commissioners tried to widen their little empire. They were soon explaining that in their opinion not only the ordinary clerks but even temporary employees required certificates of qualification. And, of course, a new public office quickly expanded and clamoured for more staff. The departments which had conducted their own examinations doubtless found it impossible to reduce their complements although relieved of the work of carrying out such tests, but the Civil Service Commission needed an establishment to organize the selection of recruits. Within five months of its formation, the Commission had moved to a bigger office, and informed Their Lordships of the Treasury that the "new house being higher by one story, and containing more and larger rooms, will require an additional charwoman to keep it in a proper state of cleanliness, and will entail a considerable amount of heavy work not fit for females, for which it will be necessary to employ a porter, who would also act, during office hours, as an inferior messenger". The Commissioners also wanted an increase in the number of clerks, and their plaintive appeal ended up on Trevelyan's desk in the Treasury. He agreed that the Commission should have one extra clerk, two more porters, and another charwoman.

Some patrons tried to sidetrack the Commission and contrived successfully to introduce their nominees into the public service, irrespective of competence. But interest in the staffing of Government offices had been awakened, and watchful eyes were now quick to note and condemn attempts to evade the provisions of the Order in Council of 1855. A few patrons even welcomed the new regulations, for they had been bombarded with applications from place-seekers. Since the number of posts was restricted, more requests had to be refused than could be granted, and Ministers found it a relief not to have to distinguish between applicants. Nominations could now be given freely to anyone who had a claim to consideration, but with a warning that all must compete in an examination of which the final result rested with the Commissioners and in which the patron had no say.

Trevelyan had never ceased to agitate for the introduction of the whole of the proposals in the Northcote–Trevelyan Report, and he now had the support of the Commissioners in urging open competition. They might be suspect as ambitious officials, anxious to attract more work into their own hands and build up a larger staff, but their evidence on the results of the revised system nevertheless carried weight. Gladstone had committed himself in 1855 to the principle of open competition, and other politicians were coming round to his way of thinking. The annual reports issued by the Civil Service Commission convinced many Members of Parliament that further experiment in recruitment should be tried. In 1860 strong pressure was brought to bear on the Government to investigate the methods of recruitment, but the proposal had bitter opponents. Among those who objected to a motion in the Commons for an inquiry was Sir Stafford Northcote. The desirability of an inquiry into the experience gained during the five years of the modified reforms had, however, been recognized by both Houses and, despite Northcote's objections, the Government in 1860 appointed a committee to "inquire into the present mode of Nomination and Selecting Candidates for Junior Appointments in the Civil Service, with a view to ascertaining whether greater facility may not be afforded for the admission of properly qualified persons".

Reliable figures of the number of Civil Servants in the nineteenth century are available only to a limited extent, and even in the earlier years of the present century the information is scanty. The North-cote–Trevelyan Report of 1853 referred to the public establishments as "comprising a body of not less than 16,000", but the estimate excluded a large number of casual and minor workers; in 1854 a return made to Parliament showed 16,338, excluding those with no title to pension. During the Crimean War the total staff reached almost 40,000, and when the 1860 Committee was appointed the total establishment in the clerical grades seems to have been about 38,000.

Most inquiries into the Civil Service had begun with the intention of reducing numbers and costs, but Parliament, though of opinion that official complements were inflated, was not this time concerned with financial economies or man-power cuts within the departments. The 1860 Committee addressed itself to the question of recruitment. Although he had deprecated such an inquiry when first proposed, Northcote agreed to serve on the Select Committee, and he took an active part in the questioning of witnesses. Most of those who gave evidence agreed that patronage, accompanied by qualifying examination, was preferable to patronage with no educational test at all; but some felt that the system still failed to produce men of the kind the Service required.

As an example of what had happened in previous years under the system of uncontrolled examination, the Committee referred in its report to the Registrar-General's Office, set up in 1836, where "a great number of those appointed were very objectionable on account of age, on account of their broken state of health, and on account of their bad character and want of proper qualifications". One of the staff had been imprisoned as a fraudulent debtor, another was detected in robbing the department, and a clerk was unable to associate with others because of his state of health and had to be given a separate room. The Accountant was removed for inefficiency; the Deputy Registrar did not attend the office for fifteen months before his appointment was cancelled as unnecessary; and the duties of the solicitor were also absorbed elsewhere.

The Civil Service Commissioners submitted a long paper on their work, and stated: "As far as our personal experience enables us to judge we think that as regards clerkships in the public service, the best method of obtaining the most competent persons for the situations is by general competitive examination." Between the date of the Order in Council of 1855 and the end of 1859 the number of nominations was 10,860; 8,039 of these nominees did not compete against any other candidates. Where competitions were held, an average of four entries per vacancy was received. In the first year of the Commission's work, more than half the candidates examined failed to pass the educational test.

The Commission had its critics. Complaints were made of errors in the papers set, but the Committee of 1860 was not convinced that such errors had been "more frequent or grave than are inseparable from the transaction of all human affairs". No system of examination has ever been devised which has not been criticized as unfair to some entrants, and the Committee was informed that "candidates whose intellect and education are more than sufficient to qualify them for passing the required test, are disabled by anxiety and apprehension from doing themselves justice before the examinees". Members, however, were unimpressed.

A more successful attack on the Civil Service Commission came from Anthony Trollope, when, in his capacity as a surveyor in the Post Office, he gave evidence as one of his department's two witnesses. He disapproved of open competition, and he disliked fiercely the requirement that men to be employed on minor jobs should have to undergo a test on knowledge which was unnecessary for their work. He told the Committee:

> . . . A postmaster finding it impossible to get a clerk who would pass the Civil Service examination for certain work, asked me to procure one for him. I took great trouble and got a man exactly fitted for the work which he had to do, which was important to the public, but not of a very high quality. I got a man fit for this special work, when four or five had been rejected by the Civil Service Commissioners. I sent him from one town to another, he also was rejected because he could not spell. He would never have been called upon to spell a word. It was extremely necessary that he

should sort with rapidity, and he was a remarkably fast sorter; but he was rejected. The postmaster asked me to get another man for him; I declined, because I had no power of doing it. I recommended a considerable increase of salary, and that increase was obliged to be given; so that a higher rate of payment was incurred, and a man much less fit for that work was appointed.

A witness on behalf of another department said that the new recruits possessed "as a rule, a better education, but less intelligence and usefulness". The Customs felt that the examination "keeps out of the service the strong, hardy and sturdy young men". It reported that a tide surveyor "referring to a tide-waiter on probation, said, 'He does pretty well, sir, but he was a linen-draper's assistant'; this is certainly not the class of man of which to make a good tide-waiter".

Faced with this evidence by Trollope and others against competition for lower-grade staff, the Committee reported that "from tide waiterships downwards, your Committee cannot advocate the general introduction of intellectual competition which they regard as unsuited for officers whose principal duties are mechanical". It agreed that "the evidence laid before Parliament, scanty and imperfect as it necessarily is, makes strongly in favour of open competition", but the members recommended that further experiment should be made with such examination before this system became the general rule. Open competition, it was argued, might encourage far more candidates to study for the Civil Service than the number of vacancies warranted. In these circumstances, many candidates with good qualifications must be declared unsuccessful, and this would perhaps give rise to demands for the creation of unnecessary posts, so that such men should not be left jobless. Thus a swollen bureaucracy would be formed, expenditure would shoot up, and the public administration would fall into disrepute. The effect might then be for pressure to arise for reversion to unrestricted patronage. The investigators felt that the possibility of such a retrograde step must not be risked, so the Committee, "for the very reason that leads them to desire the ultimate success of the competitive method, are anxious to avoid such precipitancy as might possibly lead to a reaction of public feeling".

The Committee pointed out that vacancies should be aggregated instead of being competed for singly. Where candidates must compete for a single post there should be not less than five competitors, and, as a further protection, the Committee suggested a two-tier examination system. All candidates ought first to undergo a test, and as vacancies arose the field should be confined to those who had qualified and would now compete in the final examination.

Even so tepid a report, which still preserved the principle of nomination for the time being though affirming the advantages of open competition, met with much hostility. The Government refused to make the recommendations compulsory, but it circulated the report to the departments with the suggestion that the proposals should be carefully studied. Some departments were prepared to give the recommendations a trial, others completely ignored them, and the method of recruitment continued to vary from office to office, at the will of the Minister or the permanent head of the department. A few open competitions were tried as an experiment, and these showed the fallacy of the view that capable young men would not present themselves. When the Civil Service Commission announced such tests, very large numbers of candidates came forward, and the top scorers were admitted to be of a very high quality.

In the years immediately following the report of the Select Committee of 1860 demands for an extension of open competition became more insistent. The middle classes realized the value of education for their sons and now had the money to pay for it. The conditions were thus favourable to the setting up of new educational establishments, and these had a keen interest in having the Civil Service thrown open to all-comers. Yet the decision to abolish nomination did not come as the result of any great public agitation. In 1870, Robert Lowe, Chancellor in Gladstone's Government, who had long been a supporter of competitive examination, induced the Prime Minister to propose the reform to the Cabinet. Patronage in Civil Service appointments was no longer necessary for the management of the Commons and had become less valuable otherwise when so many more opportunities were available for obtaining employment in an expanding economy. The Cabinet raised no objection to open competition for all except one or two departments.

At the same time as open competition was introduced, departments were to be organized on the basis of a superior and a lower grade of clerk, with a separate class of copyists or writers. This grading had been recommended by Trevelyan nearly twenty years earlier. Most, though not all, of his proposals had now been accepted.

The Treasury issued regulations on the staffing of the offices, but the departments had their own views on the class of employee most suitable for their particular work. Some chose to have a staff composed principally of the superior grade, others favoured the lower grade for all duties. Division of work was a novelty in most departments, and a reorganization of this kind could not be carried through satisfactorily without much more guidance than the Treasury was able to give at this time. No uniform scales of salaries had been introduced, and a man on the lower grade in one department might be paid more than a man in another department which had chosen to put its staff on the superior grade. Complaints of the injustice of the arrangements and of the chaos in the departments resounded in Parliament and elsewhere, and in April 1874 the Government felt compelled to order a comprehensive review of the whole field by another Civil Service Inquiry Commission.

Sir Lyon Playfair, who was appointed Chairman, had been invited in 1854 to submit his views on the Northcote–Trevelyan Report. He had taken his seat in the Commons in 1868, but, except for one other M.P., the members consisted of Civil Servants or ex-Civil Servants with administrative experience. The terms of reference were very wide, for the Commission received instructions to consider:

> (1) The method of selecting Civil Servants in the first instance; (2) The principles upon which men should be transferred from Office to Office . . . ; (3) The possibility of grading the Civil Service as a whole . . . ; (4) The system under which it is desirable to employ Writers or other persons for the duties of less importance.

Inter-departmental transfer and the unification of the Service had at last been recognized as of first importance, as Trevelyan had always claimed they must be if progress was to be made. Now seventy years of age, Trevelyan gave evidence before the Playfair Commission in his usual blunt style. He seemed fearful that there would be a slipping back into patronage, and he denounced that system pungently. The general purport of the Northcote–Trevelyan Report was, he said, "to indicate a great evil and an effective remedy. The evil is what is known under the head of 'patronage'." He reminded the Commission of the state of affairs which had existed at the time of the report, and warned it that, without constant vigilance, abuses could readily recur under any form of patronage. "I believe," he replied to a question by a member, "that those abuses are so deeply rooted in human nature that if the existing check upon them were at all relaxed they would shoot out and flourish as much as ever." He pointed to the triumphs of open competition where it had been tried, and he claimed that "the tendency of the competitive system is to grow higher and stronger, depending, as it does, upon the strenuous exertions of the flower of the youth of the country to excel each other".

Trevelyan had misjudged the Commission if he suspected that it would be opposed to open competition. "It may well be doubted," the Commission stated, "if any examination can effectively test a man's real and permanent capacity for the business of life"; but they affirmed that open competition must continue as the system of recruitment and that any other means of staffing the public service would be intolerable. The Commission agreed that the Service needed a superior, or higher grade, a lower, or secondary grade, and a special class of copyists. Women had been employed for several years in the Post Office, and the Commission favoured their extended use in two groups for the less important duties in the Service, since not only were women cheaper than male staff, but the evidence suggested that they were more competent in certain kinds of work. It did not suggest the employment of women on ordinary clerical duties, however, "unless they can be placed in separate rooms under proper female supervision".

The Committee of 1860 had proposed a qualifying test for all candidates, with the intention of ensuring that the final selection was made from men who had proved themselves of a certain standard. The Playfair Commission recommended a qualifying test, but for a different reason and for the Higher Division only. The Division was to be small, recruited from those with a university education. In order that unsuitable men should not waste their time in studying for this Division, the Commission suggested that candidates should be tested at the age of seventeen, and only if successful in these tests should they be eligible to compete in the final examination. While all candidates should be recruited to the Higher Division by such open competition, the Commission agreed that departments must have the right to select their own men from those declared successful, and that there could be no question of an office being under any compulsion to accept a man against its judgement. The Lower, or Second, Division would also be recruited by open competition and would be a class whose members could be transferred to any office. Copyists also would be liable to work where required in any part of the Government service.

Uniform scales were laid down for the different grades for the first time. The Playfair Commission recommended that the Higher Division should be paid on a scale from £100 minimum to £400 by increments, with special duty pay from £50 to £200; thus at the maximum a man could earn £600 per annum, a not unreasonable salary for the time. For the Lower Division the Commission felt that the starting salary should be £80 per annum, by annual increments of £15 until the maximum of £200 per annum had been attained, with a possibility of a further £100 per annum for special work. The Lower Division scales were based on a six-hour day, but some offices worked an extra hour, and the Commission agreed that in the seven-hour day departments the salaries should be increased by a further £50 per annum.

The Government accepted the recommendations for the Lower Division, and the proposed rates of pay were adopted generally throughout the Service. The recommendations in relation to the Higher Division, however, were rejected. The Government agreed that a Higher Division must be recruited, that it should be small in number, and that candidates should have a university training. But it did not accept the idea of a qualifying examination at seventeen followed by a final test after the close of a man's university career; and it considered that uniform rates of pay would be inappropriate for men of the Higher Division. As the work of the Division varied so much from department to department, the head of an office should be left to assess the scales for his own staff.

Discontent grew in the Service because of the discrepancies between the departments, but successive Governments resisted requests for further inquiries until 1887. In that year a Commission on Civil Establishments was set up under the chairmanship of Sir Matthew White Ridley. Like its predecessor, it emphasized the need for the Higher Division. That Division should, it recommended, be organized into three grades, each paid on a uniform scale. The lower, or Secondary, Division should consist of two grades—a basic grade to which all recruits should be appointed in the first place, and a grade above, filled by promotion. The Lower Division had always resented the fact that if they worked in six-hour day offices they were paid £50 less than those in seven-hour day departments. The staff protested that all entered by the same examinations and that successful candidates had no choice of the department to which they would be sent. The Commission agreed that the whole of the Lower Division should receive the extra £50, deciding at the same time that all must work a seven-hour day. It heard evidence about the value of typists in Government offices and was told that some departments showed reluctance in employing them. The members of the Commission urged that typists should be recruited to take the place of copyists and boy clerks, particularly the latter, whose employment had been the subject of severe criticism.

As on previous occasions, the Government accepted the recommendations for the Lower Division but would not interfere with the Higher Division. That class had quickly made for itself a very privileged position and had become a powerful factor in government. While practically the whole of the Lower Division was recruited by open competition, many posts in the Higher Division were still filled by patronage and limited competition. By the close of the century, however, the main principles had been firmly established and open competition had been accepted as the rule. Not only had Ministers and heads of departments been reluctant to surrender their privileges, but even the staff had a vested interest in nomination. Representatives of serving officers pointed out that "they were in the habit of receiving from Ministers appointments for their sons and relations; that this method of providing for their relations had been lost to them by recent changes; that this practice was of great value to them . . ."; and that special arrangements should be made to facilitate the entry into the Service of the sons of faithful officials.

When in opposition, Members praised the system of open competition as the best and fairest means of recruiting the staff, but the same men when returned to power had hesitated to adopt it for the Service generally. The full effect of the reforms advocated by Northcote and Trevelyan and others could not become apparent for a number of years after their introduction. It was feared that, if the proposed schemes of recruitment and grading proved to be ill conceived, irreparable damage might be done to the public service. The supporters of reform prophesied that the business of the departments would be better and more speedily conducted and that savings would undoubtedly be made. The reformers, however, could not convince Parliament that the costs of administration would be reduced immediately or indeed that the economies would be considerable in later years. The House of Commons could find little enthusiasm for measures which promised no savings at once, were of doubtful value in producing large economies later, and might give rise to chaos in Government offices during the interim period of reorganization.

Many people were appalled at the thought of open competition as the method of recruiting staff, especially for the Higher Division, where men would be clothed in authority from their early years in the Service. Northcote and Trevelyan had urged that candidates should undergo probation so that the unsuitable could be weeded out, and other investigators had also emphasized the importance of this safeguard. But probation had existed under patronage and it had been farcical; and the critics did not believe that the system would be any more successful in getting rid of incompetent staff who might be recruited by examination.

Other opponents of the reforms looked at the question from a quite different standpoint. They did not deny that open competition would probably produce a body of first-class men, but the better the quality the greater the danger. Such officials would seek power, and the more able the men the greater the lust to acquire authority. Some slackness in the conduct of public administration was felt to be less dangerous than the creation of a very efficient class of Civil Servants: such men would surely tend to usurp the functions of government and replace democratic rule by a rigid bureaucratic control.

Chapter Three

THE STRUCTURE OF THE
PRESENT-DAY SERVICE

IT has been the practice in this century for a Royal Commission on the Civil Service to be set up about every twenty years. During such an interval, some men who occupied positions in the middle grades have advanced to the highest posts within the departments and are likely to have fresh ideas to put forward. There is never a time when the public does not suspect that the organization calls for revision, and a Royal Commission provides an opportunity for people interested to submit their views on the reforms which they consider necessary. Above all, it is claimed, a Royal Commission on the Civil Service gives, or should give, confidence to the country that officialdom is being kept under careful observation.

When the Ridley Commission was appointed in 1890, the non-industrial staff numbered about 70,000. Ten years later it had swollen to 145,000. In 1910, when the Royal Commission under Lord MacDonnell was appointed, the complement was estimated at 210,000 and several important changes had taken place in Whitehall. Women had entered the Service in appreciable numbers; several departments had begun to recruit professional, scientific, and technical staff; and new classes of clerical workers had been introduced. The MacDonnell Commission devoted four years to its work; as it turned out, these labours were largely fruitless.

The Commission produced Majority and Minority Reports which were in strong disagreement on certain points. All the members, however, recognized the objections to restricting the Service to a few main groups, but nevertheless they considered that the advantage lay with the maintenance of broad classes, since sub-division of work tended to lead to a proliferation of grades which created more problems than it solved. While admitting that some exceptions would have to be made, the Commission recommended that as far as possible the Service should classify its staff in three main groups for general duties: the highest class (which has been known at different periods as First Division, Class I, and Administrative); Senior Clerical; and Junior Clerical, with subordinate staff. While uniform scales of salary had been introduced for other classes, the remuneration of the highest division still varied between departments. Most offices started entrants at £100 per annum, but the Treasury and the Foreign Office paid £150 per annum and their staffs proceeded to a higher maximum. The Commission urged that the same salary scales should be applied throughout the Service and referred to the advantages of inter-departmental transfer which this arrangement would facilitate.

Members of the Commission were sensitive that a measure of patronage might be reintroduced into the Service in the recruitment of professional, scientific, and technical staff. Departments at the time chose such staff on their own responsibility, and, where there is no competition in public appointments, favouritism and jobbery may arise. The Commission agreed that tests would not be an appropriate means of recruiting specialists who, after completing a course of training and spending several years on practical work, gravitated to the Service as a career. But it emphasized that everyone with the required attainments must be considered impartially; all vacancies should be advertised and the Civil Service Commission should take a hand in the final selection of men to fill the posts.

With this exception, open competition by means of written examinations was to be the rule. One member of the Commission disagreed with this view. "It would be lamentable," he said, "if, because of allegations of Patronage, an undue fear existed of appointing to the Public Service men and women not trained in the Civil Service, but possessing in a particular degree expert knowledge obtained in the world outside." He gained no adherents on the Commission. Anything which hinted at privilege, in however slight a degree, had now become anathema. Nor was the objection only that no other method would be so likely to produce the right men for the jobs. There was a further consideration, and the head of the Treasury put it forward in a way that indicates the change in the social climate:

> I do not speak for open competition merely as such, and out of a yearning to see mere competition, but as a practical thing to make the various classes of the country understand that they have a fair chance of getting into the Service of the State and getting such benefits as there are, it seems to me practically the only thing which is safe and is not open to the grossest abuses. It is the dream of everyone to have the power of selecting his own staff—that is, of course, the dream of every individual when he begins; but in practice it would be too terrible a position for the head of a department with all his friends wishing to put their sons into his office and everybody writing to him. And the result would be too hideous, and more hideous still if it were in the hands of the political chiefs.

The MacDonnell Commission finished its work as the First World

War broke out, and the proposals in the four reports it issued could not be fully considered at such a time. Shortly after the war the Government adopted the recommendation that all members of the administrative class should be recruited on common scales of salary, a measure which a number of major departments had most obstinately resisted. These departments contended that a man appointed to a long-established office charged with duties of great responsibility should be treated specially; and they pointed out that the older departments obtained the highest-placed and presumably, therefore, the most able men from the examinations. But the war had made interchange between the departments on a large scale absolutely essential, since some public offices were overstaffed for peacetime conditions and others needed much reinforcement. Inter-departmental exchanges could not be carried out smoothly so long as differing rates of salary remained in force.

At the beginning of 1918 the Government appointed a committee under Viscount Gladstone to consider the problems of recruitment to the Civil Service after the war.[1] The Committee proposed that the Service should comprise a small administrative class, a senior and a junior clerical class, and that women clerks should be in two grades. Much thought had been given to the employment in the Civil Service of ex-soldiers, ex-sailors, and ex-airmen, and the Committee felt that posts should be made available to them on a generous scale.

Viscount Gladstone's Committee had not foreseen all the difficulties which would arise at the close of hostilities, and in 1919 another committee was appointed to "consider the scope of the duties at present allotted to the Clerical Classes in the Civil Service; to report on the organization most appropriate to secure the effective performance of these duties; and to make recommendations as to scales of salary and methods of recruitment".[2] This Committee, a sub-committee of the Whitley Council for the Civil Service, consisted of senior officials of the Treasury and other departments and of representatives of the staff associations, and therefore, unlike earlier inquiries, it was a gathering of experts. It called no long procession of witnesses to describe the system or to put forward suggestions for modifications. The Committee pointed out:

> ... this is the first occasion on which a body composed entirely of present or past Civil Servants, possessing among them a wide and varied

[1] P.P. 1918, V. 11.
[2] Reorganization Report, National Whitley Council, 1920.

experience of the Public Service, has been given the opportunity of framing a scheme for its reconstruction. . . . The necessities of war called into being new and improvised Departments of State for the conduct of administrative operations on a scale altogether beyond parallel and touching almost every branch of the economic life of the nation. The result has been a quickening of the interest taken by Civil Servants in the organization of the Service, and a fuller realization of the need for overhauling its machinery. . . . We desire, in conclusion, to emphasize the truth that forms are lifeless things without the spirit that animates them, and that no rules or regulations have any value apart from the broad and sympathetic treatment with which they should be handled and interpreted. Administration is at least as much a matter of heart as of brain. Throughout our deliberations we have striven to promote what we conceive to be the best interests equally of the State and of the Civil Servant; we have endeavoured to remedy what has appeared to us to be defective, while, at the same time, not impairing what experience has shown to be good; and in all that we have proposed we have kept steadily in view the idea of an efficient and contented Public Service.

Apart from the professional and typing classes, and some minor grades, the Service should, the Committee recommended, be grouped into four—Administrative, Executive, Clerical, and Writing Assistants. The Government accepted the proposals almost in their entirety. Their adoption gave rise to problems of assimilation which caused much dissatisfaction in the Civil Service for several years. The Intermediate Class and most Second Division clerks were absorbed into the Executive Class, but inevitably some people felt that they had been unfairly treated. The "contented Public Service" for which the Committee had hoped did not appear.

By its terms of reference the Committee had been restricted to a limited field, but in any case no committee of officials can carry the same authority with Parliament and public as a Royal Commission. In 1929 the Government asked Lord Tomlin to be chairman of a commission to inquire, *inter alia*, into the structure and organization of the Civil Service. In its report, published in 1931, the Tomlin Commission approved the grouping in general and, though the classification has often been criticized, the Service has since continued to be organized in the four main classes for general work—Administrative, Executive, Clerical, and Clerical Assistants. The nomenclature is somewhat misleading. The Government of the country is the political executive, and the Civil Service acts as the professional executive body; but it is the middle grades within a Government department which are called executives. Under Ministers, the final control is vested in the administrative class.

The main clerical classes are clear enough, but the grading within the classes tends to be confusing. No grades exist within the clerical assistant class. The clerical class consists of two grades—clerical officers and higher clerical officers—but many of the higher clerical posts have been converted into executive posts in recent years. The executive class comprises seven grades—junior, higher, senior, chief, and principal executive officer, plus two further executive grades which carry different titles in different departments. In the administrative class are six grades—assistant principal, principal, assistant secretary, and three grades which, again, vary in title from department to department.

In 1953 came another Royal Commission, under the chairmanship of Sir Raymond Priestley. The Priestley Commission's terms of reference were narrower than those of the previous Royal Commissions on the Civil Service. Members were not asked to consider the structure of the departments but to confine themselves to the conditions of service and the remuneration of officials.

For over a hundred years the remuneration to be paid to Civil Servants has been a matter of great difficulty. Prior to the nineteenth century many officials received their income from a variety of sources. "The ancient system in most, if not all, the public offices," said the report of the Committee appointed in 1836 to Inquire into the Fees and Emoluments of Public Offices,[1] "was to appoint officers either without salary, or with a salary inadequate to the value of their services, leaving them to pay themselves by the receipt of fees from the parties for whom their services were performed." In addition to scale fees, some officials received Christmas boxes and considerable gifts at other times of the year. Commissioners appointed in 1785 had recommended, after a series of most detailed investigations, that this system of payment to staff should cease. Revenue collected by an office should be paid over to a fund from which it would meet its costs for salaries and other expenses, any remaining balance accruing to the Exchequer; where the revenue proved insufficient to cover the disbursements the deficiency should be met from moneys voted by Parliament. The Committee of 1836 was concerned to see not only that this arrangement had been followed generally but also that the fees charged did not constitute an unreasonable burden on the public and had proper authority. "It appears from the Treasury minute dated 24th April, 1695," stated the Committee, "that W. Lowndes was appointed Secretary to the Treasury at a Board at which the

[1] P.P. 1837, V. 44.

King was personally present, and that His Majesty at the same time approved the table of fees for the office. . . . The late receiver of fees and the present receiver both remember an old table of fees signed 'Lowndes', which used to hang up in one of the rooms of the Treasury; we have caused this table to be searched for, but without success." At the end of the eighteenth century the Treasury had abolished all Christmas boxes and New Year gifts, but some fees were still collected and retained by the staff on the excuse of long-established privilege. In 1800 the Admiralty had laid down fixed salaries for its staff in lieu of "fees, perquisites, allowances or other emoluments whatsoever", and, in so reporting to the Committee of 1836, it made the sad comment: "We cannot help observing, that it appears doubtful whether the public business of the offices where the fees have been discontinued to be received by the officers executing such business has been carried on with the same facility and despatch as under the former system." This view did not deter the Committee from recommending that, with the exception of fees amounting to some £14,000, all money collected from the public should be paid to the Exchequer.

So long as officials obtained the whole or part of their income from fees, the total cost of the Service remained hidden. Parliament needed to provide no money at all for salaries in some departments, and where revenue did not balance expenditure it voted only the difference. Under the new arrangements Parliament saw for the first time the wages bill of the public administration. The cost seemed to members of both Houses to be enormous. Even if the fees paid into the Exchequer had been equal to the increase in the amount voted for salaries, Parliament would no doubt have thought the rate of expenditure very high. And as some fees had been abolished and others reduced, the reform had the effect of producing a large net addition. The Commons ordered further investigations. There has never since been a time when Parliament has not thought the Civil Service to be too costly and sought, more or less urgently, for economies in administration.

In proposing that officials should not retain fees which they collected but should surrender them to the Exchequer, the Committee of 1836 had submitted that "the interests of individuals which may be affected by a compliance with our recommendations shall be duly considered". But the Committee had no part in fixing the salaries to be paid. That was left largely to the head of each department, and there was disagreement on the amount of compensation. No attempt had been made to lay down common standards or to reach agreement on a uniform basis for measuring accurately the value of the work of the different classes of clerks. In some cases the income sacrificed by officials could not be readily assessed since, in addition to regular fees, they received gifts periodically, and these varied from year to year. Some departments had to base their calculations on evidence provided by the recipients of the amount of the income obtained. A chief imbued with ideas of economy assessed salaries on a low level, while other heads of departments tended to be over-generous, perhaps to justify a higher salary for themselves. Large offices usually fared worst, since a relatively small addition to the remuneration of each clerk represented considerable sums in total, and this was particularly disadvantageous to the Excise and Customs, which had huge complements for that time. The Committee made a special plea for them, pointing out that the interests of officers of the Excise should be sympathetically considered and explaining: "The continually authorized practice of taking fees in this department in addition to salaries, has, we have reason to think, caused many of those salaries to be fixed on a comparatively low scale; and we also observe that the emoluments derived to certain officers of the Customs, from the fractional sums under 6d. has always been considered as an authorized addition to their salaries."

The result of entrusting the assessment of salaries to individual departments was a hotchpotch that affected the Service for many years. A writer in the *Statistical Review* for 1868 pointed out that "892 clerks have no fewer than 90 distinct scales of salary, the lowest being £70/£90 and the highest £700/£900". Incremental scales are not, of course, confined to the Civil Service but have long been a feature of it. All except the very highest ranks of Civil Servants are paid a minimum salary on entry into a grade and proceed by annual increases until they reach the top of the scale, unless in special circumstances. In a graded service a man's salary is not assessed on the basis of his individual worth or the value of the particular duty he is performing. Everyone on the grade is paid on the same scale. Some officials undertake much better work than others of equal rank who are in receipt of the same remuneration, but that is inevitable where each grade covers a broad field of activity, as the Civil Service grades have done for many years.

The Playfair Commission, which recommended £80–£200 and £90–£200 for the Lower Division (with allowances of up to £100 per annum for some officials) was criticized by the staff for proposing absurdly low rates, but in fact other inquirers agreed generally that these scales were reasonable, and few changes of importance were made for nearly half a century. As late as 1920 the Reorganization Committee proposed that (excluding war bonus, which was payable to all officials) the salary scales should be £60–£250 for the junior clerical grade and £300–£400 for the higher clerical grade, £100–£400 for the junior executives, and £400–£500 for the higher executive group. The Committee did not deal with salaries exceeding £500 per annum, and therefore revised only the first grade of the Administrative Class, to which it awarded £200–£500. The Tomlin Commission in 1931 did not propose salaries much higher than those already in force and was a disappointment to Civil Servants. The next Royal Commission, however—the Priestley Commission—recommended considerable increases. Since then the scales have been revised more than once. The salaries as at 1 January, 1965 are shown in Appendix I.

The MacDonnell Commission stated that "it is an accepted principle with all parties that Government should be a 'model' employer", and, in referring to this statement, the Tomlin Commission pointed out that "different interpretations have been placed on this phrase. . . . We think that a phrase which lends itself to such varied and contradictory interpretations affords no practical guidance for fixing wages or for indicating the responsibilities of the State towards its employees." The Commission was satisfied "that broad general comparisons between classes in the Service and outside occupations are possible and should be made. In effecting such comparisons the State should take a long view. Civil Service remuneration should reflect what may be described as the long-term trend, both in wage levels and in the economic conditions of the country. We regard it as undesirable that the conditions of service of Civil Servants when under review should be related too closely to factors of a temporary or passing character."

When the Tomlin Commission reported, it printed an interesting statement made by a Treasury representative who repeated more or less the views which had guided the previous Commissions.

It has been held to be essential that the remuneration and other conditions of employment of Civil Servants shall be adequate to ensure the recruitment to the Civil Service of fully qualified staff and the maintenance of an efficient and healthy Public Service. . . . It would not be right to prescribe for Civil Servants rates of remuneration and other conditions of service which were out of scale with the standards normally obtaining amongst good employers outside the Public Service. . . . It has been held that the remuneration of Civil Servants should, as far as possible, be so fixed as to ensure for a considerable period of time.

This remained largely the Government attitude for more than twenty years, but such a policy could not be expected to commend itself to the staff at a time of severe inflation, and the associations represented strongly to the Priestley Commission that Civil Service salaries should not be assessed on the basis of long-term trends and that there should be no delay in taking account of improvements in commerce and industry.

The Priestley Commission dealt at some length with this perplexing subject. It pointed out the need for a Civil Service "recognized as efficient and staffed by members whose remuneration and conditions are thought fair both by themselves and by the community they serve". The Commission appreciated that this was an ideal which could never be absolutely achieved but that "the main aim must be to approach it as closely as possible", and went on to consider how this might best be done.

When disagreement arose over salaries, it had been the practice of the Treasury to seek information on the remuneration paid by outside employers and to use this data to put forward its views on what ought to be granted to Civil Servants engaged on work regarded as similar. The associations, however, complained that the Treasury seemed to choose unfortunate comparisons which allowed insufficient weight to the responsibilities of Civil Servants; and the Treasury was also accused of a tendency to ignore model employers. The associations therefore were in the habit of conducting their own researches and, not surprisingly, usually came up with very different results on the level of remuneration earned in industry. The Commission referred to this kind of conflict but phrased its comments more politely: "It seems inevitable that the associations seeks comparison among what they consider to be 'better' employers while the Treasury may seek to include a wider range." The Commission emphasized the need for objective fact-finding in the first place and recommended that figures should be obtained "from an appropriate section of representative organizations which employ staff on broadly comparable work", both the Treasury and the staff giving prior agreement to the comparisons which should be used.

The Civil Service, the Commission felt, should not be among the employers who offer the highest rates of remuneration but among those who pay somewhat above the average: salaries should be "not lower than the median but not above the upper quartile".

As a result of the Priestley Commission's recommendations, a Civil Service Pay Research Unit was established soon afterwards and charged with the duty of assembling information from outside employers. The Unit is an independent body. The material it collects is submitted to the two sides and is used as the basis for negotiation on salaries for all grades other than the highest. Where agreement cannot be reached, the dispute is referred to the Civil Service Arbitration Tribunal.

It is of interest to see how Civil Service remuneration has risen since 1955.

	1955 £	1965 £
Permanent Secretary	4,500	8,265
Deputy Secretary	3,250	5,885
Principal	1,185–1,570	2,259–3,087
Assistant Principal	492–885	965–1,606
Senior Executive Officer	1,165–1,265	1,995–2,414
Executive Officer	302–830	614–1,483
Clerical Officer	192–595	399–1,038
Clerical Assistant	177–458	326–810

Most officials are on an incremental scale. The practice has been discontinued of requiring a certificate that an official has performed his duties satisfactorily before the annual increase is granted and the increments are now practically automatic. Each year, however, a report is made on an official's performance. The arrangement was for these reports to be kept strictly confidential, with the exception that anyone marked below a certain level had to be informed in the hope that he would pull himself together. Since 1965 all officials are advised of the nature of the comments passed on them by their supervisors.

The incremental scales are very long for some grades. The executive officer at eighteen, for instance, enters at £614 in London and advances by £55 per annum until he reaches £865, then proceeds by further annual increments to the maximum of £1,483 at the age of thirty-six (unless he is promoted in the meantime). Civil Servants can work out their probable earnings for years ahead, allowing for good luck in the way of advancement, and they know the salaries of their colleagues, since the scales are published for all to ponder.

The newcomer to a department finds that the pushful atmosphere not uncommon in private enterprise is absent from most Government offices, where life, if not leisured, is at any rate rarely rushed. The description of a public department as a place where officials make tea all day long for one another is pleasant but untrue. Much, though by no means all, of the work is of a kind which calls for quiet deliberation and keen concentration, and which cannot be done at high speed without taking chances of a kind unthinkable in a Public Service. Private enterprise is usually engaged in the manufacture, sale, or distribution of goods or the provision of profit-making services, and departments which undertake such work for the Government are organized on the same lines as business firms and are no less expeditious in their operations.

It has long been charged against public offices that they are badly run and stupidly outmoded in their methods. Fifty years ago the MacDonnell Commission pointed out that much of the delay in the departments "should in truth be regarded as part of the price paid for the advantages of public discussion and criticism of public affairs". A Committee also commented in 1944 on the complaints made that the Civil Service was dilatory in the performance of its duties:

> While the faults commonly attributed to it are not the monopoly of the Civil Service, it may be that conditions of the public service tend to foster particular weaknesses and to throw the limelight of publicity upon them to a greater degree than elsewhere. The faults most frequently enumerated are over-devotion to precedent, remoteness from the rest of the community, inaccessibility, and faulty handling of the public; lack of initiative and imagination; ineffective organization and misuse of manpower; procrastination and unwillingness to take responsibility or to give decisions. We recognize that these defects exist in some measure—though not so generally or in such degree as is often alleged. . . .

Except in particular fields or in special conditions, Government departments cannot in fact work as quickly as commercial organizations, and the principal reason is perhaps the need for equality of treatment. What the department gives to one it must give to all, if the circumstances are the same. Every official learns that he must never fail to record fully what he has done and why he has done it, unless this is self-evident, and that accuracy comes before speed in any job. He must be consistent and he must be thorough.

The officials in the branch of a department dealing with the application of sections of an Act will know the leading precedents which have been created, and no difficulty will arise in settling any case which is clearly covered by a previous decision. That is more or less routine, and such work can be disposed of quickly by subordinate or relatively subordinate staff. A correspondent's claim may, however, be covered partly by one decision and partly by another, and raise a point which has not hitherto been considered fully. It will take time to make a summary of precedents which bear on the question at issue, so that a ruling may be sought from a senior official. No one can really judge how long such a job ought to require. A man may spend weeks in searching into past precedents of his department and their history, and finding out whether other departments have come across the same problem. If the matter is of importance, reference may in the end be necessary to the Minister, but not before a number of officials have been consulted and have made their comments. The final ruling will govern any parallel case, unless the precedent can be shown to be wrong or unless conditions change later in such a way as to make amendment desirable. No one is permitted without authority to vary decisions even slightly, lest inconsistency should spread through the department. The alteration of a well-established precedent may be a formidable job.

Few officials in responsible posts ever lack a mass of files on their desks. Most Civil Servants in the higher grades have a heavy back-log and could keep themselves fully occupied for a long time if they did nothing more than clear up the old cases in their cupboards. Files with slips marked "Immediate" or "Pressing" or "Most immediate" must take precedence, and those not so adorned sink to the bottom of the tray. Unless a file has some mark of urgency on it, the tendency is to regard it as of lesser importance. It is difficult for the staff, especially the subordinate members, to be impressed with the need for speedy action in the handling of ordinary official business when they see cases which have been on their rounds for months or years.

Chapter Four

RECRUITMENT

In the years preceding the First World War the British Civil Service had been formed into a unified administration acknowledged to be the superior of any in the world. But like all Civil Services it was frequently the subject of attack: officials were called lazy and arrogant and arbitrary, and the newspapers of the time tilted at the swollen bureaucracy.

A return of the established staff of the Civil Service at 31 March, 1914, showed a total of 167,628, including employees in Ireland. The principal departments were as follows:

Admiralty	10,948
Board of Trade	2,470
Colonial Office	145
Customs and Excise	8,649
Education	1,810
Foreign Office	158
Home Office	3,259
Local Government Board	708
National Health Insurance	1,784
Ordnance Survey	926
Post Office	123,668
Prison Commissioners	3,679
War Office	1,415

Five years later, in 1919, the established staff numbered 245,855, and the temporary staff of 147,350 brought the total to 393,205.

Normal recruitment to the Service had been suspended almost entirely during the 1914–18 war, and could not be resumed for several years after it because of political pressure. For the first time men had been conscripted to the armed forces of the nation, and the Government recognized that it owed a duty to those who had sacrificed for their country, especially the disabled.

Several committees considered the procedure to be adopted for filling posts. Large numbers of temporary staff had been employed, including many women. There was comparatively little difficulty in the choice of women for establishment from the ranks of this war-time staff: either they sat for an examination or were chosen by means of a selection board. The position of men was very different. Many of them were ex-soldiers, ex-sailors, and ex-airmen who had entered the Civil Service on leaving the fighting forces. They demanded permanent employment from the Government, and their champions claimed that, even though they might lack educational attainments of the kind ordinarily required from candidates, the ex-service men should be retained. Nor would it be enough to reserve for these men the existing vacancies, it was argued; all vacancies in the clerical grades should be given to ex-service candidates and for a number of years there should be a complete ban on the recruitment of other entrants by examination.

In the end the Government agreed to hold special examinations for ex-service men, and nearly the whole of the vacancies were earmarked for them for several years; later, half the vacancies were reserved for such candidates in some grades, and a smaller proportion in others. A number of those who failed in the relatively simple examinations, or who did not bother to compete, received permanent employment, though without right to pension. Not until ten years after the end of the First World War could the Civil Service Commissioners restore open competition to recruit staff to all classes of the Civil Service. During these years the Service absorbed many candidates who were unsuitable.

The lesson had been learned and was well remembered when the Government set up a committee in 1944 to consider Recruitment to Established Posts in the Civil Service during the Reconstruction Period after the Second World War. The Committee expressed itself strongly: ". . . perhaps we may say that all who have been familiar with the Civil Service during this war are deeply conscious of the unhappy effects of unplanned recruitment immediately after the last war, and of the failure to maintain sufficiently high standards of qualification". It firmly rejected the idea of earmarking all vacancies for ex-service candidates, making the comment:

> The interest of the nation in the efficiency of its Public Service has also to be considered. This interest requires that the Service shall have the best candidates it can get; and to impose anything like an exclusive ex-Service preference must adversely affect the standard by seriously reducing the potential field of candidates. Nor does it stop at this. Once the Government is committed to such a preference, it ceases to be possible to pay as much regard to the suitability of the individual as is desirable in the national interest. This is what happened last time. The Public Service could not a second time afford the experience of the inter-war period without harm to the whole community.

But the Committee appreciated that many men and women had lost their opportunity since 1939 to enter the Civil Service because of the emergency and agreed that ex-service candidates must be treated generously. It recommended that a minimum of three-quarters of the vacancies in the administrative class should be reserved for ex-service men, two-thirds in the executive class, and one-half in the clerical class, and that 15 per cent of the posts should go to temporary staff; but it urged that at the same time open competition should be resumed for the filling of the remainder of the vacancies.

Special examinations—reconstruction examinations—were held to recruit from ex-service personnel. For the clerical class candidates were required to prove full-time education up to sixteen, and for the executive class up to seventeen, or to possess suitable educational qualifications otherwise. For the administrative class, only candidates with a good university degree, or able to satisfy the examiners that they would in normal circumstances have been likely to obtain First or Second Class Honours, could take part in the competitions.

The main reconstruction examinations were completed by 1949. The Civil Service Commission, however, has not reverted to the system, so long held out as an example to the world, of written examinations to recruit the major part of the staffs of the departments.

The first of the clerical grades, that of Clerical Assistant, has about 5,000–6,000 vacancies a year. It is mostly recruited from young people between the ages of fifteen and twenty by means of examinations designed to test common sense and accuracy; but some candidates are accepted on their educational record. Older men and women are also recruited to the Clerical Assistant Class, though not in such large numbers. The work of the class is described as "routine clerical duties, including the preparation, verification, and scrutiny of straightforward documents, statistics, records, etc.; simple arithmetical calculations; simpler forms of registry work; simple correspondence of stock letter and printed form types". Anyone who makes a routine inquiry of a Government department may receive a duplicate letter in which some additions or deletions have been made. Such stock letters are likely to have been dealt with by a Clerical Assistant who is handling the same kind of thing by the hundred.

The Clerical Class is recruited in a number of ways. The main part of the several thousand recruits needed each year comes from boys and girls between the ages of sixteen and twenty. Some of them are appointed on the results of their performance in the G.C.E., and some by means of written competitive examinations. In recent years older people have been able to compete for a proportion of the vacancies and a number of posts is reserved for those who have served in the Forces or in the British Overseas Civil Service.

Nearly a quarter of the non-industrial staff of the Civil Service (excluding the Post Office manipulative workers who are in separate categories) is employed in the clerical class. Clerical Officers do much the same kind of work as clerks elsewhere—they deal with the less complicated correspondence, draft letters for the higher staff, calculate salaries and wages, check accounts, and so on. They form a kind of utility class for the Service. Some of them spend a good deal of their time in chasing files around and in collecting information on which more senior staff take decisions.

The avenue of promotion for clerical officers is partly to higher clerical posts but also to the executive class, which has developed far more than any other in recent years. The executive grades perform duties described by the Civil Service Commissioners as follows:

> Members of the Executive classes do a wide variety of interesting work and there is ample scope for many kinds of ability and temperament. Within the limits of general government policy members of the class have to deal with the problems of people in all walks of life and with the affairs of all sorts of business and other concerns. Executive Officers can and should refer matters of special difficulty to their seniors, but their work is not routine and they have to use their discretion on matters calling for intelligence, judgement, and resource . . . Individual work includes such things as granting licences . . . awarding insurance benefits, assessing difficult taxation, checking purchase tax, handling confidential reports on staff, etc.; organizing and managing work includes the control of a Department's registry and filing section, or of a section compiling statistics . . . or of a small office, such as an Employment Exchange. . . .

Entrants to the class start in the basic grade of Executive Officer. About 300 posts are offered annually to boys and girls between the ages of $17\frac{1}{2}$ and $19\frac{1}{2}$. No written examination is held: instead, applicants are required to have five G.C.E., passes, which must include English language and two passes at "A" level gained on the same occasion (or Scottish or Northern Ireland equivalents). A selection board interviews the candidates with such qualifications and makes its choice of those regarded as most suitable for the vacancies.

Twice a year competitions are held with age limits $17\frac{1}{2}$ to $23\frac{1}{2}$ in which both school-leavers and graduates may compete for executive posts. Those with the necessary educational qualifications are seen by a selection board which assesses their suitability and awards about 200 posts at each competition.

The executive class is therefore recruited from a wide educational range, and it is the aim of the Civil Service to attract a larger proportion of university graduates to the Executive Class.

The graduate with First or Second Class Honours, however, who thinks of the Civil Service as a career hopes to enter the highest class —the Administrative Class. That class can absorb only a very few direct entrants—the average per annum has been about fifty in the Home Service and twenty-five in the Foreign Service (the Foreign Service is now amalgamated with the Commonwealth Service and the Trade Commissioners Service in the new Diplomatic Service which came into operation on 1 January, 1965).

The Commissioners insist on a very high standard for candidates to the Administrative Class. The Civil Service is sometimes described as consisting of "thinkers" and "doers", with the administrative groups as the planners and the remainder as the doers. Under Ministers, the administrative staff is responsible for the policy-making within the Government departments, and so far as Civil Servants wield power it is in the hands of this class.

Recruitment to the administrative class of men and women of high intellectual calibre has always been of importance. The duties of the administrators in the Home Service are described as follows:

> The members of the Administrative Class advise Ministers on the formation of policy and the preparation of legislation to give effect to it, and under their instructions are responsible for the general directions to ensure that Government decisions are put into effect. They are the chief source of advice to Ministers on current Government business and assist them in their Parliamentary duties by preparing answers to their letters and to Questions asked in Parliament, as well as providing material for use in Parliamentary debates.
>
> They are responsible for the broad organization and direction of the business of Government and for managing the work of Departments. They are concerned, for example, with administering departmentally the various Acts of Parliament in so far as policy decisions are required from time to time on the working of these Acts.
>
> Members of the Administrative Class represent the Minister of their Department in negotiation with other Governments, other Departments, outside interests, and members of the public.

The old system of selecting men wholly on the basis of written examinations has been entirely abandoned. During the past sixteen years entry to the basic grade of the Administrative Class—the assistant principal grade—has been by means of what are known as Method I and Method II.

Candidates under Method I take an examination which consists of an essay, an English paper, and a general paper. Those who succeed in this qualifying test are interviewed by a board which may award up to 300 marks. The candidates compete in a written examination in optional subjects chosen from a comprehensive list of the main honours courses at universities. The maximum mark in this examination is 700, and the order of merit depends on the number of marks awarded at the interview plus the number gained in the optional subjects.

Method II is reserved for candidates who have gained First or Second Class Honours in the year in which they come forward (or expect to win them). Such candidates sit for a preliminary examination of the same kind as that undertaken by Method I aspirants, but from that point onwards there is a vast difference in the procedure.

The candidates under Method II who have passed the qualifying examination are tested by a team of two or three assessors, one of whom may be a psychologist. These tests were at first undertaken in a house in the country during a week-end, and the names "house party" or "week-end" are still used though the tests are now held in London over two or two and a half weekdays.

The assessors who deal with Method II candidates have before them the educational record of each man and woman as well as reports from personal and professional referees. The tests fall into three broad categories.

The applicants are presented with a set of papers describing an administrative "case" which, although imaginary, has a substantial basis in fact. After studying the papers, the candidates are asked to write an answer to a question of principle or policy. The next stage is for the group to form itself into a committee and consider a number of aspects of the central theme. Each candidate serves in turn as the chairman or as an ordinary member of the committee. When acting as chairman he is allotted a problem to expound and the assessors watch how a man or woman succeeds in guiding the committee.

The exercise is intended, among other things, to provide evidence not only of intellectual quality but of practical ability and judgement, and to demonstrate the effectiveness of candidates in taking the lead in a company of equals and exercising control over the course of the deliberations. The assessors observe how a candidate conducts himself in discussion under the chairmanship of others.

Candidates are also examined to find out whether they possess facility in handling words and their breadth of interest in general affairs is probed, and each applicant must show that he is at least competent in straightforward arithmetic.

Once through these phases, the candidate is interviewed by the assessors individually. One assessor is concerned with the quality of the candidate's mind; a second pays special attention to how a man or woman has passed his or her time since leaving school or university and why he or she has sought a post in the public service. If there is a psychologist among the assessors he deals with temperament and personality.

Some people inevitably flop in the early stages and the assessors may recommend that such entrants should not waste time by going farther. The remainder of the candidates have a session before a Final Selection Board which makes the final decision whether a man or woman should be accepted or rejected.

When the Government decided that as an experiment Methods I and II should be adopted exclusively for direct recruitment to the basic grade of the administrative class, there was a good deal of criticism of a system which relies so largely on the personal opinion of the selectors. It was pointed out that no place existed for the outstanding man who could pass examinations brilliantly but might do so badly at an interview that he was failed. The Civil Service, it was argued, had in the past put its faith in competitive scholastic examinations, and by so doing had built up an outstanding organization.

Most people, however, were prepared to agree that Method I had great advantages. After all, clever men who wanted to secure posts in the top grade ought to be able to score at least a sufficiency of marks before a selection board to succeed if their examination results were high.

Method II was much more severely criticized. Here everything depends on the views of advisors and selectors. Method II, it was claimed, might lead to the choice of applicants who conformed to a familiar pattern and looked as if they would snuggle comfortably into the framework of Whitehall and not cause trouble by showing any originality of mind. The fear was expressed that there would be a tendency to favour the man who came from the right college, had influential referees to support his application, and whose face happened to fit.

In view of these forebodings, much interest was taken in the report by the Civil Service Commissioners on the experience gained by the two methods between 1948 and 1956 (Cmnd. 232). About one in ten of the applicants who entered for Method I during the period was declared successful, and about one in fifteen by Method II. Of the 300 candidates chosen by Method I, about two-thirds had served for two years or more in a Government department. Of this 200, twenty-three had to be given a further trial before the Civil Service felt justified in agreeing to their establishment, and five had their appointments terminated.

Of slightly more than 100 assistant principals who had been recruited by Method II and had completed at least two years in a department, only five required an extended trial before being passed as suitable for permanent employment, and not a single one had his or her appointment terminated.

In the light of this report, the Government decided that Methods I and II should continue to be the sole means of recruitment of direct entrants as assistant principals. We have not, however, necessarily reached the end of the experiments on the best way to find the men and women who will subsequently occupy the chief posts in the public service.

Chapter Five

DEPARTMENTAL ORGANIZATION

THE principal Minister of a department may be a Secretary of State (as in the Ministry of Economic Affairs, the Home Office, the Foreign Office, the Scottish Office, or the Ministry of Defence), or he may have a distinctive title (such as Chancellor of the Exchequer or Lord President of the Council).

Most major departments have in addition one or more Ministers of State, who rank in authority next to the political head, and all departments have at least one Parliamentary Secretary. Ministers of State usually supervise a section of the departmental work and some Parliamentary Secretaries also interest themselves keenly in official affairs, while others confine themselves almost entirely to Parliamentary duties proper. Every senior Minister has a Parliamentary Private Secretary. The P.P.S. is unpaid and his duties do not extend to the work of any Whitehall office but are restricted to Westminster.

The nomenclature is not without its difficulties. A Secretary of State ranks higher in the hierarchy than a Minister of State; Parliamentary Secretaries also hold office in the Government and will be expected to speak in one House or the other on behalf of his department. The Parliamentary Private Secretary, however, is not included in the administration and never speaks in Parliament or elsewhere as a representative of the Government.

Where the Minister is a Secretary of State the Civil Service head of an office is an Under-Secretary; in other departments he is usually known as the Permanent Secretary. It is rather confusing that the Deputy Under-Secretary in the Foreign Office should be higher in rank than the Under-Secretaries of those departments where the Minister is not a Secretary of State. Similarly, the Under-Secretary of, for example, the Home Office is the permanent head of his department, whereas in most departments Under-Secretaries are much less lofty beings. While departments differ in the titles they confer on the most senior officers, however, the same salaries are paid to the chief permanent official. For convenience, the organization of a department where the Minister is not a Secretary of State is followed in this chapter.

The Permanent Secretary is the principal Civil Service adviser to his Minister, and through his hands will pass nearly all the work of the office which is submitted to the political head. In a major department the Permanent Secretary has under him one or two Deputy Secretaries with responsibility for certain parts of the work of the office; they are likely to deal direct with the Minister on such work, consulting the Permanent Secretary only at their discretion. Below Deputy Secretaries in the hierarchy are the Under-Secretaries, each in charge of a number of divisions of the department. While the higher ranks of the administrative class have different titles in the offices headed by Secretaries of State, the ranks of Assistant Secretaries and downwards in the administrative class are the same in practically all departments. A division under an Assistant Secretary may consist of three or four sections, each controlled by a Principal. He submits the more important work for the decision of his Assistant Secretary, from whom it will in turn be passed to an Under-Secretary, if it is of sufficient consequence. Most Assistant Principals are young men and women who have been recruited by examination to the Civil Service administrative class and who are undergoing training. They give general help to the Principal to whom they are attached and learn the mysteries of Civil Service procedure. Such is the normal pattern of the managerial or controlling staff of a Government department, but it is not invariable. Although division, branch, and section have been used in this description, some offices are divided into sub-departments while others prefer to make the branch the larger unit and the division the smaller one. There is no consistency in such things.

The other main clerical classes of the Service—the executive, clerical, and clerical assistant classes—work under the administrators. A Principal in charge of a section may have two or three Senior Executive Officers whose work he supervises, and each of the senior executives will probably have under him a number of higher and junior executive officers. The section may also comprise clerical officers, or it may be that the whole of the section will be staffed by members of the clerical class and that no executives will be employed in it. The grading is the subject of constant debate within the departments. The clerical class representatives have claimed in the past that there is no real need for an executive class, since the clerical grades could undertake all duties except those of the administrative class; the executive class representatives for their part have proposed that the scope of the executives should be further widened; and spokesmen for the administrative class have emphasized the necessity for the most important functions to continue to be confined to their members. Some departments employ clerical staff on duties which other offices would grade as executive, and administrative staff in a number of departments probably perform duties which are elsewhere considered to be appropriate to the class below. The lines of demarcation tend to become blurred.

A plan of the organization is usually widely distributed within a department so that the staff may be aware of the way in which the work of the office is planned. As no two departments are organized alike and as some are very different indeed from others, it may be more useful to draw up a section of the plan of an imaginary department rather than show the organization of an actual department. A schematic plan is reproduced in Appendix II which shows how the chain of command might run in a mythical Ministry of Films. The plan is provided only to indicate some features which are common to most departments and to facilitate reference to Civil Service practice described in later chapters of this book.

The Ministry of Films might have been created as a result of a decision that, in places badly served by cinemas, the State should construct or acquire cinemas and operate them directly or through agents. Other functions, some of which are at present performed by existing Government departments, are assumed to have been brought within the scope of the imaginary new office, and its duties are taken to be: To exercise a general supervision over film production; to produce theatrical films of a kind not ordinarily available from commercial sources or not available in sufficient numbers; to conduct negotiations with other governments on matters relating to films; to commission and produce non-theatrical films; to co-ordinate facilities required by commercial companies from Government departments for the production of films; and so on.

It will be seen from Appendix II that the Minister of Films has the assistance of a Parliamentary Secretary, as is the usual practice. These two Ministers look primarily to the Permanent Secretary and Deputy Secretary for advice, though the three Under-Secretaries will be called in from time to time to the Minister's office to give their views on matters with which they are directly concerned and will associate their Assistant Secretaries in the discussions as required. The Chief Producer, shown as ranking with the Under-Secretaries, will also be consulted by both Ministers and will take with him to such meetings his Producers, who are equal to Assistant Secretaries in rank. The Legal Adviser, the equivalent of an Under-Secretary, will be brought into questions where there is a legal aspect and will watch all legislation in order to protect the interests of the department.

One Under-Secretary is shown as in charge of expenditure and staffing; the Finance and Accounts Branch is in the charge of an Assistant Secretary, under whom is a Chief Executive Officer with a staff of Senior, Higher, and Junior Executive Officers, concerned with financial control, contracts, statistics, etc. The Accounts Branch also is controlled by a Chief Executive Officer; he is responsible for payments and receipts, and working under him are accountants and assistant accountants. The Assistant Secretary for Establishments and Organization has three Principals, one for staff above the level of Senior Executive Officer, one for other staff, and a third for general matters, including Organization and Methods work. The staff of the Principals consists of clerical and executive officers, some of whom will have been trained in parliamentary procedure. The work of the Under-Secretary in charge of finance and establishments in this Ministry goes direct to the Permanent Secretary, not to the Deputy Secretary.

The second Under-Secretary is responsible for administration in relation to film production, and his Assistant Secretaries divide this work between them, though each will know a good deal of the work of the others, since there cannot be watertight compartments in activities of this kind. The staff will keep in touch with commercial producers, conduct negotiations with other countries regarding the import and export of films, and ensure that supplies of raw film stock, cameras, lighting equipment and so on are made available if the film trade has difficulty in obtaining them.

The third Under-Secretary is in charge of distribution and exhibition. His immediate staff is composed of specialists, the equivalent of Principal Executive Officers, who are in charge of areas—Southern England, Northern England, Scotland, and Wales. They are expert in both theatrical and non-theatrical films, but some will have more experience in one branch than in the other and their knowledge will be pooled. The staff of the sections is mainly technical, including some clerical officers but no executive officers. The Chief Producer and the Producers are men with practical knowledge, and under them will be assistant producers, assistant directors, and technicians, such as script writers, cameramen, film editors, negative and positive cutters, make-up men, continuity girls, and so on. The film directors and assistant film directors will probably be employed on contract for each piece of work and not be permanent members of the staff.

Since the Ministry has to do a great deal of checking of film bookings and film takings, it employs a large number of clerical assistants. Next in number will come the clerical officers. They are the hewers of wood and drawers of water, and few letters will reach a Government department which men and women of this grade do not handle at some stage or another. The department will have a pool of typists and shorthand typists under the control of a supervisor, who will see that the junior officials have typing service as required. In some departments only officials of Under-Secretary rank and upwards have a personal secretary; in others the barrier is somewhat lower. A good deal of the work of Civil Servants is hand-written; some of it consists of short minutes which it is probably as quick to write as to type and, even where a long minute is called for, many Civil Servants still prefer to draft it in their own handwriting and send it to a typist rather than dictate.

The number of Principal Executive Officers and above in a department does not necessarily give any clue to the total complement of an office, since the nature of the work governs the grading. The subordinate staff of the Treasury, for instance, represents a much smaller proportion of the whole than the subordinate staff of, say, the Ministry of Pensions and National Insurance, where there are large blocks of mechanical and routine work which can be left to minor grades. But the mythical Ministry of Films has been assumed, for the purpose of this exercise, to have a staff of just over 500 non-industrial Civil Servants.

An office of this size would not rate a Permanent Secretary and a Deputy Secretary were it not for the succession of high level negotiations with foreign governments. Where films are concerned, there is likely to be a good deal of talk about presenting the national image and not relying too much on importing productions from overseas.

A list of the Government departments which employed 1,000 or more on 1 April, 1964, is shown in Appendix III which, for purposes of comparison, also includes the figures for 1961. Twenty-seven departments have a staff more than 2,000, thirteen exceed 10,000, and seven employ over 25,000 officials. The Ministry of Defence has a complement of over 100,000, and is by far the largest of the departments. The importance of an office is not to be measured only by size. The Treasury employs fewer than 1,500 people.

The average cost per head of the non-industrial staff is about £1,000 per annum, and the total expenditure on salaries exceeds £660,000,000 a year. There is hardly ever a time when the number of Civil Servants and the cost of the departments is not attacked in Parliament and the newspapers.

In 1848 Parliament was demanding that the complements should be cut back to the 1797 level, but, though some reductions took place, the movement was towards an expansion of the Service. In the latter half of the century the number of officials grew steadily as the result of the responsibilities undertaken by the State for health, agriculture, and education. Further social measures prior to the First World War led to large additions, and the 1914–18 war meant great expansion in most offices. A period of contraction after the war was followed by increases consequent upon the extension of social schemes of improvement, and by 1926 the Civil Service non-industrial staff almost reached 300,000. In the next ten years the Service did not show much change in numbers, and on 1 April, 1935, the staff of 304,000 represented an increase of about 1,000 a year on average since 1926. From 1936 the increase was considerable each year until the outbreak of the Second World War:

1936 : 317,206	1938 : 362,644
1937 : 337,707	1939 : 387,377

During the hostilities, as was to be expected, the numbers advanced sharply:

1940 : 454,745	1943 : 710,636
1941 : 554,427	1944 : 704,395
1942 : 657,331	1945 : 704,646

Departments contract slowly after a war, for the clearing-up process cannot be done quickly without a risk of making bad bargains for the State. The reductions are never made as speedily as expected, nor are they of the extent that the public thinks should be possible. This is the experience in every country. During wartime the Government starts up services which, for one reason or another, it is decided must be maintained in peace. The welfare State requires huge staffs of officials.

Since 1945 the fluctuation in non-industrial complements has been as follows:

1946 : 684,500	1961 : 641,900
1949 : 706,200	1962 : 663,900
1954 : 654,800	1963 : 677,800
1958 : 637,200	1964 : 692,158

The break-up of the 1964 figures by grades shows:

Administrative (Home)	2,632
Administrative (Foreign)	776
Executive	75,835
Clerical	130,395
Clerical assistants, etc.	70,879
Typing	27,385
Inspectorate	2,770
Messengers, porters, etc.	33,902
Post Office manipulative	216,193
Professional, scientific and technical (with ancillary staff)	129,709

Of the latest number about a third (233,870) are women. In the latter part of the nineteenth century, when women had fewer opportunities to obtain acceptable employment, Government departments were inundated with applications for posts, but except in the Post Office women were not accepted for clerical work in large numbers. The use of typewriters throughout all Government offices, despite the die-hards who preferred hand-written letters and copying presses, brought an increase in the number of women employees, but in 1914 only about 7,000 women were employed in departments other than the Post Office. During the First World War women had necessarily to be entrusted with clerking work because of the shortage of male workers and the increased volume of business, and by the end of the hostilities some women had shown that they could successfully hold positions in the middle ranges, and a few had climbed to high rank. In 1919 the number of women in the departments had jumped to 170,000. Many of them had no wish to remain in employment, either with the State or any other employer, but of those who wished to continue in Government service comparatively few received appointment except in the subordinate grades. Even there the number of posts open to women was severely limited in consequence of the pressure to find situations for ex-service men. The only posts on which women could depend were those in the typing grades.

The Reorganization Committee of 1920 favoured wider opportunities for women, and ten years after the issue of its report women numbered 76,930 out of a total staff of 306,154, and were to be found in most grades. Direct entry to the administrative class examinations was, however, denied to them until 1931, when the Tomlin Commission recommended that women should be permitted to compete with men for practically all posts on equal terms. Since that time no bar has been placed in the way of the employment of women in any part of the Service, except where the work is obviously inappropriate (such as the outdoor posts in the Customs and Excise, positions in overseas territories under the Colonial Office, and some parts of the Defence Department). Women are now paid on the same salary scales as men.

In the highest class—the administrative—women are poorly represented, with about 200 out of some 2,600 in the Home Service and about one out of forty in the Diplomatic Service. The proportions increase in the executives, where a sixth of the staff are women. In the clerical class women number just under half. Relatively few women are included among the professional, scientific, and technical staffs, even in the lower grades.

The reformers of the nineteenth century pressed for the employment of a small body of well-educated men of high intellectual calibre, and when the Service was reorganized other staff were entrusted only with very minor work. For a very long time the higher grades had in their own hands all the duties which called for the exercise of judgement, even in a limited degree. A department consisted of administrative officers with clerks (intermediate class clerks, second division clerks, and assistant clerks). The lower clerks did little more than find the files, put them in good order and, after the administrative officer had made his decision, record what had been done; and even the superior grades of clerks had very little authority and could not conduct correspondence on their own responsibility unless on relatively routine matters.

Such a position could not be maintained as the volume of business increased, and new arrangements had to be made for the handling of official work. If the administrative class had continued to undertake practically the whole of the responsible duties within the department, the expansion of that class would have had to be very considerable and, as it is much more highly paid than the other classes, the wages bill of the Civil Service would have reached even more gigantic figures. The subordinate groups pressed for more scope, partly because people do not like to be kept on duties much below their capacity, but principally in order to substantiate claims for increased remuneration.

The present arrangement, whereby the staff is grouped into four main classes recruited at ages to fit in with the educational system of the country, proved capable of considerable adaptation to meet the needs of the last war and its aftermath; but there have been many suggestions that the system has outlived its usefulness and that a new approach is needed. The Priestley Commission was unfortunately not asked to consider the structure of the Service.

The parliamentary business of a public office remains largely in the hands of the administrative class, which is also responsible for taking most of the major decisions, under Ministers, and for general managerial functions. The executive class, however, now undertakes many duties which would previously have been considered clearly the work of administrators. In the first half of the nineteenth century, Ministers could deal personally with nearly all the work of their departments, and even in the later years of the century an energetic Minister could read most of the important papers. By the close of the century the higher, or administrative, division had, however, begun to decide many matters which had hitherto been left to Ministers. The increase in the volume of business made it essential that responsibility should be delegated more and more. Especially since the last war, the trend has been to allocate to the executive class much work of a high quality which the administrative class would at one time have claimed as its own.

The administrative class, which consisted of 4,402 in 1948, had fallen to about half the number ten years later. In the past five years, however, the administrative class has expanded, and in 1964 was 3,400.

The executive class, around 50,000 in 1948, had increased by nearly half in 1964, but the clerical class has fallen from 166,000 to 130,000, and the clerical assistants from 95,000 to 70,000. The administrative class is about 0.5 per cent of the total non-industrial establishment, which is roughly the same proportion as before the last war. The emphasis seems likely to be on the development of the executives so far as the general classes are concerned, with a select cadre of administrators at the top engaged in departmental policy work and the higher direction. Many more specialists are now being employed in scientific and technical grades.

Chapter Six

DELEGATED LEGISLATION

DECENTRALIZATION has already taken place to such an extent that in 1964 only about a quarter of the non-industrial staff was stationed in and around London, and further transfers of headquarters staffs are envisaged in the next few years. The Civil Servants working in the regions may be looked on as unduly inquisitive, a bit obstructive, rather stuffy, and not very bright, but for the most part the public regards them tolerantly, with pity rather than anger. The real fury is reserved for "the gentlemen in Whitehall", who are sometimes scorned as scandalously backward and dilatory, sometimes condemned as altogether too smart and efficient, and nearly always denounced as meddlesome, power-hungry, and arrogant.

Some thirty years ago Lord Hewart, the then Lord Chief Justice, made a swashbuckling attack on legislation which vested authority in departmental Ministers and placed their actions beyond the jurisdiction of the ordinary courts of the land. His book, *The New Despotism*, and others published about the same time created a great deal of alarm among the public, who protested that their hard-won liberties were being filched by ruthless and ambitious officials. Many critics joined in the hunt and delighted to refer to "Government by officialdom" and "the twilight of Parliament", and to suggest that the Legislature had become no more than a rubber stamp for the departments and that Ministers were dominated by their Civil Service staffs.

In 1929 the Government appointed a Committee on Ministers' Powers "to consider the powers exercised by or under the direction of the Crown by way of (*a*) delegated legislation and (*b*) judicial or quasi-judicial decision, and to report what safeguards are desirable or necessary to secure the constitutional principles of the sovereignty of Parliament and the Supremacy of the Law". In its report, issued in 1932, the Committee remarked: "Parliament is supreme and its power to legislate is therefore unlimited. It can do the greatest things; it can do the smallest. It can make general laws for a vast empire; it can make a particular exception out of them in favour of a particular individual. It can provide—and has in fact provided— for the payment of old age pensions to all who fulfil the statutory conditions; it can provide—and has in fact provided—for boiling the

Bishop of Rochester's cook to death."[1] Parliament can delegate to others the right to make regulations, rules, and orders, and has conferred such powers on Ministers under an increasingly large number of Acts of Parliament during this century, and especially since the end of the First World War. Such Instruments have the force of law. They may be quite trifling or they may most seriously affect the interests of large numbers of people; there may be no redress—if a legal point arises, the right of appeal to a court may be denied or reference to the courts may be permitted only within a specified period of time.

The Committee on Ministers' Powers received much evidence against the system of delegated legislation, but it reported that such delegation "is both legitimate and constitutionally desirable for certain purposes, within certain limits, and under certain safeguards".

Delegated legislation has grown enormously since that report appeared. No one really believes that such legislation could ever be abandoned, or that Parliament could so organize its business as to pass the enactments which would be necessary if Ministers lacked the authority to draft Statutory Instruments. Neither Ministers nor members nor officials are prophets who can foresee the future, and some amendments to most statutes are inescapable. Only when experience of a scheme has been gained are the snags revealed, and even when an Act has been current for several years a change in the regulations may prove to be necessary for the sake of clarity and fair dealing.

Statutory Instruments made under delegated powers must be laid before one or both Houses of Parliament, but there is no consistency in the arrangements. A Minister having drafted or made an Instrument under one statute may be required to lay it before Parliament and, if no Member objects, nothing more need be done; but an Instrument made under another statute may have to be the subject of an affirmative resolution before it can be brought into operation. Some Statutory Instruments must be laid before both Houses, while other Acts are complied with if the Instrument is presented to the Commons only. A Minister may have the right under one statute to bring an order into force at once and obtain authority, express or implied, from Parliament later, while the same Minister may under

---

[1] The Committee explains the reference in a footnote as follows: "It is ordained and enacted by authority of this Present Parliament that the said Richard Rose shall be therefore boiled to death without having any advantage of his clergy. 22 Hen. 8, c. 9."

another statute be required to wait for a period before an order equally or more urgent can become effective.

Although rules and regulations and orders were submitted in increasing numbers year by year, Parliament had no suitable machinery for examining them until 1944, and it was left to individual members to keep an eye on the mass of documents which flowed in from the departments. The Committee then set up has been appointed by the Commons each session since that time.

The Statutory Instruments Committee meets frequently, usually each week during the parliamentary session. Departments which submit an Instrument on which there is any doubt may be called on for an explanation, and any Instrument may be the subject of a report to the Commons if it comes within the scope of the very wide terms of reference. The Committee referred to the inconsistency in connection with the laying of rules and regulations. "Your Committee," the report reads, "have been impressed by the apparently illogical diversity of the periods during which action is to be taken in respect of regulations, rules or orders laid before the House. They have noticed that the various periods include 20, 21, 28, 30 and 40 sitting days, 40 days excluding prorogation or adjournment over 4 days, and one month with no requirement that any part of it shall be at a time when Parliament is sitting." Such inconsistencies still survive.

Nor has this been the only complaint. In more than one session the Committee has pointed out that a Statutory Instrument ought to specify the precise authority under which it is made. "They are not in a position to report to the House upon an unusual or unexpected use of statutory power," the Committee commented tartly, "unless they can identify the power which purports to have been received." Judging by the strong pressure for the setting up of such a Committee, it might have been expected that lots of iniquities on the part of the departments would be exposed. It may be the knowledge that the Instruments are subject to scrutiny which has made the departments circumspect, or it may be that they were never so irresponsible as some people affected to believe. Whatever the reason, the Committee has not found it necessary to make many criticisms to Parliament in recent years on individual Instruments. In the 1962–3 session, the Committee referred only five such Instruments to the House of Commons.

Many of the 2,000 or more Statutory Instruments issued in the course of a single year are of quite a routine character. A handful taken at random from the number issued in a month in 1964 included the following:

Housing (Management of Houses and Buildings in Multiple Occupation) (Scotland) Regulations
Seed Potatoes (Retail Sales)
Building Societies (Designation for Trustee Investment) Regulations
Training of Teachers (Grant) Amending Regulations
Scarborough Water Order
Hydrocarbon Oils (Restrictions on Mixing) Regulations
Composite Goods Order
Import Duties (Temporary Exemptions) No. 7 Order
Wages Regulation (Made-up Textiles) Order
Wages Regulation (Retail, Newsagency, Tobacco and Confectionery) (England and Wales) Order

A large number every year consists of orders for the closing of highways in various parts of the country, either permanently or temporarily. Another group relates to variations in wages as a result of the decisions of boards of different kinds.

The majority of the orders are quite short, often no more than a single page. Where a Statutory Instrument is lengthy and intricate, it is usual to provide an explanatory note explaining in simple language the scope of the order or regulation.

Such explanations are useful, for the wording of the Instruments is not always easy to follow at first glance. For example, a recent Statutory Instrument reads: "In this Order the expression 'the specified date' means the 4th September, 1964, provided that where, as respects any worker who is paid wages at intervals not exceeding seven days, that date does not correspond with the beginning of the period for which wages are paid, 'the specified date' means, as regards the worker, the beginning of the next such period following the date." Another in the same batch is careful to explain that "Flat means a separate set of premises, whether or not on the same floor, constructed for use for the purposes of a dwelling, or forming part of a building from some other part of which it is divided horizontally."

Few people ever need to look through the mass of Statutory Instruments, but all the regulations are diligently studied by experts, and any mistake is soon spotted and will be widely publicized in trade journals. An ambiguous description may lead to troublesome and expensive litigation, and the officials who write the regulations therefore try to cover any possible misunderstanding of their intentions: " 'dispose of' and 'obtain' respectively include offer or agree to dispose of or obtain", spells out one Statutory Instrument so that there will be no doubt whatsoever; another lays it down that "It shall be deemed to be night when, between the hours of sunset and sunrise, any unlighted aircraft or other unlighted prominent object cannot be clearly seen at a distance of at least 5,000 yards." Meticulous definitions often form the longest part of a Statutory Instrument. It is apocryphal, however, that a draftsman who provided in a Statutory Instrument for "pedestrian, horseman, pedal cyclist, motor cyclist, motorist" found that a householder who took his dog for a walk was ruled to be none of those but "a man in charge of an animal".

The power to make rules and orders and regulations need not always be exercised by Ministers in person; Under-Secretaries and above in the official hierarchy, or even Assistant Secretaries, may make regulations on behalf of the Minister under some statutes. Whether or not the Minister actually signs the Statutory Instrument, the officials of his department prepare it. Generally, officials represent to their chiefs the need for obtaining authority by means of rules and regulations. It is a common belief that Civil Servants want too much and that Ministers give way to their demands for arbitrary power much too readily, but in fact no Statutory Instrument ever slips through without close scrutiny in Parliament and out.

Even when an order does not require an affirmative resolution of one or both Houses, it must go to the Select Committee on Statutory Instruments. There is the tendency now to insert in new Bills the condition that orders shall not be made without the prior approval of the Lords and Commons. The relative clause included in a statute may be in some such terms as the following: "The power to make orders under this section shall be exercisable by statutory instrument, and before making any such order the (Minister) shall lay a draft thereof before each House of Parliament, and shall not make the order until a resolution has been passed by each House of Parliament approving the draft." This may seem an adequate safeguard against any hasty or ill-considered action on the part of a department, since under such legislation members of the two Houses have the opportunity to consider what is suggested and no order is valid until an affirmative resolution is presented to the Lords and the Commons.

Some Statutory Instruments must be submitted to an independent body before they are laid before Parliament. The Minister of Pensions and National Insurance, for example, must present certain types of regulations in the first place to the National Insurance Advisory Committee. This is a desirable precaution in respect of a department whose services affect every person in the country, since all are now insurable; but there must be a limit to the number of bodies which in effect supervise the work of Government departments prior to the submission of Statutory Instruments to a Committee of the Commons and subsequently to one or both Houses of Parliament.

The powers given to Ministers by way of delegated legislation are immense. Some Acts clothe a Minister with immunity in almost any circumstances. He may set up tribunals under statute whose decisions are not subject to any court, and he may himself be a court of appeal against the decision of others.

Where disputes are not subject to the normal legal process the statute may lay down the method of settlement or may give some freedom to a department to make its own arrangements, along lines approved by Parliament. Some of the arrangements are quite elaborate.

If provision is made for appeals to be lodged against an official decision, experience proves that it will be widely used, at least in the early stages. A minor example is the number of appeals in respect of family allowances. This is the chain: first, the insurance officer gives his ruling, and, if the applicant is dissatisfied, there is the right of appeal to a local tribunal which considers all the evidence again; if the matter is still contested, the applicant can put his grievance to the National Insurance Commissioner. Ten years ago the appeals numbered some 7,000 per annum. As decisions were handed down on different kinds of cases, however, a series of interpretations was built up and formed a code so that the volume of appeals dwindled. In 1960 the number had been reduced to around 1,800, and in 1963 was only slightly over 1,200. Further reductions are likely to be made as time goes on, but the appeal machinery must remain in existence. No one can foretell what new set of circumstances may be pleaded by some ingenious and aggrieved person who feels she has been unjustly denied a family allowance.

Not all official decisions are subject to appeal. Many statutes leave the absolute right of decision to a Minister who may be entitled to give his ruling without hearing the parties to a dispute. If a Minister is required to hold an inquiry he may be authorized to appoint one of his own staff to undertake the work rather than an independent arbitrator.

The question of the authority vested in Ministers has been the subject of controversy for many years. The Government set up a Committee on Ministers' Powers, under the chairmanship of Lord

Donoughmore, to examine whether the system required revision. In a long and interesting report made in 1932, the Donoughmore Committee said: "It is unfair to impose on a practical administrator the duty of adjudicating in any matter in which it could fairly be argued that his impartiality would be inverse ratio to his strength and ability as a Minister. An easy-going and cynical Minister, rather bored with his office and sceptical of the value of his Department, would find it far easier to apply a judicial mind to purely judicial problems connected with the Department's administration than a Minister whose heart and head were in his work."

Several countries, of which France is the best-known example, have in operation a system of administrative courts. Such courts, presided over by judges specially trained for the duty, listen to appeals against departmental decrees and decisions and have earned a high reputation for the fairness with which they decide on the issues submitted to them. The Donoughmore Committee looked at the French procedure and agreed that "it does give protection to the French subject against arbitrary acts of the public service". The Committee, however, did not favour the setting up of similar machinery in this country, but it suggested, among other things, that when a Minister ordered an inquiry, the report of his inspector should be published, unless in exceptional circumstances. This proposal by the Committee in 1932 was largely ignored.

At the time the Donoughmore Committee was appointed, the number of tribunals and inquiries was relatively small in Britain. Not only did Ministerial inquiries increase but permanent tribunals charged with the responsibility of adjudicating on some particular group of activities grew very rapidly after the end of the last war, and demands were frequently made that the whole system should be reappraised.

The state of the law made it difficult for anyone to institute legal action against a Government department. So much criticism was made about this situation that in 1947 the Crown Proceedings Act was passed to make it possible for the Crown to be sued in tort. Even so, however, departments were still able to avoid claims for damages in the courts unless an action was brought within one year. This protection was removed by a further Act seven years later—the Law Reform (Limitation of Actions, etc.) Act, 1954. Slowly, therefore, the departments were becoming less invulnerable in some things; but other demands for reform were steadfastly resisted.

Tribunals had been appointed to deal with a vast range of subjects

—valuations, national assistance, the health service, town planning, transport, schools, and so on. Some of the tribunals were admitted to be highly efficient, but others were thought to be lacking in fairness in their approach to the problems submitted to them and inconsiderate in their treatment of applicants. The clamour grew that the whole system should be subjected to another close examination so that acceptable standards could be established and that some measure of control should be regularly exercised to ensure that undesirable practices did not creep in.

Most tribunals are composed of members nominated by a Minister, sometimes after consultation with representative bodies (such as the universities, the medical profession, or the trades unions). The members are generally professional men who give part-time services.

Although the proceedings of such tribunals were sometimes the subject of adverse comment, the special inquiries conducted by Civil Servants were much more severely assailed. People felt that officials might be tempted to reach a conclusion known to be acceptable to Whitehall, whatever the weight of the evidence.

So much protest was made that in 1955 the Government agreed to set up a committee to consider the problem—the Committee on Administrative Tribunals and Enquiries, under the chairmanship of Sir Oliver Franks. The Committee reported in 1957 (Cmnd. 218). Any idea that it would suggest sweeping away the system was exploded, for the Committee stated: "We regard both tribunals and administrative procedure as essential to our society." The Committee, however, had several important safeguards to suggest.

It felt that, instead of employing inspectors appointed by individual Ministers to conduct special inquiries, the Government should authorize the Lord Chancellor to form a body of inspectors and that this inspectorate should be employed full-time and come under his control.

The Government did not accept this recommendation. Its adoption would, it was thought, interfere with ministerial responsibilities which ought not to be surrendered, and the Government also saw an advantage in maintaining inspectors attached to different departments who acquired expert knowledge and were acquainted with policy.

The Franks Committee, having examined the work of a large number of tribunals, considered that the tribunals on the whole worked reasonably well but could be improved in certain respects. It recommended that a Council on Tribunals for England and Wales and another for Scotland should be appointed with the duty of advising "on the detailed application to the various tribunals of general principles of constitution, organization and procedure" along certain lines which the Committee enunciated. The new Councils should also keep a watchful eye on the work of the inspectors who conducted special inquiries. The Committee also felt that, where an official inspector made a report after holding a public inquiry, the Minister should publish the contents when the final decision was reached. The Government reacted favourably to this recommendation and it has become the rule that reports are published.

In 1958 a Bill was introduced in Parliament to provide for the adoption of a number of proposals made by the Franks Committee and this measure was passed as the Tribunals and Inquiries Act. Under the provisions of the Act, a Council has been appointed to maintain observation on the work of the tribunals, and it has already made some pungent strictures on certain aspects of procedure. The members of the Council are appointed by the Lord Chancellor and the Secretary of State for Scotland.

A step forward had therefore been made in relation to tribunals and special inquiries held in public, but there still remained the question of administrative decisions taken within the departments—decisions against which there was no provision for appeal. It was claimed that no one really knew what was happening behind the walls of the Whitehall offices and that gross injustice might be done without the citizen having any remedy. These criticisms had grown in volume especially after the notorious Crichel Down affair, where it appeared that a decision was based on an inadequate or misguided summary of the facts. The disclosures in the Crichel Down Report,[1] published in June 1954, of the treatment of a departmental case caused consternation. They gave support to some of the most devastating criticisms which have been made in the past of the work of the Civil Service.

In November 1953 the then Minister of Agriculture and Fisheries, Sir Thomas Dugdale, appointed Sir Andrew Clark, Q.C., to "enquire into the procedure adopted (a) in reaching the decision that land at Crichel Down should be sold to the Commissioners of Crown Lands; (b) in the selection of a tenant by them; and the circumstances in which those decisions were made".

Sir Andrew Clark reported that the Air Ministry compulsorily acquired some 725 acres of land at Crichel Down from a number of owners about 1937. In 1949 it decided to transfer the land to the Ministry of Agriculture under the Agriculture Act, 1947, and the

[1] Cmd. 9176.

Ministry handed over the land to the Agricultural Land Commission. This Commission was advised by the Lands Service, a branch of the Ministry, and executive functions were for all practical purposes carried out by the Dorset Agricultural Executive Committee. In 1950 the Ministry formed the view that the land should be equipped and let as a single unit, the cost of equipment being estimated at that time at about £20,000. Various people, including the former owners, had written previously to the Dorset Agricultural Executive Committee about acquiring the land and been informed that they would be sent particulars if it were to be put on the market. About half the land formed part of the estate of the father-in-law of Lieut.-Commander Marten; the latter offered to buy back this land or the whole of the acreage. He expressed his disagreement with the proposals for equipping and letting, and his complaint was forwarded by an M.P., to the Minister of Agriculture.

The officials concerned, however, had made up their minds that the proper course was to let the land as a single unit after equipping it; and they were quite entitled to reach the conclusion that this was the best method of obtaining increased production. Having so decided, the Ministry suggested to the Permanent Commissioner of Crown Lands that the 725 acres should be purchased and, after equipping, be let to a single tenant. The Permanent Commissioner agreed to the purchase at £15,000, the cost for equipping being then estimated at £34,000. A firm of estate agents which acted for the Commissioners recommended a tenant who was willing to pay £3 per acre per annum.

Applications from other prospective tenants which had been overlooked were brought to the notice of the estate agents in March 1953, and the Permanent Commissioner of Crown Lands was informed. He wrote to the estate agents that they must decide what to do "at least to appear to implement the promises made to them", and an Under-Secretary at the Ministry who saw the correspondence said they should consider "whether there is anything that could be done with a view at any rate to appear to be implementing any past promises". In his report, Sir Andrew Clark stated that the Under-Secretary "admitted that the idea of doing something to appear to be implementing promises which there was no intention to implement was so improper that it ought never to have been considered for a moment. It may be that this was more a case of failing to give proper consideration to what he was writing, than of any deliberate intention to devise some scheme to mislead the other applicants. . . . In fact the applicants were never informed of the true position, but nothing was ever done by the Ministry to mislead them."

Among other comments in his report, Sir Andrew Clark expressed the view that the true facts and considerations had not been fully brought to the Minister's notice by his officials; that certain information should have been presented in a proper brief; that the Commissioners of Crown Lands could have advertised the tenancy; and that there was "a most regrettable attitude of hostility to Lt-Commander Marten" by certain officials. "There was no excuse whatever for this attitude," Sir Andrew Clark stated. "Lieut.-Commander Marten acted perfectly properly throughout and was merely endeavouring to stand up for what he conceived to be his moral rights. This attitude was engendered solely by a feeling of irritation that any member of the public should have the temerity to oppose or even question the acts or decisions of officials of a Government or State Department."

Civil Servants had been often enough represented as doing just whatever they liked, with no concern for the cost involved; as deciding just how much a Minister ought to be told and how much should be kept back from him; as existing in a state of muddle and incompetence; and as treating the public with disdain. But anyone who had written such a story as Crichel Down would have been dismissed as an idle romancer.

When the Commons debated the matter, Sir Thomas Dugdale accepted responsibility for the errors disclosed in the report and tendered his resignation. He dealt with the accusation that his officials had wilfully misled him. "Although there were certain inaccuracies and deficiencies in the information given me when I took my decision," he said, "I had the main facts before me, and my advisers were certainly not guilty of wilfully misleading me. I underline the word 'wilfully'." He then disclosed that a committee consisting of two ex-Civil Servants and a distinguished industrialist had reported to the Prime Minister on whether the officials concerned should be transferred from their existing duties to other posts. "There is no defined set of rules by which the confidence of the public in the administration of Government Departments can be secured and held," their report stated.[1] "Incorruptibility and efficiency are two obvious requirements. In the present case corruption has not been in question; inefficiency has. Beyond that it is difficult to particularize. But the present case seems to us to emphasize one further factor which

[1] Cmd. 9220.

may be less self-evident but which we regard as of the highest importance. In present times the interests of the private citizen are affected to a great extent by the actions of Civil Servants. It is the more necessary that the Civil Servant should bear constantly in mind that the citizen has a right to expect not only that his affairs will be dealt with effectively and expeditiously but also that his personal feelings, no less than his rights as an individual, will be sympathetically and fairly considered. We think that the admitted shortcomings in this respect are the main cause of such loss of public confidence as has resulted from the present case."

So widespread had been the protests at what had the appearance of being an attempt on the part of the Civil Service to minimize the disclosures in the Crichel Down Report that some assurance needed to be given that the gravity of the issues had been understood. In closing the debate in the Commons the Home Secretary said: ". . . there has been no attempt on the part of the Civil Service to cover up the faults that have been disclosed. . . . The Service, as a service, is as shocked by the errors brought to light as anyone else. Their pride in their service, and its reputation and tradition for fair dealing and unfailing rectitude, makes them as determined as anybody that these errors should not recur."

A few weeks later the Permanent Secretary of the Treasury, in his capacity as head of the Civil Service, drew the attention of all grades of officials to some of the lessons of Crichel Down. Writing in the name of the Lords Commissioners of the Treasury, he said: "The circumstances that led up to this report[1] have brought forcibly to Their Lordships' attention the need for constant vigilance to ensure respect for the rights and feelings of individual members of the community who may be affected by the work of departments. The confidence of the public in the administration of Government departments depends upon this vigilance."

This sounded all very well but the public remained uneasy that any department should have been able to act in this way, and wondered how many other blunders which never came to light might be committed. Strong representations were made that the Government should set up machinery for the review of such departmental decisions. A number of Scandinavian countries have long had an official, known as the Ombudsman, to whom any citizen may apply if aggrieved by a departmental ruling and a similar system is in force in New Zealand.

---

[1] i.e. the Report of the Committee to consider whether certain Civil Servants should be transferred to other duties.

The Ombudsman is able to call for the official files and make up his mind whether an injustice has been done or whether inadequate consideration has been given in any matter.

The Labour Government has accepted the need for a Commissioner to investigate complaints against the decisions of departments and to report the result of his findings to Parliament, and so ten years after Crichel Down the system is to be introduced as a means of giving protection to the citizen against harsh or irresponsible treatment.

Chapter Seven

THE MINISTRY OF FILMS

THE imaginary Ministry of Films has been assumed to employ administrative, executive, and clerical staff as well as specialists, a pattern which is familiar in most Government departments. Members of all the main grades may become involved, at one stage or another, in a single "case"—any set of official papers, usually enclosed in a file cover, is called a case. A file is a "new case" when it first starts, a "current case" while action is being taken on it, a "pending case" while awaiting developments, and a "dead case" when nothing further remains to be done. Years later dead cases will be destroyed or, if the matters with which they deal are of sufficient interest, the more important parts will be deposited in the Public Record Office, to be made available after a considerable time to future historians. The period is normally fifty years. It has often been suggested that the period is too long, but much importance has always rightly been attached to the fact that Civil Servants must be able to draft their minutes in the knowledge that, unless quite exceptionally, no one outside official circles will see the file until long afterwards. A Committee on the Preservation of Departmental Records ten years ago considered the question again, but decided against making the interval less than fifty years lest "the 'unselfconsciousness' of the writer should be impaired by the thought of too early publicity".

A case begins in the Ministry of Films with a letter from the owner of a theatre in Rexall (once used as a music-hall), who offers to sell it for conversion into a cinema. His letter is delivered with hundreds of others to the Registry of the Ministry. Registry clerks skim expertly through the morning's mail, which may not vary a great deal in subject. Every day a large number of correspondents will complain that the Ministry's films are disgracefully directed or produced, or that they are badly lighted, or that the scripts are poor and the *décor* unimaginative, and, above all, that the acting is atrocious. Commercial producers also receive letters of this kind, but many people who would not complain to a commercial company will protest furiously to a Government department. A public office can always be shot at: the cost of the films produced by the Ministry is, after all, met from taxation, and the taxpayers have a right to express their views on how their money is being spent.

The morning mail will contain suggestions for films that the Ministry ought to put into production and there will be numerous scripts submitted for consideration. It will be strange if aspirants to a film career do not seek the assistance of the department in one way or another. Some correspondents will denounce the Ministry for failing to foster more educative types of films, and others will point out that films should be of entertainment value and not suggest evening school. Since the Ministry owns a number of cinemas, the people who attend them will draw attention to improvements in facilities that should be made or object to some alteration which has been carried out. No cinema will please all the patrons. If there has been a breakdown in the film projector in a Ministry cinema, the department will be almost certain to receive letters pointing out that the apparatus is always failing, that this never happens in commercial cinemas, and that it is obviously a sign of the ineptitude of Civil Servants.

When the Registry clerk reaches the letter from the owner of the Rexall Theatre, she will first of all find out if he has written before to offer the building; such correspondence may be called "formers", or "previous papers". If the clerk discovers earlier papers about the possible sale of the theatre she will add the letter to the file. If her inquiries confirm that this is the first communication on the subject, the clerk will enclose the letter in a buff-coloured cardboard file, number the file, and write a few words to describe the contents— "Rexall Theatre—Offer of Sale". The file will be traced by its number and the letters which indicate the subject—35786/48 preceded by C.A., for "Cinema acquisition".

A record will be kept in the Registry of the name of the owner, the theatre, and the subject of the letter. Then the clerk will find out if there is any reference in her registers to former correspondence about the Rexall Music-hall which might be useful, even though it does not deal with a proposed sale. There is a file about the question of showing films on Sundays in the theatre. As it contains a plan of the theatre, she decides to send it with the new case. The offer to sell the theatre is a matter for Section 5,[1] which is responsible for acquiring cinemas on behalf of the Ministry of Films.

In a well-organized Registry the operations of filing and numbering and searching for earlier papers do not take long, and the clerk will have dispatched the case to Section 5 by mid-morning at latest. It is her job to know the distribution of the work within the department, and experienced registry clerks acquire a knack of picking out the

[1] See Appendix II.

right official to deal with a particular inquiry. From now onwards the Registry should be able to put its hand on the file at any time and produce it when required. But papers go astray in all departments: they are locked in somebody's cupboard, or tied up with a number of other files dealing with a different subject, or an official takes a case home to study.

Some departments place all new papers at the top of their files, so that the earliest letters are found at the end; others attach new papers at the back, so that the file reads like a book, the first chapter, as it were, starting at the front of the file. The arrangement whereby letters are tagged to the left of a file and internal minutes to the right, or vice versa, is not uncommon in the older offices. Each system of filing papers has its champions and its critics. The staff of an office is unhappy for a long time if, because a new chief is appointed with his own ideas of filing or because the existing arrangements have become inappropriate for one reason or another, a familiar system is replaced. It is like having to learn to read upside down.

In an office staffed by clerical, executive, and administrative staff most cases will go first to a clerical officer, though special arrangements will be made for the obviously important letters to go at once to higher authority—a letter, for example, from another department over the signature of its Permanent Secretary will be sent straight off to a senior official; or the subject may be one that is recognized immediately as requiring exceptional treatment because of its urgency or significance. The letter from the owner of the Rexall Theatre will arrive in the tray of a clerical officer in Section 5. If he did not think he could deal with it, he would pass it to his senior; but there are few things which a good clerical officer will not feel that he can handle competently, at least in the early stages.

Mr Jones, the owner of the theatre, writes in his letter that he understands the Ministry of Films is looking for a cinema in Rexall. His theatre is, he says, in an excellent position and could be readily adapted for the exhibition of films. Mr Jones remarks that there is bound to be much competition to acquire so valuable a property, and he expresses the hope that the Ministry will send someone to discuss the matter without delay. The clerical officer will look through the file which the Registry has attached and which deals with the application for Sunday opening. It will show that the local authority had ruled that the theatre could be licensed for film exhibition only if a non-inflammable projection box were constructed with access to the open air as a way of escape for the operator.

If the Ministry of Films has been looking for a cinema in Rexall the clerical officer ought to know about it, as his section is concerned with all such proposals. He is pretty sure that the owner is wrong and that the Ministry has not been seeking a place in Rexall. Since he may have thirty or more cases on his desk, he will perhaps be tempted to reply at once that the Ministry is not interested and is therefore not prepared to make any offer. While that would enable him to turn to his other work, he is much too cautious to take such risks. It is just possible that, although his section ought to know if the Ministry is thinking of a cinema in Rexall, some plan is at a very early stage and Section 5 has not been advised. If so, Section 14, which deals with Southern England, will be bound to know what is afoot.

The clerical officer sends the file round to Section 14. If it were an urgent matter, he might telephone, but he will want to have a written statement by Section 14, if time permits; information given over the telephone can be recorded, but it is better that each section should write its comments on the file. The clerical officer does not see any urgency about the Rexall letter, so he sends the file to the Regional Organizer who deals with Southern England.

Section 14 knows nothing about a search for a cinema there at present and thinks that several years will pass before it becomes Rexall's turn. Section 14 is, however, willing to examine the proposition, but as the Rexall Theatre is small and could not on the face of it be converted into a cinema which would seat more than 400 people, Section 14 doubts whether an investigation would be justified. The clerical officer in Section 5 will agree that nothing further need be done but will consult his executive officer. It will be decided that a short letter be sent merely saying that the Ministry has not been making inquiries about a cinema in Rexall and is not at present interested in having one there.

A day or two later another letter may come from the owner, remarking sarcastically that the Ministry has grown so enormous that one part is ignorant of what the others are doing. Mr Jones is quite certain that the Ministry is searching for a cinema in Rexall and has already made extensive inquiries in the district. He expects his offer to be considered reasonably and quickly. The clerical officer knows that Mr Jones is wrong. People who write to Government departments are sometimes mistaken and sometimes unreasonable, and in regard to films, over which there can be so many opinions, Section 5 may get more than its fair share of ill-informed correspondents. In such circumstances the danger is that the officials will come to look on all correspondents as foolish or ignorant.

The clerical officer knows that one Government department seems much the same as another to members of the public with a grievance, and he suspects that the inquiry has emanated from another Government office, though it may have come from anywhere. So the official starts asking questions around likely departments and may find that the Ministry of Defence knows all about it. That Ministry has been searching not for a cinema but for a storage depot in Rexall for the Air Force and has considered the theatre. It is, however, not well situated for the purpose, and the Ministry of Defence does not feel that it is very suitable for anything at all.

A reply on the lines that Mr Jones ought to get his facts right before he starts sending sarcastic letters might have been tempting to the clerical officer in his first few months in the department, but not now. He has become too much part of the system to feel aggrieved that he wasted time over the case, and that his time and that of other Civil Servants could have been saved if the owner had not jumped to conclusions on insufficient evidence. The clerical officer replies that he is advised that another department had considered the theatre and that the Ministry of Films for its part is not interested in acquiring the structure. He may show the letter to his executive officer, but such a case will not go higher. The clerical officer has protected himself. He does not say what department had considered the theatre and he writes he is "advised" just in case there may be some later question about the Defence Ministry's activities. It has been made clear to Mr Jones that the Ministry of Films does not want the theatre —it is "not interested", the clerical officer writes—and the file is now marked off to the Registry where it will be retained until it is required again or can safely be destroyed.

Two years later the Research Branch of a major department will perhaps write to the Ministry of Films. It explains that an experimental establishment is being constructed on the outskirts of Rexall and that the building workers will be accommodated in a hostel. No cinema exists in the vicinity of the proposed site. When the new buildings are completed the hostel will be maintained for the casual workers; in addition, a large number of houses will be erected for occupation by the permanent staff of the establishment. Since the Research organization expects difficulty in attracting building workers and, later, permanent staff, it would be helpful if the Ministry of Films were to provide a cinema in Rexall.

The clerical officer who dealt with Mr Jones previously has now been moved to other work, and his successor in Section 5 who receives the letter, via the Registry, from the Research organization, has probably never heard of Rexall, far less the Rexall Theatre or Mr Jones. But the records are there. Nothing is left unrecorded in a Government department, and the Registry will have attached the previous papers, C.A.35786/48, which were last current two years before. As he reads the letter from the Research organization the new clerical officer will know that the case is not for him. A cinema is costly; the Ministry of Films is allowed to acquire only a certain number within a fixed financial limit each year; and many places ask the Ministry to provide cinemas. This case will, the clerical officer knows, go much beyond his level for decision. A number of people will be at once advised in the department, not because there is anything for them to do immediately, but so that the request should be known to them and so that Ministry funds will not be earmarked for other cinemas until the Rexall proposal has been fully examined again.

Section 14 will be instructed to consider the proposal in detail, and the case may remain with it for several weeks while inquiries are being made. The section will have particulars of all the cinemas in Rexall and will calculate the number of people who attend each week. It will obtain much more information from the Research organization on future plans, such as how many staff the new establishment will require on completion, and whether expansion is probable in later years. The case will then come back to Section 5 with the suggestion that the next step is to find out what other housing accommodation will be built. This is a matter for the local authority, but the Ministry of Housing and Local Government may have the information; if not, that department can readily obtain it. So the Ministry of Films will write to the Ministry of Housing and Local Government, and a reply will come explaining the developments which are foreseen. The Board of Trade may then be approached, since that office is responsible for the location of industry and may have long-term plans which are not yet known to other departments.

Section 5 will send the information to Section 14, and that section, which deals with cinemas in Southern England, will prepare its report, accompanied by relative statistics. The estimated income and expenditure for cinemas of such-and-such seating capacity which might be erected in Rexall will be worked out, together with an estimate of the position if the present theatre is converted for use as a cinema. Allowance will be made for the effect of television on attendances, for the drawing power of other attractions, and for the fact that, as many of the research employees are likely to be young, a large proportion will be tied by family responsibilities. There will also be numerous unmarried men and women, who might be expected to have spare money to spend on cinema entertainment. The salaries of most of the employees will be low rather than medium, and the demand will therefore be for the cheaper seats. Much of the survey will be of a kind which any commercial company would undertake if considering the opening of a cinema.

Rexall Theatre is still available and the Ministry has considered it for conversion. Inspection confirms that the theatre, while it could be converted into a cinema at a price much lower than the cost of a new building of the same seating capacity, would never be satisfactory and could not provide a new cinema of the size recommended. The recommendation is that, unless it is essential to make use of an existing building, the Ministry should face the cost of new construction. All this and much more will be included in the report. The Regional Organizer will work out the trading results as closely as he can on a number of assumptions, though he will not pretend to be a prophet. Public taste is often quite unpredictable in entertainment, but the officials will have much material, gathered from their experience elsewhere, on which to base an intelligent forecast.

One point which does not affect a commercial company will have to be borne in mind by the Ministry of Films. The Act which confers powers on the Minister to acquire or construct cinemas also gives him authority to make payments to cinema owners in a district who are adversely affected by the operation of a new Government cinema. The Minister is not under any obligation to reimburse the owners for the losses or any part of them that arise from the competition of a Government cinema, but he may pay compensation, and he would not turn down a claim if he were convinced that it was a reasonable one. This possibility must be taken into account in working out the cost of the Rexall proposal.

If a new cinema in Rexall were likely to meet running expenses and leave a fair margin of profit after allowing for capital expenditure the Ministry would not need to intervene; private enterprise would supply the service at its own risk. The Ministry of Films is not empowered to provide cinemas which commercial firms are willing to sponsor, and it operates cinemas only where there is a demand which cannot be met by normal trade interests. Unlike a commercial firm, the Ministry does not turn down a proposal because of the likelihood, or even the certainty, of a loss. It is not in film exhibition to make a profit. If a cinema is required, if the Ministry has the money available, if it has not exceeded the number of cinemas which it is permitted to acquire in a particular year, and if it cannot induce a commercial undertaking to supply the need, the department may feel that it should go ahead even though the loss may be very heavy. Before reaching a decision to open a new cinema in any area the department considers which town will derive most benefit, and its standards are different from those of industry. A cinema accessible to the farming community would be valuable if it stops agricultural workers from leaving farms which are understaffed; such a cinema might therefore be more favourably examined by the Ministry than a proposal for a cinema in a town with a large force of unemployed which cannot be found work locally, and which the Government is anxious should move elsewhere to take up jobs.

The investigators into the Rexall proposition will perhaps conclude that another cinema in the town would be justified; that no commercial company will provide one because of the anticipated trading results; and that it is a matter for decision where the Ministry's funds can be spent to best advantage—Rexall's claims must be considered against others. The three Regional Organizers have full information on the position in other areas, and they express the view that Rexall must rank low on the list. If it is given priority, this can only be because of the intervention of the Research establishment. The report will be sent to the Chief Executive Officer in the Finance Branch, who will examine the financial aspects more fully.

All the work up to this point has been done by executive or specialist staff. Now the case will go to the Assistant Secretary in charge of Finance, who will make his comments and send them to his Under Secretary. The case will be discussed between the Under Secretary in charge of Finance and Establishments and the Under Secretary in charge of Cinemas and Distribution. They are satisfied that other places have a greater need; on the evidence before them, Rexall's turn might not come for three years or more. On the other hand, the Ministry is anxious to help the Research establishment. In the end, they decide that the Research people must solve their own problems and that the Ministry of Films would not be justified in making an exception in favour of Rexall and putting it to the top of the list. The Ministry has an advisory council to help on film problems, but the two Under-Secretaries feel that this is a matter on which the advice of the council is not required.

93

A reply is sent to the Research establishment explaining that the Ministry of Films cannot divert its funds to Rexall when there are other areas with much better claims. If, of course, the Research organization is willing to finance a cinema from its own resources, the Under-Secretary adds to the letter, the Ministry of Films will be very happy to make all the arrangements. When that letter has been dispatched the case will come back to the clerical officer in Section 5. On the file is a further letter from Mr Jones, of the Rexall Theatre, asking when the Ministry will make an offer, and it is the clerical officer's job to reply. That official will see that a possibility exists that a cinema will be provided in Rexall in the near future, but only if the Research organization pays for it; in any case, however, the theatre has been ruled out for conversion. Mr Jones will therefore be told that the Ministry is still not in the market for the property.

The Research organization, for its part, will explain that it cannot finance a cinema from its own funds, which are all earmarked for other purposes, and will ask that it should be advised at once if there is any chance that the Ministry will acquire a cinema in Rexall at a later time. The file will go to Section 14 to note what has happened and will then be marked away for retention in the Registry. It does not remain there for long. Mr Jones will not take kindly to the decision that the Ministry does not want his theatre. If a commercial company had been in the place of the department and decided against making an offer for the theatre, a clerk would have replied to Mr Jones's first letter saying that the company's decision was against the proposal, and that would perhaps have been the end of the matter. Mr Jones would have been silent or, if he had written again to the company, he would have received an answer by return of post repeating that the theatre was not required. But where a Government department is involved a member of the public does not give up easily. If public money is around, everyone thinks he ought to share it. Mr Jones will write to his local M.P., pointing out that the Ministry of Films has the job of acquiring cinemas, that Rexall needs a cinema, that it is just sheer folly or prejudice on the part of officials to turn down his theatre, and that something ought to be done about it.

M.P.s are accustomed to this kind of correspondence. They will usually hand the letters to the Parliamentary Secretary of the department concerned when they meet him in the House, or will post the letter to the Minister with a request for the facts. The member for Rexall may send on Mr Jones's letter with a covering note inquiring whether Rexall is to have a Government cinema and, if so, why the theatre has not been chosen for conversion. This will be a "Minister's case" and will receive priority at all stages in the Ministry. The correspondence will not circulate in an ordinary buff-coloured file; it will be enclosed in a file of distinctive colour, perhaps brick red, so that it will stand out on an official's desk and be immediately recognized at a glance as calling for urgent attention. Such a file will normally be dealt with by the assistant secretary in charge of a branch, for a Minister's correspondence, even though it relates to some trivial matter, must be treated as if it were of vital importance and of real urgency.

A Minister need not defend himself to a member of the public who writes to him unless he wishes to do so, but, unless the circumstances are quite exceptional, a Minister can be required to explain his decisions to Parliament. An M.P.'s representations are always given the most thorough examination in a department. The Minister will not as a rule wish the M.P. to ask a question in the House, though there may be times when publicity in Parliament would not be unwelcome. In general, however, the Minister and his officials will go to great lengths to convince Members that every case has been most carefully handled and that nobody can possibly have reason for the least complaint.

The Research organization may again be approached by the Ministry and asked whether there is any likelihood that it will change its mind about supplying funds for a cinema; further surveys may be made; inquiries will perhaps be addressed again to the Board of Trade and the Ministry of Housing and Local Government to ascertain whether any factors have been overlooked. Only when these points have been cleared will a reply be drafted and eventually reach the Deputy Secretary or Permanent Secretary, from whom it will be passed to the Minister or Parliamentary Secretary for signature. The letter may explain that the Minister has examined the Rexall project sympathetically but that other places have a stronger claim on the department's financial resources, which, as the member knows, are limited; it is estimated that several years must elapse before the Ministry can consider a cinema in Rexall, and, this apart, Mr Jones's theatre is unsuitable for conversion, according to the technical opinions which the Ministry has received, or would be unsatisfactory after conversion since it would not provide a cinema of the necessary size.

This example indicates why some letters do not receive replies as quickly as correspondents expect. Everything is checked and rechecked. Nothing is taken for granted and snap judgements are anathema. An official must be able to defend his actions and be prepared to demonstrate to his superiors, and to his Minister if so required, the steps by which he reached his conclusion. Letters from Members of Parliament are given precedence over practically all other work, yet a Minister told the Commons that in his department the *average* length of time taken to reply to letters from M.P.s was "about fourteen days".

The allocation of work between the departments is a vast and complex problem. An apparently straightforward question may involve three or more departments. The member of the public who makes some proposal relating to birds, for example, may involve the Home Office, the Ministry of Agriculture, the Ministry of Land and Natural Resources, and the Ministry of Health.

Chapter Eight

REVENUE DEPARTMENTS

GOVERNMENT departments and agencies numbered about a hundred a century ago, but the main work was concentrated in a relatively few offices, such as the Treasury and the Exchequer—at that time separate—the Home, Foreign, and Colonial Offices, the defence departments (Admiralty, War Office, and Ordnance), Customs, Excise, Coast Guard, Post Office, Privy Council, Trade, Forests and Works, National Debt Office, and the Audit Office. Only the defence departments, the Customs, Excise, Coast Guard, and the Post Office employed more than a few hundred people.

The latter half of the nineteenth century saw the establishment of new central offices responsible for local government, education, and agriculture; the First World War gave birth to the Ministries of Labour and Pensions as well as an additional defence department— the Air Ministry; between the wars ministries were set up for Transport and Health. During and after the Second World War we have seen the creation of a number of departments varying in size and influence, such as the Ministries of Fuel and Power, Defence, Food, National Insurance, Housing and Local Government (previously the Ministry of Town and Country Planning), and, more recently, the Ministries of Economic Affairs, Technology, Land and Natural Resources, and Wales.

It is rare for any Government department to vanish completely. Some, such as the Ministry of Aircraft Production, the Ministry of Home Security, the Ministry of Information, and the Ministry of Supply have been swallowed by other departments or have had part of their duties absorbed by another office; their names have disappeared, though their functions are continued, at least in part; or they have been linked with a larger department which tacks on the old name (or the process may be reversed—the Ministry of Pensions, for example, was much smaller than the Ministry of National Insurance but the amalgamated department is the Ministry of Pensions and National Insurance).

Amalgamations are always resisted by somebody. There are bound to be critics in Parliament and the Press who protest that the merging of two departments means a less efficient service than the separate offices provided. But at least as voluble are those who

D

complain when new Government offices are set up and voices are raised about the proliferation of departments. Whether in favour of larger or smaller units for public administration, however, the critics are usually at one in thinking that the costs of administration are too high, and that expenditure ought to be reduced.

Considerable savings can in general only be made by suppressing a service, and that is never easy. Whatever the facility which has been supplied by a Government department, some section of the community will have learned to depend on it, and a formidable array of institutes, societies, clubs, unions, and associations will rise in wrath at any suggestion of discontinuance.

Officials cannot by themselves suspend any service, nor would one expect the men engaged on a job to take the initiative in narrowing its scope. Not all officials will wish to extend the duties of their branch, for they may prefer to jog along quietly without any additional responsibilities. The tendency of most Civil Servants is, however, probably to widen the area of their particular activity and to support the introduction of new and associated facilities. Every service is capable of expansion, and every service can be made better. Officials always see neglected fields which they know could be ploughed with advantage, and perfection is never attainable. No man worth his place will ever be satisfied that he could not bring about great improvements if he had more staff and further funds. The departments impose their restraints on the over-enthusiastic and the perfectionists, and especially on those who see expansion in terms of personal prestige or promotion for themselves.

Departments "are established in obedience to law or public opinion and to meet the necessities of social conditions". A department created to undertake a new service nearly always takes over some work from older offices or completely absorbs a number of small agencies. When, for example, the Ministry of Lands and Natural Resources was formed with the intention that it should acquire freehold urban land needed for building or rebuilding and lease it back to developers, it took over at once some functions from the Ministry of Housing and Local Government and from the Ministry of Agriculture and Fisheries.

The Government can establish any new departments it wishes, provided that Parliament provides funds. The number of Ministers is at the discretion of the Government within the prescribed statutory maximum. The ceiling for salaried Ministers in the Commons remained at seventy for many years but the Labour Government on taking office decided to seek an increase to ninety-one.

While several new Ministries have come into existence in the past twenty years, a much larger number of Government or semi-Government agencies have been created during the same time. They depend wholly or partly on financial aid from the Government and receive their funds from the department which Parliament agrees should act as paymaster. A single department may have as many as a dozen specialized agencies entirely under its control or to some extent acting according to its directives. Some of the agencies perform duties of a kind which Government departments could probably do equally well, but others are charged with responsibilities which could not be shouldered so readily by Civil Servants working to inflexible rules. Such organizations, however, sometimes tend to assimilate certain parts of Government procedure, and not always the best of them; and a few of the agencies are more hidebound than any department.

Under Ministers, the co-ordination of the Civil Service is the duty of the Treasury, which ranks first among the Government departments. It has two Joint Permanent Secretaries, who are equal in rank: one of them holds the post of the Head of the Civil Service at official level. The Parliamentary inquiries of the latter half of the nineteenth century emphasized the importance of co-ordination by a single department, and the Treasury gradually assumed a commanding position over the whole of the Service. Having once obtained overriding authority, the Treasury has clung firmly to its privileges. The Playfair Commission suggested that the Treasury should be assisted by a small committee or council composed of heads of other departments; this body was to be consulted on matters that related to Civil Service problems generally. The Treasury, however, managed to steer clear of such interference.

The Ridley Commission recommended the setting up of a committee comprising the heads of four of the departments and a representative of the Civil Service Commission, which with the Treasury would have "power to entertain all questions affecting establishments, including pensions and all proposals for increased expenditure". When a consultative committee something on these lines was set up in the last decade of the nineteenth century, it did not last long. The failure arose, the MacDonnell Commission commented, "partly because of the misgivings with which the Treasury authorities of that day regarded such an innovation". The MacDonnell Commission recommended the creation "within the Treasury and subject to its administrative orders of a special section for the general supervision and control of the Civil Service". The Treasury accepted this recommendation, one which did not lead to any interference with its working by interlopers from other departments.

An Order in Council of 22 July, 1920, gave the Treasury its powers of control: "The Treasury may make regulations for controlling the conduct of His Majesty's Civil Establishments and providing for the classification, remuneration, and other conditions of service of all persons employed therein, either permanently or temporarily." Before that time, however, the Treasury had exercised supervision over the departments, but the Order formalized its position.

Any Treasury which does the job of keeping a watchful eye on expenditure must expect to come under fire, for somebody will always be aggrieved that his brainwave is rejected or his plans curbed. The complaints against the Treasury which mounted after the war were, among other things, that it exercised too strict a control over the gradings and numbers of staff, showed itself too inflexible in its attitude to new schemes of expenditure, and was altogether much too concerned with detail. While services which had been in operation for years were allowed to pass unchallenged after they had outlived their usefulness, it was claimed, the Treasury resisted promising developments. Counting the candle-ends, as Gladstone recommended, had remained a major preoccupation in Treasury Chambers.

In 1949 the Treasury loosened its grip to some extent on staff complements and, following the report of a Committee on Treasury Organization in 1950, it accorded the Whitehall departments a larger measure of delegated financial authority. But the attacks on the Treasury still continued year by year.

In the 1957–8 session, the Estimates Committee examined the system of control exercised by the Treasury and reported to Parliament (H.C.254) that "it would be idle to pretend that your Committee is left without some disquiet". The Estimates Committee recommended that "a small independent committee, which should have access to Cabinet Papers should be appointed to report upon the theory and practice of Treasury control of expenditure".

The Government did not accept this advice, but in 1959 the Chancellor ordered an internal inquiry to be undertaken by officials, under the chairmanship of Lord Plowden, and with assistance from people unconnected with the public service and possessed of special knowledge and experience. In 1961 a report on "The Control of Public Expenditure" was published by this group (Cmnd. 1432). The members from outside alone put their names to it, since Civil Servants cannot publicly tender advice to Ministers.

So far as the Treasury officials were concerned, the group, after making complimentary remarks on how well the staff had carried out their duties, went on to recommend a major reorganization of the department. This was put in hand quickly, and functional branches were set up to deal with financial and monetary policy; public expenditure and resources; and co-ordination of economic policy.

In the wider field, the group had suggestions to offer on national planning, but the responsibility for the economy as a whole still rested in the hands of the Chancellor subject only to the Cabinet. Since then, however, the Ministry of Economic Affairs has taken over the duty of planning and projection of real resources and is responsible for medium and long-term programmes to protect the balance of payments and for the development of the economy generally. The authority of the Chancellor has thereby been curtailed, but he is still the Minister who has to see that funds are raised, and the departmental officials in the Treasury also retain the right to supervise the expenditure of all Government departments, though considerable modifications have been made in the system of control.

Most of the nation's income is collected by the two revenue departments—the Customs and Excise Department and the Inland Revenue Department—which come under the instructions of the Chancellor of the Exchequer, who is their chief Minister. The detailed control in each department is in the hands of a board of officials, under a chairman who receives the same salary as, the Permanent Secretary of a major department. Co-ordination is undertaken by Treasury officials. It is their task to present to the Chancellor the forecast of the nation's income, examine how further revenue may be raised, if necessary, and advise on the costs of measures which may be proposed.

Professional accountants often express dislike of the way in which Government departments keep their accounts. The Government's financial year runs from 1 April to 31 March, and at 4 p.m. on the latter day public offices close their accounts for the year. No further new expenditure will be made as a charge on the financial year which ends on that day, and any revenue which comes in after that day will be credited to the next financial year.[1] A Government department does not prepare a balance sheet on the same lines as a commercial company. Its accounts are kept strictly on a cash basis: one part shows what a department has paid out during a financial year under a few main headings, and the second part the total it has received

_____
[1] But transfers between Government departments continue for several months.

during the same period. The accounts make no provision for creditors and debtors, nor do they include capital assets. A department may on 31 March have commitments of several million pounds to commercial companies but, since it has not paid out the money, it ignores this liability. Nor, though it may know that large sums of money will be paid to it within a few days by debtors, does it include provision in its accounts for such income. The accounts are concerned only with expenditure and revenue which have matured, and are not prepared with a view to the presentation of the financial position in the round. This arrangement has always had critics who urged that the Government accounts should be drawn up on the same lines as commercial accounts. The proposal has been examined many times in the past century. A very thorough investigation was made ten years ago by the Crick Committee, which reported against any alteration, and in 1961 the Committee on the Control of National Expenditure, which also considered the point, stated that "the case for continuing the present system seems to us powerful. To change it would be a formidable legislative and administrative task." So the old system has prevailed against all attacks. Where a department is engaged in profit-making operations, however, cash accounts are supplemented by trading accounts.

The Treasury keeps a constant watch on the outgoings of Government departments. Early in the calendar year it knows, within very narrow limits, the total amount of expenditure which the Exchequer will have to meet by 31 March. By the beginning of January it has also received estimates from all departments of the expenditure they expect to incur during the new financial year starting on 1 April, as well as estimates of the amount of revenue likely to accrue from existing taxes and duties if continued on the same basis for the new financial year. A comprehensive statement can therefore be submitted to Ministers in January to show the estimated expenditure and revenue for the year ending on 31 March, and this may forecast a deficit or a surplus; simultaneously, the Treasury will be in a position to estimate the expenditure and revenue during the coming financial year, on the assumption that no changes in taxation will be made; and here again the result may show a plus or a minus. Where there is a surplus the Chancellor may decide to give tax reliefs or reduce the national debt; if there is a deficiency, the Chancellor can insist on a reduction of the estimates of expenditure for the new financial year or decide to raise new revenue by adding existing taxes or by introducing additional taxes. Or the Chancellor can present an unbalanced Budget, if he and his Cabinet colleagues consider that this is the proper course.

Where reductions are essential, officials will indicate the financial effect of cutting out or modifying different services; if concessions are to be considered, the cost of bringing down the rate of income tax or raising allowances, or of varying the purchase tax, or taking some of the duty from tobacco, beer, wines, spirits, will be worked out in detail, so that the Chancellor may have all the material he needs on which to make his decisions. Where additional taxation has to be imposed, there will be statistics on the result of an increase in the rate of existing impositions or the introduction of new levies, again accompanied by memoranda to which dozens of specialists may have contributed.

During the course of the years a great mass of information has been collected on the effects not only of existing types of taxation, but of different measures which have been proposed from time to time and rejected as unworkable or unfair or otherwise undesirable. Some taxes may have been adopted in one form or another in the past and abandoned later because of public reaction or because of administrative difficulty or high costs of collection. But the Treasury and the revenue departments will not by themselves be able to provide all the facts which the Chancellor needs on these and other points. The nation's Budget has become part of the system by which the country's economic life is guided and is therefore much more than a financial measure.

The departments intimately concerned with trade and industry will have contributions to make from their own knowledge or through their connections with commerce. Outside interests will need to be consulted on particular aspects and no one withholds information which the Chancellor requires for the purpose of framing his Budget. Many people may know or suspect that an inquiry is being made on the effect of some specific tax or duty, but nobody can be sure what what the final decision will be, for preliminary investigation is likely to be undertaken in numerous directions. Reductions or increases in respect of certain duties and taxes may be examined again and again, though always rejected in the past; the earlier objections may no longer apply or may not now be so weighty.

From all parts of both Houses advice will flow to the Treasury Ministers. Representations will be made by the Federation of British Industries and the Trades Union Congress, and practically every other organized body in the country will have views which it will present forcibly. The Chancellor will have met deputations who make plaintive pleas for tax reliefs designed to benefit their particular interests, or adduce reasons why the State should supply funds for the support of some activity dear to their hearts. Few days throughout the year will pass without some correspondence which contains suggestions on what the Chancellor ought to do, some of them no doubt very wild. Party headquarters will have their own opinions. What may be possible at the beginning of a Government's life may be ruled out as politically dangerous if an election is not far off. The home situation will affect the choice in some matters, and in others the probable international repercussions may be the decisive factor.

The Minister of Economic Affairs, who ranks number two in the Government, is now in effect an overlord in everything affecting the country's economy, and has therefore a predominant part in shaping the lines of the main Budget, or any supplementary Budget of the kind introduced in the autumn of 1964. The Chancellor, however, retains the responsibility for presenting the financial measures to Parliament, and is in charge of the administrative machinery.

Officials will not be the sole advisers to Ministers, but they will be among the principal experts to be consulted. The Inland Revenue and the Customs and Excise, as the tax-collecting agencies, will be invited to give their comments on new ideas, and proposals that may seem simple enough often turn out to bristle with difficulties from a practical point of view. Ministers are known to have complained that reforms dear to their hearts have, when put to the departments, floated back with the polite observation that the execution of some programme would involve doubling the staff. And, of course, there is nearly always someone in a new government who puts forward proposals which have been considered again and again and rejected as administratively undesirable. Ministers may well suspect at times that the over-cautious bureaucrats invent obstacles.

In this book, it is the normal annual Budget which is described. It is a lengthy measure, which includes a large number of financial resolutions, some of which are included to correct anomalies or ambiguities discovered in previous Finance Acts. Not all the amendments which the departments might like to see included can form part of a single Budget without overloading it. The Chancellor must decide how much can reasonably be covered in each year's Budget, and some proposals which are agreed to be highly desirable must await their turn in the future.

The Government will use its majority to pass the important parts of the Budget, but the Chancellor is likely to agree to some changes, usually of a minor kind, during the stages of the Finance Bill. The general debates on the Finance Bill will continue throughout April to about the middle or end of July.

While some divisions of the Treasury are primarily concerned with the oversight of the collection of revenue, others control the expenditure of the departments and their staffing and maintain general supervision over the working of the Service as a whole. Because of the high responsibilities carried by the Treasury, it has a much larger number of senior posts than other departments.

Attached to the Treasury are the Parliamentary Counsel, who draft Bills for the Government departments, and the Treasury Solicitor, who is in charge of the legal work of the public service. The Director of Public Prosecutions arranges for the conduct of Crown cases in courts, either by his own staff or by counsel who are specially employed. The Treasury Rating and Valuation Branch assesses the amount to be paid to local authorities in respect of Government-occupied property; the Crown is not subject to rates as a rule, but an amount in lieu, equal to the sum which the Treasury Valuer agrees would be reasonable for rates if the Crown were liable, is paid to the local authority for buildings in official occupation.

Other departments which, although not part of the Treasury, come under the control of the Treasury Ministers are the Mint, the Government Actuary, the Government Chemist, and the National Savings Committee; and in the nature of things Treasury officials are closely involved in the work of these offices. The Civil Service Commission is in a different category. The Commissioners have been given a very large measure of independence, but they are bound to act on Treasury directions in recruiting for the Civil Service.

For the year ending 31 March, 1964, the total tax revenue amounted to £6,648,611,000, of which the Inland Revenue Department collected £3,711,550,000, and the Customs and Excise Department £2,765,928,000. Next to the Post Office and the Ministry of Defence, the Inland Revenue has the largest staff of all Government offices (88,000). Most of them are employed in assessing income tax, surtax, and death duties, and in collecting the amounts due. In the department's headquarters in Somerset House the Registrar-General keeps the vital statistics of births, deaths, and marriages, and all wills must be deposited there. The department is also responsible for stamp duty and undertakes the stamping of documents direct or through the Post Office as its collecting agent. While revenue stamps of high value are either impressed on a document by the Inland Revenue Department or are printed separately from postage stamps, stamps of lower value, marked "Postage Revenue", may be used either for franking letters or for receipts or stamping documents up to 6*d.* When stamps are used for postal purposes, the income accrues to the Post Office; when used for revenue purposes, the income belongs to the Inland Revenue. It must remain a mystery what precise proportion of "Postage Revenue" stamps are used on receipts and documents and what proportion are placed on letters, postcards, parcels, and so on. An attempt is made to arrive at a division so that the Post Office and the Inland Revenue Department will each be credited with the appropriate amount of income, but no one will confidently affirm that the result is anything more than a good guess.

The Customs and Excise Department follows somewhat the same organizational pattern as the Inland Revenue Department. It has a board of officials who act as commissioners and a directing staff of administrative officers at headquarters. Customs and Excise officers are stationed throughout the country, some assessing the amount of duty, others responsible for its collection. The waterguard has its inspectors engaged in the prevention and detection of smuggling, one of the oldest of the department's services. The tide-waiters of last century, referred to earlier, have been absorbed into the present waterguard service.

Income tax is in a class by itself. The regulations under which it is administered are very complicated, and a host of clever people search industriously for new interpretations or for some means of taking advantage of an unforeseen gap. One of the most confusing taxes to the public is the purchase tax, which people find it difficult to accept patiently. The vexatious anomalies are constantly publicized, and, while there may be excellent reasons for the rulings given by the department, it has failed to make them understood. For example, it was ruled that a postcard in two colours with a line of print such as "Sending you greetings" should be charged at one rate; but where the line of print was omitted the rate of tax should be increased fourfold.

Both the Inland Revenue and the Customs and Excise employ staff which fall within the normal classes in Government service, but much of the work requires specialized knowledge and many of the employees, though recruited by the Civil Service Commissioners, are organized in departmental grades. Tax inspectors, collectors, and examiners in the Inland Revenue Department, and waterguard personnel, investigators, and surveyors in the Customs and Excise Department, are some of these departmental groups. After appointment, a number of departmental staffs must study for a professional qualification.

The General Post Office is also run by a board, but, unlike the Inland Revenue Department and the Customs and Excise, which are controlled by Treasury Ministers, the Post Office has its own political head—the Postmaster-General. Until recently, Post Office profits were surrendered to the Exchequer, but by the Post Office Act of 1961 the finances of the department were separated from those of the central Government almost entirely. In most ways the Post Office is now similar to a nationalized industry, such as the Coal Board and the Gas Council. It remains formally a Government department and is represented in Parliament by its Minister, but the Post Office retains its own revenue, which is paid into a Post Office Fund. The department meets its expenditure from income and is under obligation to pay the equivalent taxes to which industry is in general subject and is expected to work to a target of 8 per cent. These arrangements are exceptional. They were introduced because it was claimed that the Post Office would not work effectively within the rules which are imposed on other departments and must be free to operate on a semi-commercial basis.

Every member of the public comes into contact with the Post Office. Most figures in relation to the department are astronomical. It handles about 11,000 million letters and postcards a year, nearly 2,500 million consisting of football pools traffic; issues around 600,000,000 postal orders, a figure also affected by the pools; and sells money orders to the value of around £250,000,000 a year. The Savings Bank holds nearly £2,000,000,000 in over twenty million accounts and has some 100,000,000 transactions annually. But the really impressive figure is £1,120 million as receipts from and payments to the public. It represents an average of £22 a year for every man, woman, and child in the country.

Apart from what may be termed departmental work proper—the sale of postage stamps, the transmission of letters, postcards, parcels, and telegrams, and the provision of the telephone service—the Post Office acts as the agent of the Government in the payment of old-age, widows' and other pensions and allowances. It sells savings certificates and defence bonds and some Government stocks and will arrange for annuities. It issues dog, gun, radio, and television licences and, through its 25,000 branches, acts as the grand distributor of documents on behalf of a large number of Government offices.

The Post Office is accused of having fallen behind in organization, and being a laggard in introducing new methods. It still makes substantial profits overall, but a number of its services are remunerative. The ordinary letter post more than covers the cost of operation and telephones make a handsome profit, but a number of other services are run at a loss. The Post Office cannot, as a commercial undertaking might do, promptly cut out unprofitable activities. It is partly a social service. Telegrams, for instance, must continue to be accepted though the loss on the service is considerable and it would be resented if the charges were increased to the high level necessary to balance the expenditure.

Overseas services could not be operated efficiently without prior agreement between the Post Offices of the world. So far as telecommunications are concerned—telephones, telegrams, radio, and television—the International Telecommunications Union, which has its headquarters in Geneva, is the central agency, and lays down standards and imposes controls which are accepted by members throughout the world. The Universal Postal Union, with its headquarters at Berne, is the controlling body. Each country carries the letters of other countries free of charge, retaining the revenue which accrues from correspondence posted within its frontiers. This may not work out altogether fairly, but in general one nation sends as much postal matter as it receives, and the discrepancies are not considered to be serious enough to justify accounting. The administrations, however, charge each other for the parcels they transmit or deliver, since here the position is different. Where there are large immigrant populations, the number of parcels sent back home is likely to be much larger than in the reverse direction. West Indians in this country, for example, post far more parcels to the West Indies than are dispatched from there to Britain.

It is often said that British postage stamps would be more artistic and attractive if so much of the space was not taken up with the head of the sovereign. Other countries print their names on postage stamps, but Britain has never done so. We were the first country to introduce adhesive postage stamps, which for over a hundred years have been printed with no other indication of origin than the head of the reigning monarch. The British Post Office is unique in this respect and has always successfully resisted demands that the name of this country should appear on its postage stamps.

Chapter Nine

SECRETARIES OF STATE

A POLITICAL post which once ranked very high in the formal ranking of the Cabinet may be given a lower precedence for one reason or another. It was, for instance, long the practice to include the Home Secretary among the first half-dozen in the Ministerial hierarchy. In the 1964 Government, however, he had to be content with eighth place, though his office is the oldest of the principal secretaryships.

Public business, which had previously been conducted on behalf of the Sovereign by a secretariat of clerics under the direction of a single officer, was divided between two representatives of the Crown early in the seventeenth century. By the middle of the century one became responsible for home and the other for foreign affairs. From these Home and Foreign Offices of three centuries ago have developed all the departments of today.

The Home Office particularly has always been the breeding ground of departments, and few of the present public offices have not absorbed some service which has been first nurtured under the Home Office. "Although particular duties have been allotted to each secretary," stated a Parliamentary Committee of 1837, "the whole secretariat was, and now is, one officer, any one of the secretaries being competent, and having authority, to discharge the duties assigned to his colleagues." Certain duties can be undertaken only by a Principal Secretary of State, and when one is out of the country or otherwise unavailable arrangements must be made for the work of the absent Minister to be performed by another so that current business will not be held up. A number of Home Office documents have no force unless they bear the signature of a Principal Secretary. The Post Office must, for example, have a warrant signed by a Secretary of State before it may open any letters which have been entrusted to it for delivery.

From its early days the Home Office has been a fashionable department and a powerful one. When by Order in Council of 1870 recruitment by open competition to posts in the Civil Service became general, the Home Secretary of the time succeeded in excluding the Home Office from the new arrangements and for many years its administrative staff continued to be recruited by nomination and to be paid on a scale higher than that in most other public offices. In the past the department had the reputation of providing very pleasant conditions, with a volume of business which was believed not to place a particularly heavy burden on most of its officials. Internal affairs which are not specifically assigned to other departments come under the Home Office, and because of this the range of its activities is very wide.

Not all new departments which have taken over functions started by the Home Office have inherited its prestige. The Home Office, with its ancient traditions and its close association with the Throne, still holds a very special place. Police, prisons, fire service, and matters relating to the internal security of the country come within the jurisdiction of the Home Office, which also acts as the channel of communication between the imperial Government and Northern Ireland, the Isle of Man, and the Channel Islands. Candidates who have a choice of departments often express a preference to be posted to the Home Office, which, although not now a leisured department, can offer the attraction of varied and highly interesting work.

During the war the Government created a separate department, the Ministry of Home Security, for civil defence, but these duties have now fallen upon the Home Office proper and absorb a considerable part of its staff. Where local authorities refuse to provide for such services the Home Secretary may make other arrangements for the work to be carried out, as he did in June 1954 when Coventry City Council disbanded the local civil defence organization, and in 1957 in St Pancras.

At each of the chief seaports and airports the Home Office posts immigration officers, who check on all passengers arriving by plane or ship. At the passport examination of British subjects these inspectors can sometimes be seen with a book in which the names of undesirables are recorded. Should his name happen to correspond with that of a wanted man, the most respectable citizen will be subjected to keen scrutiny and may well experience a qualm of misgiving. The principal duty of the immigration branch is to examine overseas travellers who wish to enter this country, a job which inevitably gives rise to some criticism. The immigration officer must take the immediate decision whether to permit a passenger to land or whether to keep him on the wrong side of the barrier until further inquiries can be made. Mistakes occur, of course, but travellers are rarely denied entry or detained without good reason. The treatment accorded to aliens at seaports and airports is always a matter of much interest to the public. Few countries regard an administrative break-down or an error of judgement in such a matter as very serious, but Britain has always prided herself on showing courtesy to all who wish to come here and Parliament has never lacked Members eager to rush to the defence of anyone who appears to have been treated unfairly or with less than the utmost consideration on arrival in this country.

Once foreign nationals are admitted they come under the control of the Aliens Branch of the Home Office, and if they apply for naturalization after a minimum residence of five years, it is the Home Office which conducts the investigation into their suitability as citizens of this country and decides whether to recommend the application. When magistrates consider that a man or woman should be deported, the Home Secretary makes the decision, and if other countries ask for the extradition of one of their nationals the arrangements for his return are made by the Home Office, provided the courts are satisfied that a *prima facie* case has been established.

The Police Act of 1964 has altered the arrangements for police forces in some ways, but does not affect the long standing practice by which the Home Secretary is directly responsible for providing the Metropolitan Police Force in the capital—a quite special position which does not apply to other parts of the country. Outside London, Watch Committees or Standing Joint Committees are responsible for the police forces in their area, but the Home Secretary must be satisfied that the service in England is adequate and that the forces are working efficiently. Senior appointments are subject to the Minister's sanction. He has Inspectors of Constabulary to advise him on all aspects of police work. These inspectors are men of standing with practical experience in police administration, and are available to give assistance to local authorities. Reports on the efficiency of the police forces are submitted by the inspectors to the Home Secretary. Fifty per cent of the cost of police establishments is met from central Government funds administered by the Home Office, and the Minister can withhold the financial grant until he is convinced that necessary improvements have been carried out when so recommended by the inspectors.

The Home Office has its corps of inspectors to confirm that the fire services of the country are well run, and to report and advise on the organization of local brigades. Any major deficiencies may lead to the appointment of a commission of inquiry on behalf of the Home Secretary.

Inspectorates are a feature of the Home Office. In addition to those for police and fire forces, the department employs a number of men and women to keep a watch on the arrangements for the welfare of those children in need of care, who are in approved schools and elsewhere; and another group of inspectors is concerned with the prevention of cruelty to animals. The control of explosives, and of their storage by those authorized to hold stocks, are entrusted to a further corps of inspectors. Everything connected with dangerous drugs must be the subject of detailed supervision, and the Home Office employs inspectors to see that proper records are kept of the use of the specified drugs, that they are always in the custody of trustworthy persons, and that the laws governing distribution are strictly complied with. The branch is a small one which is not often mentioned: it is the smuggling of drugs or the conviction of drug pedlars which the newspapers publicize. The work of the Dangerous Drugs branch of the Home Office is not of less importance, though it is much less exciting.

Prisons, borstals, remand centres, and detention centres are run under the authority of the Secretary of State. The policy to be followed in relation to these institutions must be reviewed in the light of experience and of public opinion, opinion which has changed greatly in recent years. The probation of offenders and the after-care of those released after serving sentences are questions on which views are divided, and are among the topics on which the Home Secretary must expect some discussion in Parliament each session. And, a perpetual cause of disagreement, the question of vivisection is likely to be raised with the Minister who is responsible for authorizing experiments on animals.

Among his heterogeneous duties, the Home Secretary answers for the operation of the State-controlled public houses and restaurants in Carlisle and some areas in Scotland. Licensed premises under Government control are a legacy from the First World War and are an experiment which has never been extended, though it has often been proposed that the State should increase its activities in so profitable a field—the Carlisle establishments are very prosperous undertakings and had a gross trading income of over £400,000 for the year 1963 and a net profit of half the amount which it paid over to Exchequer. But if some people would like to see the experiment widened, others feel it wrong that the Government should be directly involved in such traffic.

The Home Secretary is the link between the Throne and the subject, and is the channel of communication betw n the Sovereign and the Church. Petitions from the public to the monarch are dealt with by the department, which forwards them to the Palace with its suggestions for answers; if approved, the Home Office sends the reply, explaining that this is by command of the Queen. Royal licences and charters are issued by the Home Secretary on the authority of the Crown.

From funds voted by Parliament the Home Office makes a miscellaneous series of financial grants, including one for the training of marriage guidance counsellors. Similarly, the Home Office meets certain expenses of the Women's Voluntary Services, which trains its members as auxiliaries to the main civil defence services and also assists in various welfare and emergency services for the benefit of the community.

Advice to the magistrates is issued from time to time as required by the Home Secretary, but he is not responsible for the High Courts. The separation of authority as between the Legislature as the lawmakers, Government as the executive, and the judiciary as the interpreters of the law is one which all parties agree must be strictly preserved. The salaries of judges, unlike nearly all other servants of the Crown, are not subject to approval by Parliament each year, for the independence of the courts must be made apparent, and one way of doing so is by removing the authority for their remuneration from the normal Parliamentary procedure. Parliament cannot interfere with the judges in the exercise of their judicial functions, but Parliament can, of course, change the law if the judges give an interpretation of a statute which Parliament did not foresee or intend.

The administrative and clerical work of the courts is performed by Civil Servants, who are subject to the rules which govern the employees of the other departments. Any legislation relating to criminal law is steered through Parliament by the Home Secretary, who has the ultimate responsibility to the Throne for the tranquillity of the kingdom and may call on the armed forces to quell disturbances.

The Home Secretary was until recently responsible for the efficiency of the police and fire services in Wales, while other Ministers answered in Parliament for health, agriculture, education, etc., in the Principality, and the Minister of Housing and Local Government answered for general Welsh affairs. Previous administrations resisted the demand for a full Minister to be wholly concerned with all Welsh problems, but in 1964 a Secretary of State for Wales was appointed with a seat in the Cabinet.

This new appointment brings Wales into line with Scotland,

which has had its own principal Minister—the Secretary of State for Scotland—since 1855. The Scottish Secretary has several Junior Ministers to assist him in the administration. A reorganization took place in 1962 and the work of the Scottish Office is now divided into four main branches: Agriculture and Fisheries; Development; Education; and Home and Health.

Among the group of departments involved in the overall direction of the economy, the Ministry of Economic Affairs is a newcomer. As mentioned earlier, it has the duties of framing and supervising the plans for economic development and undertaking the general co-ordination necessary to implement programmes of economic growth, and for keeping an overall control over the allocation of physical resources. The regional organizations for industry come under its directions.

The Ministry of Technology, also formed in 1964, is charged with modernizing industry so that production will expand, and the department has a special interest in industrial techniques and technological progress. The Minister guides the atomic energy programme and co-ordinates scientific research so far as it affects industry, and in this field works through a number of scientific councils and committees. The Government has its own research establishments, but also finances research by outside bodies and maintains close liaison with institutes set up by industry to investigate particular problems. The State allocates grants to some fifty such institutions.

In the past, the Board of Trade has been a kind of depository for activities which could not be conveniently fitted in elsewhere. The President of the Board of Trade—the Board never meets—is nearly always included in the Cabinet. He has a wide range of duties which extends to nearly the whole of industry and commerce in some degree. The Board of Trade is charged with the protection of the public against monopolies and the administration of the Resale Prices Act and other similar legislation comes within its scope.

The department operates the Export Credit Guarantee scheme. A branch of the Board deals with the incorporation of companies and their management and mismanagement. From its funds, the Board makes grants to the Council of Industrial Design, which seeks to encourage good design in industry, and to the British Travel and Holidays Association, which is engaged in attracting visitors to this country.

The Patent Office is a sub-department of the Board of Trade: its operations call for specialists and round it circulates a little world of inventors of all kinds, of artists and draughtsmen, skilled in making patent drawings, and of agents expert in the preparation of specifications.

The Board of Trade was once responsible for fuel and power, but this duty has now been passed to the Ministry of Power. The Ministry is in charge of the nationalized coal, gas, and electricity industries; the members of the operating boards are appointed by the Ministry who lays down policy. The department maintains a research institution in connection with safety in the mines, and an inspectorate of the Ministry satisfies itself on working conditions of mine and quarry workers. The Ministry of Power is also responsible for steel and oil, and is concerned with the efficiency of heavy industry in general.

Of the departments within the Trade, Industry, and Transport group, the Ministry of Labour, created in 1916, is among the largest, with a staff in excess of 20,000. The labour exchanges throughout the country are the best-known part of the Ministry's work and absorb the greater part of its man-power. Unemployment is no longer the problem of pre-war years, and the task now is to make the best use of the available resources and fit workers into the vacant jobs. Training and re-training are an important part of the Ministry's functions and will increase as automation and mechanization extend in industry.

Everything which relates to man-power and all aspects of employment are within the purview of the Ministry of Labour. It maintains contact with the employers' associations and with trades unions, and, when industrial disputes arise, its conciliation officers are ready to intervene to try to obtain a settlement acceptable to both sides. Wages boards for a number of industries are appointed by the Minister.

The Factory Inspectorate, previously under the Home Office, now forms part of the Ministry of Labour. Although working conditions have naturally improved vastly since the first factory legislation in the early nineteenth century, the primary work of the inspectorate still lies in enforcing the basic requirements of the law. The inspectors, however, also give advice and information on safety, health, and welfare.

The Ministry of Agriculture and Fisheries has also undergone considerable changes. A Board of Agriculture was established nearly seventy years ago and at the beginning of the century the Government set up a Fisheries Branch. In 1919, Agriculture became a full Ministry.

Shortly before the Second World War, a separate organization was developed to look after food supplies in view of the emergency which was foreseen, and in 1939 had its own Minister of Food, with a staff of more than 40,000, many of them experts on loan from commercial companies. The Ministry of Food was merged in 1954 with the Ministry of Agriculture and Fisheries. The department maintains a strategic food reserve at a cost of some £13,000,000 a year. It turns over its stock regularly, selling supplies to traders and replacing the food with fresh purchases.

The Fisheries Branches of the Ministry conduct research into the problems of fishing in the sea and protect the fishing waters from poaching, though the ships which police the sea are operated directly by the Navy. Fishing has a special importance for Britain. If fishermen leave the industry because the rewards are too meagre or for other reasons, the country may be short of experienced sailors, and both the Navy and the merchant marine have in the past been able to look to the fishing industry as a reservoir from which to recruit trained men. Moreover, fish is one of the few goods which this country can obtain in abundance without the expenditure of foreign currency.

Government expenditure on fishing grants and services amount to over £8,000,000 a year, but by far the greatest part of the Ministry's costs are in respect of agriculture. The department provides grants and subsidies to the extent of about £100,000,000, and the agricultural price guarantees are more than twice as much annually. There is a vast range of subsidies and grants—for lime, ploughing and cropping, livestock rearing, attested herds, hill cattle and sheep, silos, farm improvements, and so on.

Agricultural subsidies are always a perplexing problem. An annual review takes place at which the Ministry and the farmers negotiate the amount to be given for specific kinds of production. The Government undertakes to make deficiency payments for wheat, rye, mixed corn, and barley; it has guarantee schemes for pigs, sheep, and cattle; and it subsidizes eggs, and makes payments to the Potato Marketing Board.

Transport is a good example of the kind of switching and reswitching which occurs between departments. When the Ministry of Transport was set up in 1919 it had no responsibility for sea transport, which remained under the Board of Trade. In 1939 the Government formed the Ministry of Shipping, and two years later Shipping and Transport were amalgamated under the title of the Ministry of War Transport. At the end of the emergency the department retained much of the same functions but dropped "War" from the description. Then, in 1949, a separate department was formed to take over civil aviation. It had a very short life. In 1955 the Ministry of Transport absorbed civil aviation and assumed authority for the control of transport on land, sea, and in the air. This arrangement did not prove wholly satisfactory and civil aviation was again divorced from the Ministry of Transport, and all aviation matters came under a Ministry of Aviation in 1959.

The Ministry of Aviation has often been under fire for some decision or another since its establishment six years ago. It has been responsible for the provision of aircraft, civil and military; air safety, navigation and traffic control, and most things relating to air services. The boards of the air corporations, British Overseas Airways and British European Airways, are appointed by the Minister of Aviation, and their operations are subject to his directions. He also appoints the Air Transport Licensing Board and the Airports Authority set up to operate the State-controlled airports.

Complaints were made that the Ministry of Aviation had failed to plan the work of the aircraft industry effectively and shown a lack of foresight in gauging what kinds of machines should be manufactured for civil and military purposes. The public may sometimes excuse faulty judgement in planning, but no one can ever find any defence when a Government department is inefficient in its contractual arrangements and the taxpayer makes a bad bargain which could have been avoided.

A great outcry arose, therefore, over the disclosures about a series of contracts for the equipment of the Mark I Bloodhound missile and for the associated ground-launching equipment. The first intimation of the affair came to light in a short paragraph submitted about the Ministry of Aviation by an official attached to a Parliamentary Committee. "The Ministry," he wrote, "negotiated prices on the basis of prime cost estimates provided by their technical costs officers with addition of overheads based on accountants' recommendations. I observed, however, that the sum total of amounts included for direct labour and overheads in the agreed prices, relating to production up to 31 March 1961, exceeded by 70 per cent, or £2.5 m., the total direct labour and overhead costs for that period for that period as prescribed by the Ministry's accountants, although the accountants' figures had been available when the prices were fixed." The Committee was alarmed at these comments and called witnesses from the Ministry of Aviation and elsewhere. It discovered that millions of pounds had apparently been overpaid and proposed to the House of Commons that a detailed investigation seemed to be required into the circumstances. The Government therefore set up a special inquiry under the chairmanship of Sir John Lang, and the subsequent report of the investigation, published in July 1964 (Cmnd. 2428), revealed an extraordinary state of affairs. The estimates of cost which the department had agreed for the contracts were so widely astray that the allowance for overheads turned out to be 558 per cent for the ground equipment and 630 per cent for the missiles. The fault for this fantastic blunder, submitted the inquiry, lay in the failure of the Ministry to make use of information which existed within the department and would have enabled the miscalculation to be seen. The report referred bluntly to "a lack of direction and drive in making the best use of the Ministry's resources". The contractor subsequently agreed to refund over £4,500,000 of the profits which had been made under the contracts.

The Ministry of Aviation has suffered a curtailment of its responsibilities, and so, too, has the Ministry of Transport, which was until recently in charge of shipping policy and shipbuilding on behalf of the Government. The Minister of Transport, however, still covers an enormous field. He is responsible for the construction of highways, in conjunction with local authorities, for road transport, for safety on the roads, and for research on new methods of building motorways and associated subjects. The Ministry of Transport is the licensing authority for public service vehicles and has offices throughout the country to consider applications for additional and extended services.

The Minister appoints the members of the nationalized transport boards, such as British Rail, British Transport, Inland Waterways, and a number of boards concerned with docks. Though these are largely autonomous bodies, he exercises a general oversight over their work and prescribes the policies to be adopted. It is the Minister who has to satisfy Parliament on the way in which the transport boards have carried out their duties.

M.P.s like to delve into everything where public services are involved. Ministers, however, are protected to some extent from questions about nationalized industries. A Minister does not answer in Parliament for the day-to-day working of the industries for which he is responsible: it is agreed that the boards should be allowed to get on with their jobs without any fear that points of detail will be challenged in the legislature.

An M.P. will, for instance, be ruled out of order if he tries to cross-examine the Minister of Transport in the House on why the 8.28 was so late in reaching Victoria Station on the previous Tuesday that the passengers failed to make the connection with the nine o'clock boat train and were in consequence put to much inconvenience and expense. That is not a ministerial matter.

Not everybody agrees that it is right for such questions to be disallowed, but Parliament has accepted that the nationalized industries must have a measure of freedom from the kind of inquisition which is common enough so far as Whitehall departments are concerned. Ministers are felt to have enough to do in answering questions on the policies pursued by the boards which they have appointed. It was in the past sometimes difficult to make the distinction between policy and the day-to-day running of the services and complaint on the point still arises from time to time.

Parliament has for generations insisted that where public money is involved, there must be full accountability, but the Parliamentary Committees which examine other Government expenditure are precluded from venturing into the field of the nationalized industries. A separate Select Committee is appointed by the Commons each session to deal specifically with the work of those industries, but it does not probe into their activities in quite the same way as the Public Accounts Committee and the Estimates Committee scrutinize the operations conducted by the Whitehall departments.

Chapter Ten

OVERSEAS DEPARTMENTS

THE Foreign Office, like the Home Office, strenuously resisted the idea of open competitive examination for the recruitment of its staff until after the First World War. The establishment of the Diplomatic Service remained very small for many years: in 1831 it consisted of sixty-six persons, costing £130,050 plus £9,950 for house rent, and in 1868 it cost only £131,175 plus £10,920 for house rent, although its numbers had grown to eighty-two. While the department opposed open competition, candidates for posts in the foreign service had to undergo an examination, which in the middle of the nineteenth century consisted of Latin, French, German, some history and geography and law. Nominees could, if they wished, take part of the test after they had served for a time in an overseas post. If they chose this alternative, they must at the second examination "draw up a report on the general commercial and political relations" of countries where they had resided and "on the internal polity and administration, the social institutions, and the character of such countries". The salary on entering the Diplomatic Service was £150 per annum in the nineteenth century. It remained the preserve of rich men's sons and, until after the First World War, candidates had to possess a private income of £400 per annum for the first two years of their service. The caste system survived in a strict form in the Foreign Service long after it had ceased to be a prominent feature elsewhere in the Civil Service.

Until reorganized after the First World War, the Foreign Service consisted of: (1) Foreign Office staff in London, (2) diplomatic staff in posts overseas, (3) consular staff, and (4) commercial staff. The Foreign Office staff and diplomatic staff were made interchangeable in consequence of criticism, but between the wars the consular and commercial services continued to be looked upon as quite inferior, and transfers from them to the diplomatic side seldom occurred. Such a vulgar activity as trade seemed to Foreign Office officials to be beyond the pale, and as for consular work this consisted to a considerable extent of dealing with British subjects abroad who had got into difficulties, and was a duty regarded as unworthy to be ranked with the high responsibilities of the diplomat. The argument went on for twenty-three years before the services were fully integrated. The story provides an excellent example of how privileged a position the Foreign Office held in conducting its own affairs in the face of much protest from the public. The arguments against a unified service read strangely now.

The reform was one of the decisions taken in 1943 when the Government decided that changes were required in the Foreign Service generally. The White Paper issued in that year proposed a number of alterations. "Among the criticisms which have been brought against the Diplomatic Service," stated the White Paper, "the view has been expressed that its members lead too sheltered a life, that they have insufficient understanding of economic and social questions, that the extent of their experience is too small to enable them properly to understand many of the problems with which they ought to deal, and that the range of their contracts is too limited to allow them to acquire more than relatively narrow acquaintance with the foreign people among whom they live." If even half these criticisms were justified, the Foreign Service needed overhaul, and the White Paper, without giving any hint whether it regarded the strictures as justified, went on to suggest revisions intended to make the Foreign Service more democratic. Candidates with suitable qualifications were to be enabled to obtain vocational training at the expense of the State, and such an arrangement would, it was hoped, open up the service to men and women who had been excluded from it because of the cost of studying languages abroad.

It was proposed therefore that successful candidates, however recruited, should study at the cost of the State; such candidates should go abroad for a period of eighteen months, during which they should learn two foreign languages and study other specified subjects. At the termination of this period they were to undergo a qualifying test in their subjects, and a selection board set up by the Foreign Office with one representative of the Civil Service Commission should then decide whether the recruits should have their appointments confirmed. Those so chosen should serve a probationary period of one year in this country; half the time was to be spent in the Foreign Office so that recruits could study the organization and make themselves familiar with the general lines of the work, and half in the study of economic, industrial, and social questions, during which time they would be attached to other departments, visit centres of industry, and so on.

Such a scheme would have been very costly and it would have required a considerable increase in the complement of the Foreign

Office. Even if the money had been available, the reforms could not have been adopted in full, for the Civil Service Commission found itself unable to recruit sufficient candidates of the high quality demanded.

In 1964 the Foreign Office had a staff of about 2,500, partly stationed in London, and partly in over ninety foreign countries. The personnel was divided into more or less watertight compartments: Branch A, the senior branch, corresponded to the administrative grade of the Home Service; Branch B included officials equivalent to the executive and clerical classes in Whitehall; and Branches C and D were for typists, security staff, porters, etc. The newcomer to Branch A started on A 9 and, if he had the qualifications and ability and was exceptionally fortunate, could reach the top grade of an ambassador to a great power.

Branch B officials had more limited opportunities. Starting as the equivalent of a junior executive officer, however, a man could rise to one of the chief posts of his Branch, which were comparable to Principal Executive Officer in the Home Service and carried a salary of over £3,500 per annum.

Britain was represented overseas not only by Foreign Office staff but by representatives of the Commonwealth Relations Department and by Trade Commissioners who came under the Board of Trade. Certain aspects of this organization came under much public criticism and in 1962 the Government set up an inquiry "to review the purpose, structure, and operation of the services responsible for representing the interests of the United Kingdom overseas, both in Commonwealth and foreign countries; and to make recommendations, having regard to changes in political, social and economic circumstances in this country and overseas". The Committee on Representational Services Overseas was under the chairmanship of Lord Plowden.

The main recommendation of the Committee, which reported in 1964 (Cmnd. 2276), was that a unified service should be formed to include the personnel of the Foreign Service, the Commonwealth Service, and the Trade Commissioners Service. The proposal was accepted by the Government and the combined service, called Her Majesty's Diplomatic Service, came into force on 1 January, 1965. The new Service has common recruitment and conditions of service and conducts British representation throughout the world on an integrated basis. The Foreign Office and the Commonwealth Relations Office in Whitehall, while remaining separate departments, draw their staffs from the unified service.

Instead of Branches A and B, such as the Foreign Office had in the past, the Diplomatic Service consists of a number of grades—Grade 1 is the rank of ambassador and Grade 10 of a clerical officer. Some of the grades are classed as administrative and some as executive and a number are divided between both classes.

The importance and complexity of the work done at overseas posts and in the parent departments in London has grown enormously. In 1962 the Foreign Office received some 75,000 telegrams and sent out more than double that number, while the incoming correspondence amounted to 270,000 and the outgoing to 665,000 items. The Plowden Committee stated that it was not entirely satisfied that the systems of control "are fully able to ensure that the effort is correctly directed towards the most important functions and areas and away from those which are now less important or have ceased to be important at all". An average of eight telegrams a day going backwards and forwards to each foreign post sounds formidable, and it would be a miracle if some of the energies had not been misdirected.

There has often been criticism that some overseas offices are over-staffed and a number of the posts over-graded, and one of the recurring complaints is that diplomats receive over-generous allowances. While the British diplomat's salary is no greater than that of his colleagues in the Home Service, he receives allowances which make his gross income higher and his net income very much higher than anyone earns in Whitehall. The man on grade No 4, holding the rank of Counsellor in the Diplomatic Service, has a salary with a maximum of about £4,000 a year, the same as that of an Assistant Secretary in London. If stationed in Paris and married with one child his allowances may amount to over £7,000. His total income is therefore £11,000, of which only £4,000 is subject to tax. The diplomat is a highly favoured person who lives in a style which is out of reach for all except a tiny proportion of the people in any country. (The salaries of the Diplomatic Service are shown in Appendix I.)

All countries agree that their representatives serving overseas must maintain an exceptional standard. The diplomat cannot live as he chooses. He is required to keep up an establishment of the kind which his Government considers appropriate for a man of his rank. The most senior grades of the Diplomatic Service are provided with an official residence and are in receipt of huge allowances so that they may offer hospitality and entertainment on a scale befitting the plenipotentiary of the Sovereign. The British Ambassador to France, for instance, in addition to his salary of around £8,000 a year, receives an annual allowance of nearly £26,000, and in Washington the *frais de répresentation* amounts to nearly £36,000 tax free.

Under the Vienna Convention, "the person of a diplomatic representative shall be inviolable. He shall not be liable to any form of arrest or detention." The British diplomat overseas is therefore protected from legal processes, as are the diplomats of foreign and commonwealth nations and some members of the international organizations stationed here. Several thousand people are entitled to diplomatic privileges in the United Kingdom and the immunity extends to minor employees. In 1964 a chauffeur attached to a foreign embassy who was involved in a fatal traffic accident did not appear at the inquest. The coroner was entitled to ask the Foreign Office to approach the Ambassador and request that diplomatic immunity should be waived and that the man should give evidence. It would, however, have been entirely at the discretion of the Ambassador whether this was done. In fact, the matter was not pursued.

Like the members of the diplomatic services of other nations, the British diplomat receives a commission on appointment to a post. The wording of the commission issued by the Diplomatic Service is is shown in Appendix IV. The diplomat is liable to serve his country in any part of the world and will have a roving career. The practice is that a man is moved every few years, probably five is the longest time he will serve consecutively in any post.

His posts will be mixed and he must expect to put in spells at some bad places. From one of the great capitals of the world, in which he has enjoyed highly civilized surroundings and been able to lead a glittering social life, he may be transferred to a city where the conditions are inclined to be primitive and amenities few and where he may have to exercise considerable self-discipline if he is not to grow stale. There can be no permanence in the arrangements, and the wandering life, passed amid a privileged circle, may be wonderful for the first few years but become a weariness later.

The diplomat will, however, have ample opportunities for holidays away from the post to which he is accredited, and will have home leave from time to time. Not all his service will be spent overseas, but probably two-thirds may consist of duty abroad.

Wherever he goes, the experienced diplomat is almost certain to meet someone he knows when he assumes duty in another capital. The diplomatic world is not very large and its personnel are often on the move. The British official who is posted to Rome or Athens is likely to be greeted by diplomats of foreign nations with whom he foregathered when he was stationed in Buenos Aires or Moscow.

An embassy has its naval, military, and air attachés, and a large post may include an attaché from the Ministry of Labour, an expert from the Ministry of Agriculture, as well as representatives of the Ministry of Aviation, the Ministry of Power, and the Ministry of Public Building and Works. Their parent offices in London will look to these men for information on specific subjects and issue instructions on inquiries to be pursued, but such representatives come under the ambassador and in the last resort are subject to his directions. He is responsible for their conduct, as for that of everyone else on the staff over whom he spreads the cloak of diplomatic immunity.

Every employee of an overseas post is supposed by foreign nationals to be an encyclopaedia on Britain: he may be a counsellor or a humble book-keeper, a press reader or a welfare officer, the head of Chancery or a cipher clerk—whatever his position, the people of the country will be astounded if he is not an expert on all phases of British life and knowledgeable on every detail of British policy. The same questions will be asked again and again. The official will become accustomed to explaining that the British Broadcasting Corporation is not controlled by the Government, though it is true that the B.B.C. could not operate without subventions from the Exchequer; the diplomat will be skilful in describing the position of the Leader of the Opposition in Parliament, quick to confute the idea that the salary of £4,500 paid from official funds to the holder of that post is a bribe to keep him from embarrassing the Government with awkward questions in the House of Commons. Nor will the diplomat be stuck if asked to explain why public schools in England are in fact private schools (though he must qualify his statement, pointing out that not all private schools for which fees are charged rank as public schools). After all, the administrative diplomat should be familiar with the system: of those recruited to the diplomatic service of the Foreign Office between 1952 and 1962 some 70 per cent were educated at public schools. A higher proportion is now coming from other schools—in 1961–4 about 50 per cent.

Embassy staff may also be asked to state the cost of training to be a barrister, the amount of the Government subsidy to the Covent Garden Opera, how one gets a ticket for (a) Wimbledon, or (b) a Buckingham Palace garden party; and there may be an earnest inquirer who wants to know how many turtles are needed to provide the soup for the Lord Mayor's banquet each November. British officials have excellent libraries at their disposal, but some questions will stump the most industrious archivist and the answer will have to be sought from London, if it is worth obtaining at all.

Many of the dispatches which flow into Whitehall for overseas posts are likely to contain facts which need only be noted and then filed away for future reference; others call for careful study and may be of such interest that further details will be sought. Some will require urgent action and may involve immediate decisions at a meeting summoned for the purpose, or go at once to the Minister to lay down a course of action.

When conferences are scheduled to take place overseas and the Minister from London is to attend, he will be accompanied by his own advisers, but the Embassy in the country where the conference is to be held will have a great deal of preliminary work to do. The Ambassador and his staff will almost certainly be asked to provide guidance on some points and, from their intimate knowledge of local conditions and the personalities on the other side of the conference table, may be able to offer valuable constructive suggestions. To the young man in the overseas service it will be an exhilarating experience, though perhaps an exhausting one, to be concerned in a conference. His days before it begins may be devoted to a succession of humdrum affairs—ensuring that the miniature Union Jack on the Rolls-Royce is replaced, making a final check on the proof of the menu for an official function, picking up the latest crop of local jokes and re-angling them for the speeches to be made by his masters. But, while his duties may be humble enough, he will feel the heady intoxication of playing some part in international affairs. As he advances in the service, the heavier responsibilities will come to him gradually, accompanied perhaps by a certain amount of weary cynicism.

The Diplomatic Service maintains its own language school in London.

As French is the diplomatic language, those in the service must be expert in the tongue. Most candidates for the Diplomatic Service have at least a fair knowledge of it before they enter the administrative Civil Service competition, but, where necessary, men and women are given a three months' course in France; the time is spent in Tours, where the best French is said to be spoken.

Some of the staff learn "hard languages"—Japanese, Chinese, Turkish, Russian, Arabic, Persian, and so on—since the Service must have a number of officials so equipped. It may need two years or more before a man reaches the required standard.

Until a few years ago the entrant to the administrative grade spent a short time in a Whitehall department and was then assigned to his first overseas post, but newcomers now receive some preliminary training. Moreover, after a few years abroad, young officials attend the Centre for Administrative Studies, recently set up in London by the Treasury, where a special three months' course is given for members of the Diplomatic Service. The course deals with economics, finance, international trade and payments, Parliamentary and administrative problems, and international and Commonwealth affairs.

The Foreign Office is responsible for the Passport Office and provides much of the money required by the British Council, which also receives financial assistance from the Commonwealth Relations Office. The Council is organized to present the British way of life to other countries, principally in cultural and artistic matters. The Council's activities and their cost—over £10,000,000 a year from the Exchequer—are a favourite target for attack in some organs of the Press. Foolish things have been done by the Council, but, however high its performance, it is bound to be criticized because of the nature of its work. The Council does not operate in the United States, where the British Information Services, with offices in Washington, New York and elsewhere, form part of the Diplomatic Service.

While the work of the Commonwealth Relations Office is similar in many ways to that performed by the Foreign Office, countries within the Commonwealth naturally receive much fuller information than foreign powers, and are consulted on many aspects of United Kingdom policy. The Commonwealth Conferences, which are held at irregular intervals in London, are attended by representatives of all self-governing countries within the Commonwealth. In a time of rapid transport, Ministers may see other frequently, but conferences at which the leaders from all the Commonwealth countries can meet round the table and examine problems are likely to be repeated whatever governments are in power at home and overseas in the foreseeable future.

The Conservative Government appointed the same Minister to take charge both of Commonwealth Relations Office and the Colonial Office and proposed that the two departments might be merged in the near future. The Labour Government, however, appointed a Secretary of State for Commonwealth Relations and another for the Colonies in 1964. As more and more countries have received independence, the work of the Colonial Office has naturally declined in volume, and amalgamation has only been postponed.

The head of the government in a colonial territory is the Governor, who is appointed by the Sovereign. Most colonies have legislative and executive councils which are responsible for local administration. The British Government may, however, suspend the constitution of a colony temporarily if it feels this necessary for the protection of life and property, as was done in British Guiana in 1964. Within certain limits, the Secretary of State for the Colonies answers in Parliament for whatever happens in a colonial territory. The most senior officials are appointed on the recommendation of Whitehall, but their salaries are a charge on the colonies in which they work.

Both in some of the colonies and in the newer independent countries there is a constant need for technical assistance and supplies. Since the last war, the British Exchequer has provided financial aid of nearly £1,400,000 for this purpose.

In 1961 the Department of Technical Co-operation was established to take over the work of giving assistance to developing countries, and in 1964 it became the Department of Overseas Development with a full Minister in charge. The department operates to a large extent through existing international agencies, such as the Food and Agricultural Organization and the World Health Organization, and the United Nations network generally.

One of the most successful pieces of work of the department is the Voluntary Aid Scheme. People who serve in overseas countries under this scheme are paid by the overseas Governments at local rates for the job, but these rates are often well below the salaries which could be earned here, and the Department of Overseas Development grants additional allowances.

Large numbers of medical officers and nurses have been sent to forty countries, as well as industrialists, teachers, engineers, architects, experts on afforestation, police, communications, and so on.

The Ministry of Overseas Development has experienced difficulty in recruiting staff to go abroad. Some candidates willing to serve overseas are perturbed that after a few years they will be thrown on the market, since every country hopes to employ its own technicians as soon as it can. Security of tenure cannot therefore be guaranteed, and this has a restrictive effect on the number of people prepared to take up posts in under-developed countries.

Men and women who enter the diplomatic service have always been able to look forward to a career to the age of at least sixty, unless in very exceptional circumstances. Although since 1943 there has been provision for the premature retirement on pension of officials who, for some reason or another, are regarded as unlikely to continue to offer good service or who, through no fault of their own, are declared redundant, such compulsory retirement has rarely been applied.

So it is not lack of security which has deterred candidates from coming forward for diplomatic posts. Between the wars little difficulty was found in obtaining first-class recruits and the number of people who present themselves for employment is still high—for the administrative grade the number of applicants to successful candidates has been running recently at about seventeen to one. The problem is to recruit men and women considered to be of the right calibre.

The Foreign Office has always been something of a law to itself. After the last war, when other departments were recruiting their staff by Methods I and Methods II, the Foreign Office decided that anyone who aspired to enter its portals must have First or Second Class Honours and be approved by "the house party". This extraordinary arrangement was soon abandoned and the Foreign Office agreed to recruit by Method I as well as Method II.

Twenty years ago a Government White Paper (Cmd. 6420) pointed out: "Among the criticisms which have been brought against the Diplomatic Service the view has been expressed that it is recruited from too small a circle, that it tends to represent the interests of certain sections of the nation rather than those of the country as a whole."

In the ten years from 1952 to 1962, of the successful candidates to senior branch of the Foreign Service, 94 per cent came from Oxford and Cambridge, and only about one in twenty from other universities. In drawing attention to this record, the Committee on Representational Services Overseas commented: "Those who represent Britain must be truly representative. They should, therefore, reflect the widening of educational and social opportunities which has occurred in recent years. This has important qualifications in the fields of recruitment, training, and conditions of service."

The new Diplomatic Service hopes to cast its net wider than the Foreign Service has done in the past, and it may be that we shall see a higher proportion of candidates from other universities.

Chapter Eleven

DEFENCE AND SOCIAL SERVICES

THE great spending departments are those concerned with defence and the social services. The Financial Secretary to the Treasury submits to Parliament each year an estimate of what is expected to be needed by way of expenditure for each civil department, but the estimates for defence are treated in a different way.

Some question or other about defence crops up in the Press almost every day. With modern weapons, and particularly the devastating nuclear bombs and ballistic missiles which the great powers control, we are bound to be keenly interested in defence and the subject has its hosts of commentators.

Earlier generations also felt themselves exposed and vulnerable to disaster, though in a different degree. At the beginning of the century, to some extent as a result of the experience of the Boer War, the country was highly critical of service policy and administration, and the Committee of Imperial Defence was set up in 1904 to advise on the protection of Great Britain and the Empire. Revised arrangements were made after the First World War and again after the Second. In 1946 the work of co-ordination of defence was entrusted to the Defence Committee with the Prime Minister as chairman. Other changes took place and in 1958 the Government ordered a widespread reorganization of the fighting services. Five years later the whole system again came under review, and the Government announced the setting up of a unified Ministry of Defence, but with the separate identities of the individual services still preserved. Integration of the services, which has often been proposed, did not meet with acceptance.

The Navy, Army, and Air Force had for a long time their own senior ministers who almost invariably formed part of the Cabinet. Under the present arrangements the fighting services all come under the Secretary of State for Defence, though each service retains its own Minister.

The Secretary of State delegates much of the day-to-day management of the Navy, Army, and Air Force to the service ministers, but he has the ultimate authority, subject only to the Committee of Defence and Oversea Policy. This committee sits under the chairmanship of the Prime Minister: in addition to the Secretary of State for Defence, its other members are the Foreign Secretary, the Chancellor, the Home Secretary, and the Secretaries of State for Commonwealth Relations and the Colonies. The Chiefs of Staff, while they come under the Secretary of State for Defence, retain, as they always have done, the traditional right of direct access to the Prime Minister.

Many people have seen at least one of the fighting services at close quarters, either in the last war or afterwards; and everyone has his own version of how they should be run. All fighting services must in the nature of things be wasteful of man-power and supplies, and this is generally recognized to be unavoidable, be the safeguards what they may. It is not this kind of expenditure of which sensible people complain, but of the huge sums devoted to the missile programme and associated activities and the many millions of pounds disbursed on aircraft which have never flown or have turned out to be much less effective than originally anticipated, or to have far exceeded the budget.

The defence expenditure in 1964–5 is estimated to be around £2,000,000,000. The system by which the fighting services obtain this money from Parliament has its roots in history. In February, the Services produce their estimates of expenditure for the year beginning on April 1. These estimates are broken into Vote A for Personnel and eleven other separate votes. Parliament must specifically approve the number of men and women in each Service, a reminder of the days when the country's elected representatives feared that the sovereign might increase the number of the standing army and so imperil the liberty of the citizens. Parliament spends two days in February on a general debate about defence and passes a resolution authorizing a ceiling figure for the complements of each Service.

So far no money has been voted from which the sailors, soldiers, and airmen may be paid. In March, however, each service asks for the approval of some of its votes. Four days are devoted in the Commons to debates on defence topics and, in the end, the selected votes are passed.

The Services thus start the financial year in April with money for only a part of their work. Not until July are the remainder of the votes passed. In the interim, each Service uses money agreed for some purposes and makes financial switches to cover the cost of other activities. Otherwise, defence work would be brought to a halt in a number of directions. The Commons reserves the right to object to transfers between different votes, but in practice the

Opposition never challenges the Government to a division on the matter.

The procedure is agreed by almost everyone to be unnecessarily complicated. The Select Committee on Procedure, which examined a question which arose over the Defence Estimates in the 1964–5 session, felt that the system called for further examination but did not make proposals. It recommended that another Committee on Procedure should consider the arrangements.

The money, once granted, is under the control of the Civil Servants subject to Ministers. The chief Civil Service post in the Ministry of Defence is that of Permanent Under-Secretary, who is assisted by four Second Permanent Under-Secretaries, each of whom is responsible under his Minister for expenditure on specific services. This arrangement is unusual, for it is the normal practice to have a single Permanent Under-Secretary, who under the political head answers for all disbursements of a department.

The Ministry of Defence is, however, so vast that it must have separate treatment. It employs a vast number of Civil Servants—nearly 52,000 for the Army, over 30,000 for the Navy, and 27,000 for the Air, and in total the department absorbs more than 100,000 non-industrial Civil Servants as well as a large staff of industrial workers. Altogether, the Minister of Defence is responsible for more than 400,000 civilian employees, as well as the men and women in the fighting services.

The recruitment of scientific staff, of which the Ministry of Defence is one of the largest employers in the country, presents great difficulties. It is a problem which other Government departments share.

Before the war, the scientific staff was divided into numerous grades, but is now organized in a few main groups—junior scientific officer, scientific officer, and senior scientific officer, with a considerable number of controlling and directing posts. The salaries are shown in Appendix I.

Security is a continuing problem in Government departments. Scientists are obviously in a better position than most other officials to obtain access to secret information, but all employees in some offices are likely to see papers at one time or another which contain valuable material, and thousands of posts are classified as "sensitive". Those who occupy them are subject to special security procedures.

After secrets had leaked some years ago, the Government announced that investigation would be made into the earlier affiliations of Civil Servants, going back even to the age of eighteen or nineteen. The British Civil Service does not necessarily bar people because they have been members of the Communist, Fascist, or any other political party, but officials whose loyalty or discretion is considered to be questionable are not permitted to see information which it would be contrary to the interest of this country to disclose to another power.

If a *prima facie* case is thought to exist against an official on security grounds, the Minister of the department submits the evidence to an advisory committee composed of retired Civil Servants and a retired trade unionist. Men and women who are displaced as suspected to be unreliable if exposed to temptation are found other positions, if possible, and most such officials can be allocated to duties where they will have no opportunity to handle confidential papers. Only when alternative employment cannot be safely offered to a Civil Servant suspected to be a security risk is he or she discharged. Between 1948 and 1954 the number of Government employees, both industrial and non-industrial, found unfit to occupy posts where they would deal with secret information was 96, of whom 24 were dismissed and 72 transferred to other work. From 1955 to 1963, the number of cases was 167 in all, of whom over a hundred had been employed on non-industrial work. Twenty-five were dismissed, 24 resigned, and the others transferred to non-secret duties.

The Government has continued to be greatly alarmed at the danger of leakages, and in 1964 it issued a warning booklet to its staff— *Their Trade is Treachery*. The publication points out that "spies are with us all the time" and describes some of the methods adopted to inveigle people into disclosing valuable information.

The Ministry of Defence is by far the largest individual spending department, but between them the offices which are responsible for the social services disburse around £3,000,000,000 a year.

The Chancellor of the Duchy of Lancaster, a minister who has a seat in the Cabinet but is largely free of any departmental duties, co-ordinates the social services.

Of this group of departments, the Ministry of Health is one of the grand paymasters. While it has important duties in international health, in food, and in nutrition, most of its work is connected with the various health services at home which make the British scheme the most comprehensive of any nation. In matters of health, the Ministry is primarily a directing and advisory department. From its funds comes the remuneration to the 22,000 doctors in the National

Health Service, to the dentists, opticians, chemists, nurses, and midwives; it finances the hospitals and specialist services, and makes substantial payments to local authorities for welfare work; it gives assistance to institutions for the aged and infirm; is concerned with home nursing and health visits; and with vaccination and immunization—the two latter are not without some doughty opponents who regard the policy as pernicious and who wage an energetic campaign against it. The Ministry of Health also has responsibility for the care of the mentally afflicted and maintains a number of services for the blind, the deaf, and the dumb.

The teaching hospitals are run by their own governors and receive contributions from the Ministry of Health, but otherwise the hospitals of England are in the care of regional boards, the members of which are appointed by the Minister. While the department extends a wide measure of autonomy to the Regional Boards, their expenditure is, as the Ministry puts it, "subject of course to the Minister's overall responsibility to Parliament". Hospitals which, when supported by voluntary contributions, could decide how to spend such money as they had at their disposal found the position very different when brought under the umbrella of the Ministry and required to submit to an audit of their expenditure.

Nobody welcomes financial control and the hospitals disliked many of the arrangements imposed by the Government. The Ministry of Health purchases supplies in bulk for the hospitals, and it is never very hard to find isolated examples where local purchase would have been speedier and perhaps cheaper than central buying. Bulk purchase is on the whole more economical, and the cost of the health service would mount if the Ministry did not negotiate for supplies in large quantities. That is little consolation to the hospital which finds that, instead of obtaining goods in its own locality and receiving them immediately, it must indent the central stores and wait patiently for delivery.

Hospital boards may protest that amateurs in Whitehall interfere with what they do not fully understand, but officials will perhaps point out that not all governing bodies have much idea of administrative procedures or even know how to organize the custody of stores. In 1952 the Government Auditor reported that the stock losses from hospital stores amounted to nearly £200,000 and that, on the National Health Service Accounts, £71,000 was for "deficiencies revealed by checks on such inventories as existed". Ten years later the Auditor could report a happier picture: stock losses had been reduced to less than £3,000, of which half was for deficiencies.

Nor are the doctors allowed to escape a measure of supervision. The Ministry of Health keeps an eye on doctors and makes inquiries of medical men whose prescriptions seem excessive or who appear to have been overfree in asking for expensive drugs to be dispensed. The direct savings by such spot checks may not in themselves be very high, but the knowledge that watch is kept must exercise a restraining influence on medical men inclined to extravagance at the taxpayers' expense. It is inevitable that the cry should resound that any check whatsoever is an interference with the professional standing of the profession. Every group has its irresponsibles, however, and the public would soon grumble if the Ministry of Health permitted itself to be deflected by criticism from checking on irregularities, real or suspected.

The expenditure on the health service has steadily increased during the past ten years. In 1954–5 it amounted to £671,000,000. For 1964–5 the expenditure is estimated to be of the order of £1,000,000,000. Further increases are certain.

Of the departments in the Social Services Group, the Ministry of Pensions and National Service has by far the largest number of non-industrial Civil Servants. The Pensions branches of the department authorize the payment of pensions, gratuities, and allowances for disablement or death arising out of war, including payments to members of the merchant navy and to civilian dependents. But the National Insurance part of the Ministry is responsible for by far the major part of the expenditure. Retirement pensions account for over £800,000,000 a year. Sickness benefits cost over £160,000,000, and family allowances—about £90,000,000 ten years ago—have risen to £135,000,000 in 1964–5.

Several Government departments are controlled by boards—for example, the Board of Inland Revenue and the Board of Customs and Excise, each with an official as chairman, and others are under the chairmanship of a Minister of the Crown. The National Assistance Board is in a different category. Its chairman is not a member of either House nor a permanent Civil Servant. The Board is responsible for investigating the needs of those in distress and affording them help as required, and it maintains offices throughout the country to conduct inquiries on its behalf. When established in 1934, it was agreed that the Board's operations should be removed from question in Parliament on details of the work and should be "taken out of politics". The annual account of its expenditure is presented to Parliament, not by the chairman of the Board but by the secretary, who is a Civil Servant.

Much of the work of the Board has been in paying allowances to people in supplement of old-age pensions. It is contended that this is an unsatisfactory position and that the National Assistance Board should be wound up. Whatever is done about raising the level of retirement pensions, some organization will still be required to look after people in need in emergency—the man whose unemployment benefit has been exhausted and the woman who has been deserted by her husband and must have immediate relief. It may be such duties will be undertaken by a Ministry of Social Security.

While several departments exercise functions in connection with specialized services performed by local authorities, the Ministry of Housing and Local Government, the successor to the Ministry of Town and Country Planning, provides the principal liaison between the central Government and the local councils. The Ministry makes payments—for 1964–5 estimated at nearly £82,000,000—in respect of the provision and improvement of housing, most of which is paid by way of contribution to the local authorities.

The Ministry of Housing has a continuing responsibility for new towns. When the Government decided after the war to set up such towns under development corporations, with loans provided from the Exchequer, the intention was that, once a new town had been completed and became self-supporting, it should be transferred to the local authority in whose area it was sited. There were, however, second thoughts on this idea. New towns grew highly prosperous and it was felt that such valuable undertakings should not be handed over to local councils. Under the New Towns Act, 1959, therefore, a central commission was formed which is responsible for the operations of the completed new towns and works under the directions of the Minister of Housing and Local Government, who may decide what part of the profits should accrue to the Exchequer. Twenty new towns have been completed or are planned.

The Exchequer meets approximately half the cost of expenditure incurred by local authorities, and has therefore an interest in ensuring that the money is properly applied. The Ministry of Housing and Local Government maintains a staff of inspectors who audit the accounts of local authorities (except in a few places).

The district auditor must investigate any complaint that is made to him regarding the expenditure of a local authority; satisfy himself that the councils have used the funds properly; confirm that the instructions from the controlling department have been observed; and bring to notice any irregularities. The auditors are appointed by the Minister of Housing and Local Government, but "they are independent of him and have duties laid upon them by Statute", with which no one may interfere.

The position of the district auditor is not always easy. Some local authorities resent their dependence on the central Government and chafe at supervision by a representative from Whitehall. The auditor must therefore be tactful, but at the same time he must, when necessary, be firm with councils, some of whose members are inclined to blame him for all the misdeeds of Whitehall and any legislation which they may happen to dislike. While technical qualifications are essential, personality is also of importance. The district auditor who lacks strength of character may become a punchball; on the other hand, the man who has no sense of proportion may turn himself into a self-righteous inquisitor, constantly querying trivialities in the course of his job.

Part of the work hitherto performed by the Ministry of Housing and Local Government is now within the province of the Ministry of Land and Natural Resources. In addition to its responsibilities for the purchase of freehold building land and leasing it to developers for building, the Ministry of Land and Natural Resources is responsible for protecting access to the coastline and the countryside, for minerals rights, and for the National Parks. Parliament decided that national parks should be established in areas of outstanding beauty, and ten such parks were designated by 1964.

The Ministry of Land and National Resources has inherited afforestation from the Ministry of Agriculture. The operational work is left to the Forestry Commission which acts under the directions of the Minister. In its latest report the Commission stated that it held estates totalling about $2\frac{1}{2}$ million acres and owned about a third of the woodland in the country. But since trees mature slowly, it may take forty years before a profit-and-loss account can be drawn up on some schemes. It is not easy sometimes to arouse much enthusiasm for such long-term projects when economy is the watchword. A Treasury witness told a Parliamentary committee in 1964 that "one would sooner see (the nation's resources) put into something which is likely to yield a return earlier". Nevertheless, the Forestry Commission has been treated generously. Far from being starved of funds, it has found it impossible to spend the amount of money which Parliament has allotted for afforestation in the past.

The remaining department within the Social Services Group to be mentioned in this chapter is the Department of Education and Science. In general, while the Minister of Technology is concerned with applied science, the Secretary of State for Education and Science is responsible for pure science and has a number of research councils to advise him. The Minister is in charge of the museums and art galleries and national collections in general, most of which have their funds directly voted by Parliament.

Education absorbs about 5 per cent of the gross national production of the United Kingdom and the cost of the services, which have grown by around one and a half times in the past decade, now run at some £1,000,000,000 a year. The proportion of the costs which is met from the central Exchequer is likely to increase in future.

After a number of experiments in raising revenue for education, a scheme was introduced in 1902 whereby the cost was met partly from the local rates and partly by a block grant from the Government. This system was superseded soon after the First World War when the Government decided to make its contribution on the basis of the number of children at school in an area and the capacity of the local ratepayers to meet the costs, the poorer areas therefore receiving more in proportion than the others.

The working of this scheme may be illustrated by taking the position as it existed ten years ago. In 1954 the payment to local authorities in respect of education was then based "on 120s. per unit of the average number (of children) on the registers", plus 60 per cent of the expenditure, less the product of a local rate of 2s. 6d. in the pound.

The legislature, however, adopted another method under the Local Government Act 1958, which provided, among other things, for the payment of a general grant—a block grant—to local authorities for a group of social services, of which Education was only one though the most costly. The grant took into account a number of factors, including the rate resources of each area, and broadly the Exchequer met about 50 per cent of the total disbursements on the group.

The system of the block grant gave local authorities some degree of freedom on how funds should be disbursed between different services, but the scheme had several disadvantages. The former system of grants related to individual services is likely to be readopted, with the Exchequer meeting an agreed proportion of the total cost of approved expenditure.

Whatever arrangements are in force, the Ministry of Education has the responsibility of setting minimum standards for education and ensuring that these are maintained by local authorities. It does so at present through its 600 inspectors who visit schools from time to time and make their reports to the Secretary of State.

The Secretary of State retains responsibility for teacher training and for educational building programmes which the local authorities may wish to undertake. He is also intimately concerned in the remuneration of teachers, though they are in the employment of the councils.

The salaries of teachers were for a number of years negotiated by the Burnham Committee, consisting of representatives of local authorities as the employers and the staff associations who look after the interests of teachers. Once this committee had reached agreement, it made its recommendations to the Secretary of State for Education, who usually accepted the advice. In 1962, however, although the Committee agreed on the scales of teachers' salaries the Secretary of State exercised his power to impose a different settlement. The conflict arose not over the total sum to be made available but the proportions in which it should be allocated between different kinds of teachers. The Burnham Committee has now been reconstructed and teachers' salaries will be fixed by another method.

It was generally conceded that new arrangements were overdue. Both the local authorities and the teachers' associations felt that a system whereby they reached a settlement only to have it rejected by the Secretary of State was nonsense. As, however, so large a part of the cost of teachers' salaries fell on the Exchequer, no prudent Government could accept any proposal that the local authorities and the teachers should be able to make an award which the Ministry must accept without question.

The revised procedure is set out in the Teachers' Remuneration Bill. The Ministry of Education, which under the old system was not a party to the negotiations in committee, will now appoint a majority of representatives on a panel of which the other members will be from the local authorities. A second panel will consist of representatives of the teachers. The two panels will meet to negotiate salaries and other conditions affecting the teaching profession. In the event of disagreement, provision is made for independent arbitration, though in the last resort Parliament will have the decisive word.

Most people have strong views on education, and the topic often figures in the newspapers. Both Houses of Parliament take a keen interest in educational affairs, and debates on the subject are often very lively. For, like publicity, education is something on which everyone is his own expert.

Chapter Twelve

FINANCIAL CONTROL

By the end of the eighteenth century Parliament had won the battle against the Crown for the control of the nation's finances, but the machinery for exercising its authority effectively had still to be created. The Government was pressed to set up a proper system of supervision of the country's expenditure. Two things were necessary in the view of the financial experts: that forecasts, or estimates, of expenditure should be presented annually which described in some detail the costs expected to be met for each service, and that, as soon as practicable after the close of the year, an audited account of the expenditure should be drawn up in a form which would enable comparison readily to be made with the forecasts.

Pitt had founded the Consolidated Fund in 1787 for the receipt of Government revenue and the financing of Government departments, but many public offices continued to retain their own income for the purpose of meeting their debts. Departments resisted the submission of estimates, and they accepted only very slowly and very reluctantly the recommendations of successive committees that all revenues should be paid to the Consolidated Fund and that no department should be able to spend funds unless voted by Parliament. By the middle of the century, however, Parliament's requirements had been met in this respect. Departments submitted estimates, though of a sketchy kind sometimes, and received their funds from Parliament through the Consolidated Fund.

There remained the question of accounting for the money which had been voted by Parliament. At the end of the eighteenth century Commissioners had been appointed to audit the public accounts, and later these Commissioners were made independent of the Treasury and responsible only to Parliament. The arrangement proved unsatisfactory. In 1866 Parliament passed the Exchequer and Audit Department Act, which placed in the hands of a new official, the Comptroller and Auditor-General, the duty of auditing all Government expenditure and reporting on any irregularities. The Act has been twice amended, but the principles remain unchanged. The Comptroller and Auditor-General receives the same salary as the Permanent Secretary of a major department, but, though he is appointed on the recommendation of the Treasury, he is independent of all control except that of Parliament. He is the servant of the Legislature and his duty is to serve as the watchdog over the taxpayers' money. His appointment is for life, subject to good behaviour, and he can be removed from office only on an address by both Houses of Parliament to the Crown. In practice, the Comptroller and Auditor-General reports to a standing committee of the Commons—the Public Accounts Committee.

Each department submits an annual estimate of its expenditure; as soon as Parliament has agreed to it this becomes the department's vote. All revenue received by the State is considered as forming part of a single fund and is paid into the Exchequer account at the Bank of England,[1] and from this account the Treasury may draw up to the total of the votes authorized by Parliament for the various departments. The Treasury alone may operate on the Exchequer account, and before doing so it has to obtain the prior authority of the Comptroller and Auditor-General, who must see that any withdrawal is in order.

When an amount is granted by Parliament it is earmarked for a specific purpose, and one of the responsibilities of the Comptroller and Auditor-General is to satisfy himself that the funds are not diverted to any other use. If Parliament votes money to the imaginary Ministry of Films to produce documentaries, that department will not be allowed to use the funds to purchase a seaside home where exhausted film producers can recuperate. This is a fantastic example, but instances have occurred where departments wished to use their funds for purposes which, although quite admirable, had not been authorized by the House. Parliament had to fight the Crown for the right to appropriate money for particular services, and it attaches importance to the requirement that departments must keep strictly within the ambit of their votes and not start up new activities without legislative approval. All departments are very conscious of the limitation, though they may occasionally slip up.

The Comptroller and Auditor-General informs the Public Accounts Committee whether, in the course of his examination of departmental accounts, he has become aware of any instances where money has been spent in a manner which is or appears to be wasteful or extravagant or unbusinesslike, or which indicates a lack of foresight. No year passes without a number of such departmental failures.

[1] Some departments meet part of their expenditure from money which they collect, but Parliament must approve such arrangements.

Parliament looks to one official in each department to take the responsibility for the proper use of the funds. Since 1920 he has almost invariably been the permanent head of the department. In theory, all departmental expenditure is by direction of the political head of an office, but the chief Civil Servant accounts for the manner in which the money has been spent. If it is the policy of a Ministry to buy, say, thousands of tons of sand, the Minister will be responsible for that policy; but the chief Civil Servant will have to answer to the Public Accounts Committee for the arrangements made for the purchase, and be prepared to defend the form of contract, the source of supply chosen, and so on. As soon as he can after the end of each financial year he must prepare an account of the expenditure of his office during the twelve months ending on 31 March, and any unspent balance of his vote at that day must be surrendered to the Exchequer. The account is not usually completed until September or October, for Government departments need several months to make transfers between themselves, often a complicated business, and to complete their audit. The account—the Appropriation Account—is signed by the permanent head of the office as "accounting officer", and, after examination and certification by the Comptroller and Auditor-General, is submitted to the Public Accounts Committee.

In 1872 that Committee considered the responsibility which rested on the permanent head of a department who signed the Appropriation Account, and the Lords Commissioners of the Treasury replied to the Committee's observations in a long minute.[1] Part of this minute is even now brought to the attention of anyone appointed to act as an accounting officer, with the comment that it is still applicable.

A clear distinction was necessary between the duties of the official who signed the Appropriation Account and the accountant of a department. The term accountant, read the minute from the Treasury, "is no doubt commonly held to describe persons performing duties of a technical character in connection with book-keeping and accounts, and possessing qualifications of a special kind; and my Lords admit that some other title is needed to distinguish between public officers whose high and responsible position in their respective departments is the principal reason of their appointment to render Appropriation Accounts.

" . . . some term should be employed which shall clearly denote the relation in which such last-mentioned officers stand towards

[1] Treasury Minute, 14 August, 1872 (H.C. 154, 1938).

Parliament as responsible for the financial administration of the grant for the services under the control of their departments, while it should at the same time avoid ascribing to them a character which properly belongs only to persons possessing a technical knowledge of book-keeping and accounts.

"It appears to my Lords that the designation of 'Accounting Officer' will sufficiently meet both of these requirements."

The official who signs the account is described as "the person whom Parliament and the Treasury regards as primarily responsible for the balance in the custody of the department, though he himself may not hold one farthing of it".

To avoid misapprehension, the Treasury further decided that "the term 'Accountant' should no longer be applied to the officers entrusted in each department with the technical business of its accounts. They propose, therefore, to alter the designation to that of 'Clerk in charge of the Accounts'." This was one of those simple solutions which solved nothing, for "Clerk in charge of the Accounts" was a title which could hardly have been expected to survive even in official circles. Government offices now employ principal accountants, chief accountants, senior accountants, accountants, and assistant accountants; but the title of the head of a department, so far as financial matters are concerned, continues to be Accounting Officer. This causes a certain amount of confusion, and the head of the office is sometimes regarded as the man who pays the messengers' salaries and spends his time in looking after the petty cash, but the title has the authority of long usage, and what survives in the Civil Service for a century does not change readily.

Expenditure from the Exchequer Account is mainly of two kinds—the Consolidated Fund Services and the Supply Services—and in 1964–5 was estimated at about £7,000,000,000. The Consolidated Fund Services include the interest, management, and expenses of the national debt, the civil list, the costs of the courts of justice, and the salaries of certain high officers. Such expenditure does not require the authority of Parliament each year. In 1963–4 the Consolidated Fund Services amounted to £817,454,549. Departments receive their funds by vote of the Commons sitting as the Committee of Supply, and these Supply Services, which are authorized year by year, cover the vast bulk of the country's expenditure.

The Supply Services are divided into Defence and Civil Estimates. Civil estimates of expenditure are separated into broad classes and each vote has a number within its class. The fifth vote in

Class III, for example, is for the cost to the Exchequer of the police, and is readily identifiable as III, 5.

The form of the estimates remained unchanged for a hundred years. They followed a pattern drawn up in 1866 from which no divergence whatsoever was permitted unless in very exceptional circumstances. It had been often represented that a style appropriate for a century ago when departments were relatively few and expenditure a fraction of what it is today had outlived its usefulness and that a complete overhaul was needed. Nobody, however, seemed anxious to interfere with a pattern which, whatever its disadvantages, had become familiar to M.P.s and a host of officials.

In 1960, however, the decision was taken to revise the form of the estimates, and the Treasury, in collaboration with other departments, began a comprehensive review and suggested considerable changes. The new form of estimates received the blessing of two Parliamentary Committees and was introduced in 1962–3 for the first time.

Among other things, each estimate now contains a table which breaks up the expenditure in accordance with the National Accounts Classification—Current operations abroad; current grants to private sector; capital grants to private sector; gross fixed capital formation at home; transactions with Exchequer, Interest; and Transactions with Exchequer, Capital.

The aim of the revision was stated to be to present the estimates clearly, so that it would be possible to exercise better control of expenditure by providing more information. In fact, the new system gives less detail than formerly in some respects. It has, however, one great advantage: in the old form, it was sometimes necessary to wade through a volume of about 1,000 pages to discover the cost of a particular activity, but under the new arrangements, though some services are still spread over a number of separate votes, the search is much less wearisome, since all expenditure on the same kind of service is grouped within a single class and the relevant votes usually run consecutively. The total number of votes remains the same as about ten years ago—around 150—but the layout has been simplified and such detail as is provided is set out more acceptably.

The classes, previously ten, have been increased by one, the last class containing a miscellaneous collection of votes, including the financial grant to the British Broadcasting Corporation, which for some reason used to be lumped under Education. The rest of Class XI consists of a legacy of pensions to the Royal Irish Constabulary and various minor payments.

The classes of the civil votes, together with the allocations for 1964–5, are as follows:

I.   Government and Exchequer, £95,091,500 net
II.   Commonwealth and Foreign, £180,016,000 net
III. Home and Justice, £158,283,000 net
IV.   Industry, Trade, and Transport, £770,947,000 net
V.   Agriculture, £350,148,000 net
VI.   Local Government, Housing, and Social Services, £2,751,739,000 net
VII. Universities and Scientific Research, £211,261,000 net
VIII. Museums, Galleries, and the Arts, £9,086,000 net
IX.   Public Building and Common Government Services, £342,467,000 net
X.   Smaller Public Departments, £7,508,000 net
XI.   Miscellaneous, £66,808,000 net

The preparation of departmental estimates involves a great amount of work and may call for a good deal of guessing. The Accounting Officer receives on 1 October of each year a document known as the Estimates Circular, over the name of the Financial Secretary to the Treasury. The Accounting Officer is enjoined, for the information of the Lords Commissioners of Her Majesty's Treasury, to forecast the expenditure to be made and the revenue to be collected by his department during the twelve months starting on 1 April of the succeeding year. The letter is a formidable document which lays down in great detail what may not be done and describes less fully what is permissible.

Although the great mass of the country's income is collected by the Inland Revenue and the Customs and Excise, nearly every Government department receives some income in the course of a year, though it may be comparatively trivial. Certain kinds of income must be surrendered to the Exchequer as soon as practicable and not used by a department of defray expenses; other revenue, however, may be taken to offset expenditure, but any amount to be so employed is fixed in advance each year for every department and must be clearly shown in an estimate.

Even if a department collects much more money than it needs to spend, it must still go to Parliament and apply for some finance. Parliament exercises control over the departments by holding the purse, and no department can dodge the duty of seeking money from the legislature. The Royal Mint, for example, spends some £4,000,000 a year in turning out about 900,000,000 coins and, as one would expect, is run at a profit. It earns over £11,000,000, but it seeks authority for a token sum—£1,000—and finances itself otherwise from its income and pays over its net profit to the Exchequer. The Post Office is in a special position: it is operated on semi-commercial lines and does not approach Parliament for money to carry out its services. But Parliament must demonstrate its supremacy: this is done by requiring the Postmaster-General to ask the Commons to vote a few thousand pounds to meet his own salary and that of the Assistant Postmaster-General. Thus, the tradition is maintained that no Government department is ever wholly independent of Parliamentary supervision.

Revenue is described as Appropriations in Aid in Government accounting. The Appropriations in Aid of the Supply Estimates in 1964–5, including Defence, are estimated to amount to £825,700,000.

Under the revised arrangements for estimates, although the total number of votes has remained the same as about ten years ago, the sub-heads have been reduced by around a quarter. Also, instead of budgeting for the cost of services to within a few pounds, as in the past, the practice is now to round off the figures in each sub-head to the nearest 5,000 or 1,000 or to add a balancing figure to the total. No longer, therefore, do we see some department spelling out a request to Parliament for "Three hundred and eighty million seventeen thousand two hundred and ninety-seven pounds." It was always unrealistic to expect such accuracy.

There is an exception to all the rules for estimates—the Secret Service. The Secret Service vote for 1964–5 consists, as it has done for many years, of only a few lines. It says no more than that £8,000,000 is required and that the Treasury will account to Parliament for the expenditure. In practice a statement of how the money is spent is never provided, an arrangement confined to this vote and sections of one or two others (such as the Ordnance Factories, where it is not revealed how much is being devoted to certain activities since information on the scale of the expenditure could be of value to other countries). A hundred years ago when the Secret Service vote amounted to £150,000 per annum, 2 per cent of the present allocation, a Parliamentary Committee commented that it had "of course, not entered into any consideration of the details". It has remained the practice that the legislature is content to accept unquestioningly how the Government spends the pounds voted for the intelligence services.

As an example of the new form in which estimates are prepared for submission to Parliament, the first part of an estimate has been drawn up for the imaginary Ministry of Films and is shown in Appendix V. A complete estimate would take up too much space.

It will be seen that reference is made in the preamble of the estimate to a grant in aid. Where Government departments propose to make such grants the attention of Parliament must be drawn to them specially. As mentioned earlier, grants in aid are moneys given to an organization to provide services directly for the Government or to assist in the provision of services which the Government considers it desirable to encourage. Unlike Whitehall departments, which must surrender any unspent balance at the close of a financial year, a grant-in-aid body usually receives the whole of the agreed amount and any money left over from one year may be retained for future use.

The estimates state where responsibility for expenditure will rest, and this usually means the chief Civil Servant of a department. The estimate goes on to give the headings, distinguished by an alphabetical letter, under which disbursements will be recorded and a comparison of the vote for the preceding year is included. Whatever the number of these sub-heads, the letter Z is always the prefix for Appropriations in Aid. The remainder of the information in an estimate consists principally of details of staff—the number employed with the salaries of the senior and professional staff.

It will be seen that, in addition to the cost of staff and for travelling and incidental expenses, the Ministry of Films spends money on the Purchase of Rights in Films (sub-head C); under Film Production (sub-head D) is the provision for making the few theatrical and non-theatrical films which the Ministry proposes to finance; Film Distribution (sub-head E) is for the operation of cinema vans which will present propaganda shows in various areas and also covers the cost of distributing some films to cinemas; Film Exhibition (sub-head E) includes the expenditure in running the official cinemas. The grant in aid for the Institute of Film Research and Sound Recording (sub-head G) is to give encouragement to an organization whose work may be of value to the Ministry. Souvenirs (sub-head H) covers the purchase of novelties for giving away to the public at gala film performances. No attempt has been made to make the figures realistic in the light of commercial practice. Nor has any money been shown for the construction or reconstruction of cinemas on behalf of the Ministry of Films. For that purpose, the department has a separate buildings vote.

Before an estimate reaches the Commons it has been approved on behalf of the Government. When an estimate is presented, therefore, everyone knows that it will be passed by Parliament, since the Government is committed to the use of its majority to secure the passage of the votes. The Cabinet decides in advance on the scale of expenditure for the Defence services and for some other services which involve large sums, but most estimates are drawn up without a Cabinet directive, though general instructions may be issued by the Chancellor.

By far the greatest part of the civil expenditure of the country is in pursuance of the policy agreed in past years and now accepted by all parties. Such expenditure is outside the control of the departments and only the legislature can amend statutes. A quite trifling reduction in any service is likely to cause an uproar, for every cut in expenditure offends some group, and people who are hurt do not remain silent in a democracy. An outcry arose at once when, on grounds of economy, some parts of the national collections had to be closed to the public; a reduction in the amount made available to the British Broadcasting Corporation aroused bitter criticism in the Commons and elsewhere and was described as "just one example of the many shortsighted, and yet insignificant in amount, economies in the Government's activities in the general field of information services at home and abroad". No session ever passes without some M.P. making a complaint that a worthy cause is being sacrificed through miserable cheeseparing or that facilities which ought to be developed are stagnant because of the incredible meanness of the administration.

Estimates for the year beginning on 1 April are expected to reach the Treasury by the preceding 1 December. Before the estimates arrive, however, the Treasury knows within narrow limits what the major departments will need and few estimates contain any large items which have not previously been discussed. While there can be no interference by the Treasury with the provision for statutory expenditure, there are always some services and administrative costs which can be pared, and most estimates presented to the House are probably for a lower sum than the department first proposed to the Treasury, though not perhaps much lower. The archives of Whitehall are bursting with schemes which are brought out for an airing each year and then regretfully marked away for another twelve months after the departments have had to accept the decision that the money necessary for the projects will not be forthcoming.

The imaginary estimates for the Ministry of Films might start at around £1,300,000 net and show increases in every sub-head; the Ministry considers them highly desirable, if not indeed absolutely essential, for carrying out its functions successfully. Nobody can work on a job without seeing ways in which it could be improved by pouring more money into it. The regional organizers of the Ministry of Films will point out that a few thousand pounds more would enable considerable improvements to be made. The chief producer and his assistants will be quite certain that they could produce better films if only they had another 5 per cent on their budget. Those responsible for the studio will perhaps represent that new equipment ought to be bought, while experts concerned with the distribution of films may point out that a slightly more liberal financial allocation would bring about quicker showings, since more prints of each film could be obtained. In a commercial firm the decision would normally be taken on the basis of whether further expenditure would produce bigger net profits, but the Ministry of Films lacks this yardstick in its operations. Most of its work lies in fields where commercial producers will not enter, and it will expect to make losses.

The Ministry may decide that the first requirement is to increase the number of films. The officials know that they cannot get all the money they would like, and will consider what is practicable as well as what is desirable. The estimate will be cut down after discussions within the department, and when it is sent to the Treasury the figure may be £1,200,000 net.

The Treasury for its part will stress the need for economy. It may have the Chancellor's authority to say that estimates are to be reduced and must not in any case exceed those of the previous year, unless the circumstances are exceptional. Proposals by the Ministry of Films for a few thousand pounds on this sub-head and on that will have to be abandoned until "the national finances are more healthy". The salary scales of some of the staff may have gone up, but the Treasury officials will not necessarily be satisfied that the whole of the consequential extra payments should be by way of an increase in the net vote; the Treasury officials will need to be convinced that the department has no scope for economy elsewhere. In the course of their work at the centre of the financial organization the Treasury staff acquire special knowledge, and their duty is to submit every estimate to a critical examination in the light of that knowledge and of the instructions of their Ministers. If the department and Treasury fail to reach agreement, the Treasury representatives can only say that they will advise the Financial Secretary of the position.

A departmental head, told by the Treasury that his estimates are not acceptable and that the Financial Secretary must be so advised, has recourse to his own political chief. The decision then rests between the Minister of the department, if he backs his officials, and the Treasury Ministers; should Ministers fail to agree, the Cabinet must adjudicate. Politicians in control of a department may be strong or weak, but few of them will risk earning the reputation of being unco-operative with the Exchequer or will want to have their disputes aired before other Ministers who are overburdened with urgent tasks. It is rare therefore for a departmental Minister to resist the Financial Secretary to the Treasury or the Chancellor, unless over a very large issue. For their part, Treasury Ministers will probably not be too unsympathetic to a scheme on which a departmental Minister has really become enthusiastic, provided that it is not completely outrageous and would not have serious financial effects. The Ministers will perhaps reach a basis of agreement over a talk at lunch, and will then wonder why officials cannot show some common sense and make reasonable deals without bothering their political masters. The next time an estimate from the same department is under review the likelihood is that the officials will take good care to come to an agreement somehow or another.

The estimate for the Ministry of Films may be fixed at £1,100,000 net, with an increase in the amounts for film production and film exhibition as well as in salaries, but reductions have taken place in other sub-heads. The increase in the gross total is less than the amount required to meet the higher salary bill. The forecast of revenue is £50,000 under the receipts in the previous year, and it is because of this shortfall that the net deficiency is so large. In these circumstances the Treasury would perhaps have suggested that the gross expenditure should be reduced to compensate for the loss of income, whereas the Ministry of Films would point out that the reduction is due to the decrease in the number of people who attend cinemas, that the running costs cannot be cut in proportion, and that there is no possibility of making further economies. To show willingness the Ministry has reduced the grant in aid to the Institute for Film Research and Development in Sound Recording by £500.

By the beginning of February the squabbles are over and the estimates, agreed by the departmental and Treasury officials, are in the hands of the Financial Secretary. He will have been consulted on at least the major votes at an earlier date, and little change will now be made unless an important policy decision is taken. The next stage rests with Parliament. The close examination given to every estimate, within the department and by Treasury officials, before it reaches the Commons might suggest that the forecasts are correct within narrow margins. That would be quite fallacious. The Comptroller and Auditor-General reported to the Public Accounts Committee that in 1962–3 revenue had not come up to expectations and was about £10,000,000 less than anticipated, and that the departments as a whole had underspent by around £200,000,000. This over-provision for expenditure may seem huge when one looks at the figures by themselves. When, however, they are related to the disbursements of thousands of millions of pounds in the year, the picture is different. The under-spending was about 3.2 per cent.

Even so, the surplus held in some departments at the close of a financial year is often very large. This does not necessarily mean that the estimators have been irresponsible or that the Treasury has fallen down in its scrutiny. There may be special circumstances—some activity which a department confidently hoped to expand may be reduced in volume or Government policy may have changed suddenly. The departments, moreover, make their forecasts so far in advance that precision in some allocations is almost bound to be unattainable.

On the other hand, when protests have been made that the estimates were unrealistic, Whitehall has taken note and has usually been able to improve its forecasting. A few years ago the Comptroller and Auditor-General pointed out that the underspending amounted to 6 per cent. In the following year, the departments managed to reduce the over-provision to less than half that percentage.

In the middle of February the Financial Secretary publishes a memorandum which lists the total of each of the Civil Estimates and draws attention to the reasons for the increases and decreases in the different classes. At this stage all the detailed estimates are not available. The House of Commons will require the details only when it examines the individual estimates, a process spread over four months. The rules of the House provide that "26 days, being days before the 5th of August, shall be allotted to the business of supply in each session". The last of the departmental estimates are as a rule not passed by the Commons until just before the end of the summer session.

Since Government departments must not carry over funds from one year to another, and since they have to meet liabilities before the estimates as a whole are passed, arrangements are made for funds to be provided to them to finance operations immediately the new financial year begins on 1 April. This is done by means of a Vote on Account, which the Financial Secretary presents to the House in March, for about a third of the total amount of the year's estimates. The resolution is in standard form, and is that such and such a sum should be "granted to Her Majesty, on account for, or towards defraying, the charges for the year ending on 31st March . . .". The Vote on Account for the year from 1 April, 1964, is £1,700,906,100.

Parliament gives its assent to the Vote on Account before the end of March under the Consolidated Fund (No. 1) Act,[1] and funds can therefore be released from the first day of the new financial year as may be necessary. When the Commons come to consider the detailed departmental estimates, it is the Opposition which chooses which of them shall be the subject of debate in the twenty-six allotted Supply Days, and the Government must table those votes for approval.

The whole House sits as a Committee of Supply to consider the estimates. It is the long-established right of the Commons to present their grievances and seek redress before voting supplies of money to the Sovereign, and a debate on an estimate may range over a very wide field. In a few instances only is there any real examination of the financial provisions of the estimate under discussion; but the Opposition will certainly criticize vigorously some parts of the department's policy, and the Government speakers will leap to its defence.

While most departmental estimates are passed without a debate, those selected by the Opposition may be the subject of discussion for several hours. There are departments which welcome the opportunity to obtain publicity for their work by means of speeches in Parliament, and which hope therefore that their estimates will be picked out for debate in the Commons; but most departments probably prefer that their money should be voted without comment. Departments wait anxiously to hear which estimates have been selected for discussion. When an estimate is chosen, the Minister responsible for it, together with other Government spokesmen, must be briefed by officials of the department. Civil Servants cannot intervene in Parliamentary proceedings, but several representatives of the department whose vote is being examined will be present in the Official Box, behind and to the right of the Speaker's Chair. The officials will carry much more information in their bulging black bags than has been included in the ministerial briefs, which must not be lengthy or they would be unmanageable.

---

[1] This Act contains authority for other expenditure in addition to the Vote on Account.

When a proposal for expenditure is made to the Commons, the proposer must signify to the Speaker that the Sovereign's recommendation has been given, which means that all such motions are made by one of the Queen's Ministers. The Opposition cannot therefore move that a department should insert an additional sum in its estimate. Members on the Opposition benches may feel that inadequate funds are being devoted to some object, but in order to secure a debate their only course is to move that the department should receive less money! In any case, the Government's majority will ensure that the estimate will pass unaltered.

If the mythical Ministry of Films' estimates were selected for debate, some critics would doubtless contend in the Commons that the Government ought to take over more cinemas; others that the State should never have acquired any at all and must at once dispose of those cinemas it owns. Such speakers might be followed by others who suggested that the Ministry of Films could not produce good enough feature films because it was not allowed to spend adequate amounts and that the country needed lavishly mounted features. The next participant would perhaps point out that the Ministry had at its disposal large sums of money which it spent wastefully and that the Minister would be well advised to use his funds to subsidize commercial producers instead of making films direct. There would probably be complaints that the Ministry paid too much attention to documentary films, and soon afterwards other speakers might be expected to declare that Britain had won a high reputation for such films and that the Ministry ought to concentrate far more on productions of this kind.

It may seem a waste of time for criticisms to be made when an estimate is under consideration, for the House knows that it will be passed as submitted by the department, whatever the speakers may say. The departmental Minister and his officials will, however, note carefully what is said in the debate, and suggestions which are made at that time may lead to a change in the method of providing some existing service, or to the introduction of a new service. Allowance must naturally be made for the fact that the Opposition will not be unprejudiced in its comments.

However carefully the information has been collected for the debate, some point is almost certain to be raised on which the officials in the Box have incomplete knowledge or about which they may know nothing at all. Hurried telephone calls will be made to obtain particulars from the office, where some members of the staff will have been told to remain at their desks until the conclusion of the debate. The Minister or his Parliamentary Secretary or his Private Parliamentary Secretary will perhaps call their officials to a conference, possibly held in the corridor behind the Official Box, and the new facts will be inserted into speeches where they can be used with most telling effect.

Few officials, other than exhibitionists, can really enjoy attending in the Official Box and listening to the politicians discussing a department's business at estimates time. Other things apart, the Official Box in the Commons is not particularly comfortable—it is rumoured that this is deliberate, so that officials will not go to sleep while on duty and will have no encouragement to invent excuses for crowding into the few seats in the Box on the great occasions of the House. After sitting in the Box for several hours until the end of the debate is reached, the most junior official may have a final duty before he goes home: to telephone the order of release to his colleagues who have been standing by in the office to assemble any further details which were required.

Next morning the officials who have been present at the debate may regale their friends with stories of how they produced immediate rebuttals to charges and made the rout of the Opposition a certainty. But a study of *Hansard* usually shows that some allegations have not had a complete reply from a Government spokesman—perhaps because nobody knew, or had time to find out, whether there was any effective answer; or because the officials realized only too well that the department had no convincing defence to offer.

Chapter Thirteen

SUPPLEMENTARY ESTIMATES

ALTHOUGH all estimates have been examined and agreed by the Treasury before submission to the Commons, a department is not free to go ahead and spend up to the limit of the moneys which have been voted for its work. The Treasury is in control of all expenditure. At its discretion, it delegates authority to departments for specified types of disbursements, subject to review from time to time, but otherwise every department must seek prior Treasury sanction before any commitment is made. The departments conduct a running correspondence with the Treasury about the expenditure they wish to incur, and departmental and Treasury officials meet frequently to discuss proposed schemes. An Assistant Secretary, with perhaps two Principals and subordinate staff, deals in the Treasury with the activities of a group of services. These officials exercise a close supervision over the finances of the individual projects for which they have been given responsibility and know a great deal about the detail of their operation.

There are so many checks on the control of public funds that, if evidence did not exist to the contrary, it might seem impossible that any waste could ever occur. In some departments operational divisions are responsible for the control of their own funds, subject to Treasury sanction which they themselves seek, where necessary. In most departments, however, expenditure is in the charge of a Finance Division. The mythical Ministry of Films has been shown as having a Finance Division with an Under-Secretary at its head, and this is a common pattern.

Except in the large departments, which have a separate Contracts Division, the Finance Division places the contracts for goods or services. The number and value of Government contracts is, of course, colossal, and thousands of companies and firms want to have their share of the work. Departments must take care to see that all interested and competent people have a fair chance to obtain orders on competitive terms. A Contracts Co-ordinating Committee meets at the Treasury as required and issues directions and advice to departments on all questions relating to the placing of contracts, the preparation of specifications, the terms of payment, and so on. Not all work can be the subject of competition, since some of it is of a highly specialized kind. The Ministry of Aviation missile contracts, where the overheads were miscalculated and as a result the contractor was able to make a profit of over 80 per cent, were of this type.

Strict precautions are taken against fraud. The usual procedure in a Government department is to require tenders to be delivered before a specified date and hour and placed in a locked box, which is not opened until the advertised time. All the tenders are taken out together and examined at the same time by at least three officials, who form a Tender Board. The board lists the different bids, and it is then for another section of the Contracts Branch to place the contract, after consultation with the operational division, if this is required. The lowest tender is accepted unless there are special reasons why it should be passed over, and a decision to accept any tender other than the lowest must be approved by a senior official; in the case of very large contracts the Permanent Secretary or the Minister may have to give authority.

In view of the precautions taken and the careful vetting of the staff before appointment to established positions, the number of dismissals every year for misconduct, including fraud and peculation, looks on first glance to be very high. In 1963 the number dismissed on those grounds was 540, or one out of about 1,300 of the non-industrial staff; but more than 80 per cent of the offenders—out of the 540—were employees of the Post Office, principally postmen. The possibility of engaging in large-scale fraud is very slight. The more obvious frauds—such as inserting a tender after seeing the prices quoted by other contractors—are impossible in a well-organized office, but no system can ever be entirely safe against a conspiracy. If the members of a Tender Board are all dishonest men they may give preference to one contractor to the detriment of others, though such a fraud will be bound to be discovered before very long where proper checks are imposed. Some of the delay in the finalizing of contracts by Government departments is due to the precautions taken to prevent fraudulent practice.

No department invites tenders for a new scheme until it is clear that the Treasury will agree to the expenditure. The department first of all makes up its mind what would be likely to be a reasonable figure for the work to be done, probably adds a margin to be on the safe side, and then seeks the sanction of the Treasury. The more important correspondence between the Finance Division of the Ministry of Films and the Treasury will be conducted by the Under-Secretary, the most important matters of all being reserved for the Permanent Secretary.

The idea that every department was at heart a spendthrift and could only be kept within reasonable bounds by the ever-watchful eyes in Treasury Chambers waned very slowly and has not entirely disappeared even yet.

Until a few years ago, major departments, employing thousands of people under high-paid directing staffs and with votes totalling millions of pounds, had to seek specific Treasury authority for the expenditure of quite small sums of money if within certain fields. A visitor might, for example, slip on the stairs and sustain injury to his leg. If he decided to instruct his solicitor to make a claim for the accident, the department's lawyer would perhaps recommend that the matter be settled by the payment of £150.

But the department was not empowered to agree to meet the claim. It had to write to the Treasury describing what had happened, perhaps explaining that the unfortunate man's injury was caused by a careless cleaner who forgot to use non-slip polish and promising that this sort of thing would never occur again.

It was, of course, inconceivable that the Treasury would turn down the request, but the system of seeking special sanction for such payments lingered throughout generations. The theory was that the Treasury had the duty of ensuring that all the departments kept in step. It would intolerable that it should be more rewarding to meet with an accident in Office A than in Office B! Because of the rule that payments of this kind could not be made except with Treasury agreement, a great deal of letter-writing went on. A Parliamentary Committee which examined the system was appalled by the position and, as a result of its comments, the Treasury has recently granted more delegation to the departments to make *ex gratia* payments.

No department ever likes to be caught short of funds, and every office usually manages to tuck away a comfortable margin in its vote; but circumstances change and a department may find that it cannot carry out its work without overspending on a sub-head of its vote or even on several sub-heads. The Finance Division will perhaps foresee compensating savings on other sub-heads, but it is not within the competence of a department to make transfers between sub-heads, though it may switch money between the different services provided within the same sub-head. The Treasury alone has authority to sanction transfers from one sub-head to another without the prior approval of Parliament, and then only within certain well-defined limits and in accordance with long-established practice. The Treasury cannot, for example, permit a department to provide a new grant-in-aid or to increase an existing grant-in-aid. Nor can it authorize the introduction of a service which is not within the scope of a vote, unless as an interim measure until Parliamentary authority is obtained. Where changes are necessary in estimates during the course of a financial year and are of a kind which the Treasury is not empowered to authorize, the approval of Parliament must be sought by by means of a Supplementary Estimate. The Commons can consider such an estimate at any time it finds convenient during the session. In practice, the Supplementary Estimates are normally submitted in batches in July and February.

Early in the financial year the Ministry of Films will perhaps decide that it must spend more money on souvenirs. It will seek Treasury agreement to increase the allocation from £5,000 to £15,000, on the understanding that the expenditure on Distribution will be reduced by £10,000.[1] A transfer from sub-head E to sub-head H for such purpose is within the powers of the Treasury and need not therefore be referred to Parliament. A transfer between sub-heads or between votes is known as "virement". Departmental Finance Divisions have the French word frequently on their lips, not always with the same pronunciation, and it sometimes causes difficulty elsewhere. A Minister in the course of a debate in the Commons about transfers between the different Defence votes raised the question "whether we can discuss this only by way of excess vote or by virement", and a Government spokesman interjected: "I am sorry to interrupt the hon. and learned Gentleman, but he used an expression which I am afraid I do not understand. It was 'by way of' something or other." "It was 'by way of virement'. I believe I have used a good English pronunciation for the French word," was the reply. "It is a process by which the Treasury may exchange sums voted for one purpose for sums voted for another. Normally the House takes the view that this is a reasonable procedure, and that the thing should go through on the nod." Later in the debate the Financial Secretary to the Treasury referred to "the somewhat eclectic word 'virement'."

Few departments get through the financial year without virement, unless they are exceptionally knowledgeable, unusually lucky, or have inserted an inflated amount for each sub-head in their estimates to

---

[1] But, of course, the Treasury uses its authority with discretion. If the Ministry of Films estimated £100,000 for one sub-head and £1,000 for another, the Treasury would not allow the figures to become £50,000 and £51,000 respectively.

make quite certain that they are covered against all eventualities. Transfer between votes is permitted only in respect of the fighting services and subject to report later to Parliament. Transfer between sub-heads is usually a routine matter, but not always. In May the Institute for Film Research and Development in Sound Recording may explain to the Ministry of Films that, far from being able to give up £500 compared with the previous year, it needs an increase in its grant to £5,000, since otherwise it will be unable to carry out an important piece of work. The Ministry of Films will not be readily convinced that such an increase is essential, nor will the Treasury. Only if the Institute is able to prove that the work cannot be held over until a later year and that the money must be made available or the consequences will be serious is the the Treasury likely to consent to a Supplementary Estimate. Ministers do not in general like Supplementary Estimates, nor does Parliament look on them with favour.

The Ministry of Films may be able to reduce its expenditure elsewhere so that the additional money will be available to the Institute. If it were merely a matter of switching funds from one ordinary subhead to another, it would be fairly straightforward, but a grant-in-aid is involved, and Parliament alone can give authority for any increase in such a grant. It may be decided that the Ministry should find £2,000 by making savings in sub-head F (Exhibition) and that approval should be sought for an extra £500 by means of a Supplementary Estimate. The Supplementary will be presented to the Commons on behalf of the Ministry in July and will show a reduction of £2,000 in sub-head F and an increase of £2,500 in sub-head G so that the Institute can go ahead with its work. The difference of £500 is the amount which Parliament will be asked to sanction.

Nor may this be the only time during the financial year in which the ill-fated Ministry of Films will have to submit a revised estimate, first to the Treasury and then to Parliament. In October the Ministry receives an offer of the rights in a number of old films at a cost of £70,000. It has already earmarked all its allocation under C, Purchase of Rights, and it may hesitate to ask for more. But the films it has been offered are regarded as very useful and the Ministry is anxious to accept the opportunity to add to its collection. It will discuss the proposal with the Treasury, which may be unwilling to contemplate such an increase in the total vote and suggest that the Ministry should go away and think again. So the Ministry, keen to complete the bargain and convinced that the old films will make a profit during the remaining months of the year and a further profit later, may feel that it should reduce its expenditure on Production (sub-head D) by £49,500 and provide for an addition to its revenue of £20,000. That may seem simple enough, but Government finance is not so easy. Parliament has for a hundred years kept a watchful eye on what departments do with revenue. Only the Commons can authorize a department to use extra revenue to meet extra costs, so the Ministry of Films will be unable to apply this additional income to offset the further expenditure. The unfortunate Ministry must therefore beg the Treasury to present a further Supplementary. This will be done in February, when the Treasury will submit on behalf of the Ministry of Films a revised vote, again providing for a token increase of £500. If the Ministry's predictions of revenue and expenditure are absolutely accurate, it should at the end of the financial year have a balance of £1,000, made up of two increases to its net vote of £500 each; but such estimating is not to be looked for in the world of films or anywhere else.

Although there are always some token Supplementaries in both July and February, a number of the revised estimates are for very substantial sums, perhaps because of the expansion in one of the armed forces or because of unforeseeable demands on some social service or just because someone has blundered badly. In 1963–4, the total of the Supplementary Votes amounted to £137,627,600.

During the war some departments were relieved of the troublesome procedure of main estimates and supplementaries. Parliament granted Votes of Credit for war purposes and waived the requirement that details of proposed expenditure should be shown under each sub-head. The Commons accepted the position that the presentation of normal estimates might convey valuable information to the enemy, but the House surrendered its rights with reluctance, and on the termination of hostilities the traditional system of financing the departments was resumed almost at once. When finance officers meet, they sometimes tell one another of what bold financial gestures could be made, and so easily made, in the "happy days of Votes of Credit".

Solutions have been found to most of the perplexities caused by the ordinary legislative procedure for providing money to meet the expenditure of the departments, though Civil Servants complain that the system is tedious and awkward and unrealistic in present conditions. Obviously a department which has miscalculated the cost of an existing service, or which wishes to expand a service urgently needed by the public, cannot be left without funds for its work until a Supplementary Estimate can be presented in July or the following

February. The Civil Contingencies Fund exists for such emergencies. Parliament agrees each year that the Treasury should have at its disposal a fund from which it may advance money to any department, either because the vote has been exhausted or because, although there is adequate money within the vote, some step involving expenditure has to be taken prior to the sanction of the Legislature. Amounts so advanced must be repaid to the Civil Contingencies Fund and, at the first opportunity, Parliament is approached for authority for a grant to enable the debt to be discharged. The repayments to the fund may amount to hundreds of thousands. No one could pretend that departmental finance is easy to understand or that Parliamentary procedure for voting funds is simple.

As mentioned earlier, the first allocation of funds for the new financial year is provided under the authority of the Consolidated Fund (No. 1) Act, passed by both Houses of Parliament before the end of March. When a number of complete estimates have been accepted subsequently by Parliament and authority to utilize further money from the Consolidated Fund has become necessary, Parliament passes the Consolidated Fund (N. 2) Act, and a third such Act may be required during the session. In any case, there must be a Consolidated Fund (Appropriation) Act, usually passed within a few days as one of the last pieces of legislation before the summer recess. While the other Consolidated Fund Acts are quite short and do little more than state the total amount to be released from the Fund, the Appropriation Act for the session has attached to it a number of schedules which set out the departmental estimates one by one in some detail, and any variation to these schedules must be notified.

The Commons had the first reading of the Consolidated Fund (Appropriation) Bill for 1963–4 on 27 July; the second reading took place on the following day and the Bill was committed to a Committee of the whole House. The Committee reported on the next day without amendment and then came the third reading. The finance aspect was not mentioned. The debate which ensued dealt with Representational Services Overseas, Southern Rhodesia, and Mentally Handicapped Children.

The Bill was endorsed by Mr Speaker as a money bill and presented to the Lords on 30 July. The proceedings were purely formal, since the peers do not intervene in money bills. The first and second readings took place without any debate, there was no Committee stage, and the Lords gave the Bill its third reading, all on the same day. Next day, the Bill received royal assent.

Chapter Fourteen

COMMON SERVICES

FROM the specimen estimate of the imaginary Ministry of Films (Appendix V) it will be seen that against the Ministry has been logged the cost of certain services provided by other Government departments. No payment is made for such services by the recipients, but the estimated cost is included in the votes so that Parliament may have an idea of the total cost of any office. Work performed by one department for another free of charge is known as an "allied service", and departments whose main functions are for the benefit of other Government organizations are known as "common service" departments. The principal offices in the common service group are the Ministry of Public Building and Works, the Stationery Office, and the Central Office of Information. The actual cost of the allied services which they perform on behalf of individual Government departments is not regularly published.

The Ministry of Public Building and Works is responsible for nearly all Government buildings at home and for their furnishing and also looks after property occupied by British embassies and legations. In addition to the provision of accommodation for the Government service generally, the Ministry maintains the royal palaces and parks.

Many of the ancient monuments of the country have been handed over to the custody of the Ministry of Works. Only in 1953, however, under the authority of the Historic Buildings and Ancient Monuments Act, did the department obtain power to make financial contributions towards the upkeep of buildings of outstanding historical and architectural interest which are still occupied by their owners. Separate Historic Buildings Councils have been set up in England, Scotland, and Wales to advise the Minister of Works regarding the buildings to which assistance should be given. Since the Act was passed, the department has offered financial assistance to the owners of notable houses—thirty a year is about the average. A condition is that the public obtains reasonable access to the property.

This, however, is a very minor though highly interesting activity of the department: its principal work is concerned with the accommodation of Civil Servants. Most officials are badly housed. With a few exceptions the Government buildings in Whitehall are very old and dreadfully inconvenient. Proposals have been put forward that the whole area should be redeveloped, but immense costs would be involved and nothing much has been done. Nor, of course, does the suggestion of redevelopment meet with unanimous approval since some historic buildings would have to disappear. Expenditure on renovation is sometimes higher than the cost of new structures, and the Ministry of Works shocked the public when it presented the bill for Downing Street and the old Treasury buildings. The cost of renovation was originally estimated at slightly over £1,000,000, but the expenditure came out at double this sum.

Rooms in Government offices are furnished according to the rank of the officers who occupy them. A strict standard is laid down which departments sometimes try to evade but which in the long run they are usually forced to accept. Few things have aroused so much protest on the part of the staff in the past as the dingy rooms, bad lighting, and poorly designed furniture. The improvement made in recent years has been startling; but, though the standard is much higher, one room looks rather like all the others allotted to officers of the same rank, in whatever department they may serve. British offices overseas are more luxuriously furnished, but a Civil Servant who visits a British Embassy will feel quite at home, since some of the furnishings will be exactly the same as those he left behind in his own room in London (or Birmingham or Bath or Edinburgh).

The little appurtenances of rank are dear to the heart of the official. If he is graded as a Principal, a man is likely to have a carpet of some kind, and if as an Assistant Secretary he will certainly have a passable carpet; he will also be entitled to a large-size desk, an easy-chair for the use of his visitors, and a spare table for conferences, though he may never hold any conferences. When he climbs the next step in the promotion ladder, to Under-Secretary, he will have a better conference table and he may even manage to acquire a clock for his mantelpiece. The official will be recognized as being near to the top flight of his profession when his conference table is an antique. There are said to be Civil Servants of high rank who insist on two clocks, but the most senior of all are reported to be satisfied with a single clock provided it is a museum piece. Senior officers, too, have the privilege of writing their letters on blue-coloured notepaper[1] instead of the white used by the lesser breeds. Such fruits of office, though well understood and endeared by usage to men and women who have

---

[1] In some departments the most senior officials share with their Minister the privilege of using notepaper bearing only the crest of the office, printed in red.

spent their working lives in the Service, are often a source of much annoyance or amusement to members of the public who come into contact with the system. But if the badges of office are to be treated with levity, nothing is sacrosanct in a Government department.

Arrangements by which a single department provides accommodation and furnishing for all are obviously desirable. Apart from the economies which can be made by centralizing the work and by bulk purchase of articles and materials, the procedure avoids the scramble among the departments for supplies of a higher standard on the ground that their prestige demands something better than the general run. Some twenty years ago it was agreed that the Foreign Office should have special latitude in their buildings and furnishings, but this has led, almost inevitably, to complaint that the costs are too high.

Where a department needs a new building, the Ministry of Works is responsible for making the plans and drawings, or for commissioning an architect to prepare them. It places the contract for construction with a commercial firm, and its staff supervises the work and may provide specialized services. In general, the Ministry meets the whole of the costs from its own funds in such circumstances. It must defend the way in which the work has been carried out and prove, if need be, that there has been no extravagance. But it is acting as an agent and is known therefore as the "agent department". The duty of justifying the need for a building, and a building of the particular type constructed, rests with the department which asked for its provision—the "principal department". This division of responsibility sometimes makes for a rather uneasy partnership and has caused a certain amount of confusion.

A Committee of the House of Commons asked a number of questions about the respective responsibilities of the agent and the principal department in a transaction, and the Treasury explained: "Where one Department is carrying out work on behalf of another as an agent, the principal Department is responsible for the policy necessitating the expenditure. The principal Department must define its requirements. . . . The principal Department will keep itself informed of the course of the expenditure on its behalf, but the agent Department, and not the principal Department, is responsible for the exercise of efficiency and economy in the administration of the service provided by the agent Department." Perhaps not surprisingly, the Committee did not appear to be quite satisfied with this pronouncement. When it took oral evidence on the subject it inquired whether the Ministry of Works could criticize the kind of buildings which a department wanted to have erected for its use. "To what extent," the Chairman asked a representative of the Ministry of Works, "would you say the Ministry of Works has the right to go back to a Department and say, 'Your requests are altogether too lavish?'" The representative replied that his Ministry had the right to make such criticisms and sometimes exercised it, but that the agent department could be over-ruled. On the point whether another department was justified in obtaining its own estimate of cost from a private contractor in order to satisfy itself that the Ministry of Works was doing the job at a fair price, the Ministry of Works' representative stated his office's doctrine very firmly: "I think it would be intolerable to suggest that it was the business of all the Departments to which we are providing a service to be 'testing our efficiency'. To start with, I am not quite sure how you would test our efficiency. But I should maintain that it is the responsibility of the Ministry of Works ... to make itself and to keep itself efficient ... it is not for other Departments to be testing our efficiency from time to time."

The particular piece of work which gave rise to these questions was one in which the cost of a building constructed through the agency of the Ministry of Works on behalf of the Home Office greatly exceeded the original estimated cost. Few officials either wish to arrange for their department's building contracts or think they could get the work done more cheaply or competently by sidetracking the Ministry of Works, but where printing and publicity are concerned there may be contrasting views. The public relations branches of Government departments are often staffed by people who have had considerable experience in advertising and many of whom have decided opinions on how the Stationery Office should print a poster or a booklet and how the Central Office of Information should conduct publicity.

The Stationery Office, which comes under the direction of the Chancellor of the Exchequer, has as its permanent head a Controller, who is the Queen's Printer, an ancient and honoured title; such an office has existed in this country since 1786. The department prints the Papers, Bills, and Acts for both Houses of Parliament, the Parliamentary Debates (Hansard), and the Command Papers,[1] as well as a vast number of non-Parliamentary papers and other publications. They are sold at a price which will, it is estimated, cover the costs of production, and the department is not in business to make a profit.

---

[1] The Command Papers are numbered consecutively in series. Until 1895 the number was prefixed by the letter C; from 1900 to 1918 by the letters Cd.; from 1918 to 1956 by the letters Cmd.; and since then the letters Cmnd. have been used. Such papers are technically presented by command of the Sovereign to Parliament.

Each year it issues about 6,000 publications and its sales reach 15,000,000–20,000,000 copies. Though it makes very wide use of commercial houses, the Stationery Office undertakes much of the Government printing and binding in its own establishments.

The Civil Servant needs to buy nothing at all at his own expense in connection with his work. Everything he requires is supplied at the cost of the Government. Should he need a book or map, the Stationery Office will supply it, though the process is sometimes slow and frustrating. The Stationery Office is able to buy books from publishers at the same discount as a large bookseller and, equally important to other departments, it makes no charge for the books it purchases for distribution to Government offices. So if an official asks for a book his department would not dream of sending a messenger to the local bookseller and paying for a copy from the petty cash. A central point exists in each department from which orders for books are sent to the Stationery Office as required. The stationery clerk may have been told to keep down the number and cost of such orders, and the more conscientious he is the greater may be the fury which he arouses in his colleagues.

The final responsibility will not rest with the clerk. If he agrees that the book should be ordered, he will make out a requisition to the Stationery Office and pass it for counter-signature to a more senior officer, for clerks are not usually entitled to authorize demands for such supplies. The counter-signing officer may decide to make inquiries of his own and, if he is doubtful about the need for the purchase of a book, may consult his superior. If the requisition is eventually sent to the Stationery Office, the book will be supplied, with a form on which the clerk will acknowledge receipt. He will then stamp the book at the front, at the back, and round the edges "For official use" in indelible ink, lest a wicked Civil Servant might take the copy home or sell it.

The ordering procedure will perhaps discourage an official from asking his department to get a copy of a book for him, and this may, or may not, be a good thing; or the official may buy a copy from the local bookseller at lunchtime, and thus the taxpayer's money will be saved. But though the arrangements are designed to ensure that only essential publications are ordered and that there is no over-lavish distribution within the departments, the latest published accounts of the Stationery Office show that the expenditure on books and maps in the course of a single year amounts to over £1,500,000. This may indicate the patience of Civil Servants and how determined they are to keep up to date at the cost of the Government. Or, of course, it may indicate that too many officials receive a copy of every Parliamentary and other official paper as a matter of routine distribution and that too many copies of newspapers and of expensive reference books are delivered to Government departments.

It may be difficult to obtain a copy of a new book in a Government department, but the problem is trifling compared with that of introducing a new form. Government departments are accused of taking an unholy glee in adding to the number of forms with which they are supposed to bamboozle the public. In fact, it is a major achievement to induce an office to authorize an extra form. Nothing indeed sounds more ominous to the public than an increase in the number of forms; it is invariably regarded as a confession of incompetence or arbitrariness on the part of lazy officials. The tendency of departments is therefore to make one form do the work of two or more, with the consequence that, while the number of different kinds of forms may become fewer, the size of the others become ever larger.

The expert may over-estimate the ability of the public to understand forms and produce a type of form which calls for a legal training before it can be tackled with confidence. Quite as often, however, the expert swings to the other extreme and under-estimates the common sense of the public; in trying to make his requirements crystal clear he thinks it necessary to clutter up his form with long explanations, and few people do more than skim through such printed matter. No one doubts that in all large organizations which have to collect statistics, issue permits and licences, and prepare returns, forms are inevitable. It is, however, human nature to be struck with mental paralysis when faced with an official form, or to become rebellious or even perhaps perverse. Civil Servants are probably not as a class any better in filling up forms than the average member of the public. The man who day by day is handling forms returned by citizens, and who has formed a poor impression of an educational system which cannot equip people with the knowledge to reply accurately to a "simple questionnaire", is not necessarily much more competent in filling up forms designed by others. The branch of the Inland Revenue Department which deals with Civil Servants' income tax—a special branch because of the number involved—is said to be dismayed by the mistakes of officials in making their returns.

When a department wishes to issue a publication, it cannot go direct to a printer of its choice. It employs the Stationery Office which can get the work done more cheaply than other departments, and

Parliament entrusts to it the money for most, though not all, the printing required by Government offices. The operations of the Stationery Office are vast. Its purchases of paper from the mills in 1964-5 is estimated at over £7,000,000. Unless the printing is done by one of its own printing houses, the Stationery Office orders the work from a commercial printer, to whom it supplies the paper, a more economical arrangement than asking the printer to provide his own paper. If a department wants a publicity booklet, it will not go direct to the Stationery Office. There is an intermediary—the Central Office of Information must come into the transaction.

On the abolition of the Ministry of Information at the end of March 1946 such of its work as the Government decided to continue was divided between the Foreign Office, the Colonial Office, the Commonwealth Relations Office, and a new department, the Central Office of Information. Like the Stationery Office, the C.O.I. supplies a number of services to Government departments free of charge but logs the estimated costs against them. It arranges, through commercial agents, for the Government's Press and poster advertising. Its experts write or commission the text of a booklet, if the department which initiates the proposal does not wish to do this work itself; and in any case the C.O.I. will prepare the layout. The department maintains a photographic section which is at the disposal of all Government offices, and it mounts exhibitions in overseas countries from time to time as well as at home. Official news is distributed to Fleet Street by the C.O.I., which also prepares a valuable daily summary of comment on the news for transmission to all British representatives overseas.

Public reaction to any official publicity is inclined to be one of deep suspicion. No one can escape the Government's advertising campaigns, for the operations are on a very wide scale and examples are seen everywhere. Like all publicity measures, the effect of such campaigns is often a matter of opinion rather than of established fact. "Publicity is not a science," a C.O.I. representative told a Parliamentary committee, "and its results are very often not measurable. There are, of course, always a certain number of rough, common-sense tests that one can apply. One can, for example, watch the relationship between the volume of expenditure on Service recruiting and the actual level of enlistment. Even then, of course, the other factors do not remain constant, so that one can never be absolutely sure."

It is not the function of the C.O.I. to make propaganda for any political party—each party has its own organization for this purpose. The distinction is well understood, but it is not always appreciated that the C.O.I. does not launch publicity measures on its own responsibility. Other departments which require publicity come to the C.O.I. as the Government's central production agency, and are advised of the best media to use and the cost which would be involved. The department which asks for a publicity campaign must decide whether the expenditure is justified.

Not only is the Government publicity machine precluded from boosting the achievements of any administration, but it is also forbidden to spend money in advocating the desirability of any measure which has not yet reached the statute book. Once a measure has been passed and has become the law of the land the C.O.I. may properly use its services in explaining the effect of the new legislation and in bringing its provisions to the notice of the public. It must not, however, use public money to declare that the new Act is a wonderful achievement which the country owes to the prudence, skill, and devoted efforts of the Government of the day, and which would never have been drawn up by the incompetents who form the party in Opposition. Mistakes are sometimes made by the C.O.I., and in such a field they are bound to be made now and again. Any party in Opposition is rightly watchful of the actions of the Government publicity organization. The C.O.I. walks a tightrope, and very successfully.

Everyone agrees that the House of Commons cannot devote the time to examine departmental estimates. Proposals have often been made that the Commons should adopt the practice as in America, where Congress appoints a number of committees which are responsible for examining estimates covering particular activities —defence, labour, foreign affairs, aviation and so on. No estimate of expenditure is accepted by Congress until it has been considered in such a committee, in which the same members serve year after year, becoming highly knowledgeable on the functions and operations of a particular department. This system has, however, never been favoured here. Its opponents argue that the committees become too closely involved in policy and that officials lobby the politicians on behalf of their pet schemes. Moreover, it is claimed, the American system would be in inappropriate in this country where Ministers may be questioned in Parliament, whereas in the United States there is no such inquisition in the Senate or the House of Representatives.

The House of Commons has made a number of attempts to deal

with the problem of the estimates of Whitehall departments. Throughout the nineteenth century Select Committees were set up to examine individual estimates or groups of estimates, but such committees were largely useless as a means of confirming that the expenditure on services was justified. During the nineteenth century frequent inquiries took place into the work of one department or another, but no regular procedure was instituted. In 1912 a Select Committee on Estimates was appointed with the object of subjecting departmental estimates to critical scrutiny: its operations were suspended at the beginning of the 1914 war. The protests against extravagance in Government administration during the war led to the appointment in 1917 of a Select Committee on National Expenditure, which was re-appointed each year until 1920, during which period it produced a number of highly adverse reports on the operation of departmental services. In 1921 the Select Committee on Estimates was revived; it functioned each session until, at the beginning of the 1939 war, it gave way to another Select Committee on National Expenditure. After the end of hostilities, the Select Committee on Estimates was revived and has since sat each session.

The terms of reference of the Estimates Committee are "to examine such of the Estimates presented to this House [of Commons] as may have been put to the Committee, and to suggest the form in which the Estimates shall be presented for examination, and to report what, if any, economies consistent with the policy implied in those Estimates may be effected therein." The Committee is composed of thirty-six M.P.s drawn from all parties, under a chairman who supports the Government in office but is not a Minister; although a back-bencher, he is usually a prominent member.

The Committee forms itself into a number of sub-committees identified by a letter of the alphabet. Sub-Committee A allocates the work and the other sub-committees (B, C, etc.), of which there may be half a dozen, each undertakes one or more investigations. The sub-committees do not examine more than a small proportion of the estimates. About ten to twelve reports are issued each session. Among other things the Estimates Committee in the 1963-4 session dealt with the work of Service Colleges, the Forestry Commission, Military Expenditure Overseas, Technical Co-operation, and Transport Aircraft.

The members of the Committee are not chosen on the basis of their knowledge of a subject and change frequently. While the Committee is not empowered to intervene in matters of policy, which is for the

Government to decide, it is sometimes very difficult to draw the line between execution and policy. Clashes between Ministers and the Committee arise from time to time, and sometimes the exchanges are tart.

One of the principal handicaps of the Estimates Committee is that it lacks sufficient staff to help in the work of investigation, and, since its members are not usually expert and must gain their information by reading memoranda from the departments and questioning officials, the Committee sometimes tends to get bogged down by the mass of technical material presented to it and by the volume of oral evidence given by specialists.

Hardly a session of Parliament passes without an appeal for the Committee to be supplied with more staff, who would maintain continuity, grow knowledgeable in the ramifications of Whitehall, and be able to offer guidance on the fields in which the inquiries could be best directed. In 1964–5, an M.P. who felt strongly that staff ought to be increased, referred in the Commons to the Estimates Committee as "little more than a paper tiger which Governments are too often tempted to treat with the contempt so well deserved". No Government has ever been willing to agree to equip the Estimates Committee with an adequate secretariat.

Chapter Fifteen

A CINEMA IN REXALL

WHILE officials can take no direct part in proceedings in Parliament, some of them spend the greater part of their time in assisting their Ministers over Parliamentary matters, and most administrative Civil Servants, as well as many in the middle grades, are likely to be involved in some degree during a session. It would be foolish to imagine that before an official takes any decision he wonders "what would Parliament think", but departments are very conscious of Parliamentary accountability. Everything possible must be done to ensure that, should any criticism be made in Parliament, members will be convinced that the department undertook a most thorough examination of a problem before reaching a decision.

It has been suggested that the Minister of Films has been given authority to construct or acquire a limited number of cinemas each year at a cost not exceeding a maximum sum. Were Parliament to grant such powers, it might prescribe that the Minister should submit an annual return to the House of Commons; such a return would be issued as a Parliamentary paper. The Act might lay down that the Ministry must not acquire or erect a cinema, unless it has first taken all practicable steps to make sure that no company will provide adequate film entertainment at its own risk; that cinemas may be run by the department only in those places where the total population in the area in relation to the number of existing cinemas is such and such per cent more than the average throughout the country; and that the Minister should hold a local inquiry to hear any representations if so requested by a sufficient number of objectors.

The Ministry of Films has hitherto refused to open a cinema in Rexall since other places had priority on the department's resources. The time comes, however, when the more urgent claims have been dealt with, and the Ministry is prepared to reconsider the town's position. The new Research establishment is in course of completion, business premises are being erected by commercial firms, and the local council has had plans agreed for a housing estate. Officials of the Ministry of Films will meet representatives of the local authority; consultations will take place with the other Government departments concerned—the Board of Trade, the Ministry of Housing and Local Government, and the Ministry of Works; and it may be agreed that plans should be made provisionally for another cinema in Rexall.

If so, the department will wish to seek the advice, or the approval, of the Advisory Committee. First of all, however, it will ascertain whether any commercial company is prepared to provide a cinema, for the statute lays it down that the Ministry must be sure that there is no alternative to a State-owned house. Advertisements are inserted in newspapers and trade publications, but every Civil Servant knows that this not enough. Some Member of the Commons or the Lords will probably want to know what the department has done to bring the need to the notice of commercial exhibitors. In addition to the advertisements, therefore, the Ministry will write to film companies and others, pointing out the desirability of a cinema in Rexall and inviting them to examine the proposal sympathetically. No one will expect any favourable outcome, of course, since the department should have known if there existed the faintest possibility that a commercial company would be interested. Several weeks will be taken up in making these inquiries and a little money will be expended, but these are trifles. The department has made doubly sure by going through the motions and has a good reply to any member who asks for an assurance that the Ministry has made full investigation.

Reference to the Advisory Committee will follow. The department will prepare a statement showing the inquiries which it has made and ask the Committee to consider whether in the light of this information, a 700-seater in Rexall would be justified. Members of the Committee may or may not take such submissions very seriously. Some Advisory Committees deal with subjects where members may well have useful contributions to make to a problem; others seem to exist primarily for the purpose of requiring departments to prepare reasoned statements explaining what they wish to do—which may not be without value. The Advisory Committee which examines the proposal for a cinema in Rexall will probably agree to it without discussion.

The Minister of Films can now be informed that no commercial company has been found which is willing to provide cinema entertainment in Rexall, that the Advisory Committee does not disagree with the proposal, and that the Ministry has enough money in its vote to start work on a new cinema. The Minister's authority will be required to proceed to the stage of finding out if there is opposition to the proposal in the the town. The department's view is that a new building should be erected rather than that the old theatre be converted, and that the site should be about half a mile from that theatre on a piece of vacant land on which the Ministry can obtain an option.

The Minister will have known of the inquiries which were proceeding and there will probably be nothing in the statement which is new to him. His formal approval of the next stage is therefore likely to be given at once.

Immediately the plans are published by the Ministry an outcry will arise in Rexall, for someone is bound to be adversely affected by such a proposal, and others will feel that, though the idea is good, better arrangements could have been made. The Minister will hold an inquiry, and he will formally appoint an investigator to report to him. The investigator may be a lawyer, or an expert in films, or one of the Ministry's own staff. Whoever he may be, he will be highly vulnerable: if a lawyer, critics will say that he is too much governed by legal niceties; if connected with the film industry, he will be looked on as being prejudiced in favour of either films or associated interests; if the inspector is an official, people will hint that he has received his instructions from his chiefs and dare not report anything they do not want to hear. Many people will be quite convinced that the inquiry is just a piece of window-dressing. They will point out that the Ministry of Films has already spent time and money on the scheme and must have made up its mind. It seems to them too much to expect that the Ministry, which has gone so far, will appoint an investigator who is likely to make a report detrimental to the proposal. On the other hand, the same or other people would have protested violently if the Ministry had started an inquiry without having in the first place made detailed plans; they would have complained that the Ministry's ideas were half-baked and that it should know its own mind before wasting the time of busy citizens.

Opinion in Rexall may be that the result is a foregone conclusion, but that will not prevent many witnesses from coming forward and having a day out before the inquiry. Cinema owners in Rexall will be among the objectors. They will give their opinion that no new cinema is required in the district and that it would be irresponsible for the Government to spend money on such a plan. They know that if they can prove hardship when the new cinema is constructed and in operation the Ministry will be bound to consider a claim for compensation, but any payment to the cinema owners will be at the discretion of the department, and Government departments are notoriously stingy in making *ex gratia* payments. Other entertainment proprietors will doubtless object that a new cinema must take away business from them also, and that it is unreasonable for the Ministry of Films to enter into competition with private enterprise in such a matter. Such entrepreneurs will not have even the possibility of obtaining some reimbursement for loss of profits, since the Act will provide only for compensation to cinema owners, not to proprietors of dance halls and fun fairs and so on.

Some people will denounce the cinema as interfering with the peace of the town, others will come forward to declare that a new cinema is essential if the district is to have its fair share of amenities. Evidence will be presented by the local Chamber of Trade, by the Ratepayers' Association, by individual shopkeepers, and by many others. The proposed site will win the approval of some and be roundly rejected by others as unsuitable or less suitable than alternative locations. Architects will loudly affirm that the old theatre could be readily converted, while other architects will support the objections to the use of an outmoded building.

Counsel may be briefed to appear before the investigator, and the inquiry may cost hundreds of pounds—an important inquiry may run up a bill of thousands. If a commercial company wanted to open a cinema in Rexall, it would not meet with the same difficulties as the Ministry of Films, though it might meet with others. But a commercial company would be risking its own money, whereas the Ministry is using the taxpayers' money; a commercial company would have the measurement of profit and loss, but the Ministry would not need to erect a cinema at all if a profit were foreseen, since others would take over the proposition. The entertainment proprietors in Rexall are not unreasonable when they complain of unfair competition by the Government. By commercial standards the competition is, in fact, unjustified. The department is not governed by ordinary financial considerations, and its only reason for erecting a cinema is that the town has not a sufficient quota. The Ministry will claim that public welfare must come first.

The investigator will put forward the facts clearly and summarize the arguments in his report to the Minister of Films. Some Acts provide for a tribunal which has the right of final decision, but in such a matter as the provision of new cinemas, the decision would be likely to rest with the political head of the department. When he reads the result of the inquiry, the Minister may feel that the proposal should be abandoned altogether, perhaps because new evidence has been brought forward or because of the strength of the local opposition; but before he makes up his mind he will give his departmental officials the chance to state their views. They may convince the Minister that the investigator is wrong, that he has given too much weight to certain factors, or has overlooked others; or that, even if the inspector is correct, departmental policy requires that the scheme should go ahead and that the Minister should take an administrative decision in favour of the new cinema in Rexall. The advice given to the Minister by his officials is confidential. No one outside the department will know what happens after the report is sent to the Minister, or what considerations have led him to his final verdict. The Minister will publish the report, but he will not publish the comments of his advisers.

Some officials will no doubt shrug their shoulders and tell the Minister that, if numerous people in Rexall are against the cinema, the department can readily find other places where its money will be welcome, but such pique must be rare. Other officials may feel that their judgement is in question and press their views strongly in support of the scheme merely because they have previously committed themselves to it. Possibly one or two officials will regard any public inquiry as just a formality and a waste of time and denounce it as monstrous to suggest holding up the department's plans because some silly people do not know what is good for them. But Civil Servants as a class are careful and cautious and conscientious: if the investigator has brought forward new evidence or has put a different interpretation on some fact, the officials will consider the proposal again with an open mind, and will not hesitate to suggest a complete reversal of departmental policy, if this seems to them to be justified after a dispassionate examination.

If the inquiry or the further reconsideration does not lead to any alteration in the plans, the Minister will announce his decision to proceed with the erection of a cinema on the selected site in Rexall. At once a flood of correspondence will pour into the department, and the M.P. for the constituency will also receive a spate of letters. A number of correspondents will object to any new cinema, some will protest against the selected site, and others will complain on general principles about the waste of public money. The cinema owners who are affected by the prospective competition of a Government cinema will seek the member's assistance to kill the scheme. The proprietor of the old theatre is almost certain to return to his plea that the Ministry of Films ought to take it over instead of incurring the expense of constructing a new building. The M.P. will receive few, if any, letters in support of the Ministry's plans, at least at this stage; for the present, his mail on the subject will consist principally of criticisms.

Since the inquiry took place in Rexall and affects his constituents, the Member will have kept in close touch with the proposals. He will perhaps have discussed the matter with his election agent and others in the district. Although his correspondents are mostly opposed to the scheme, he finds on inquiry that on the whole public opinion in the town is in favour of an extra cinema. He will decide that he cannot support the claim of the cinema owners that the project should be abandoned altogether. The local authority, while approving a new cinema, prefers that the site of the old theatre should be chosen, and the Member may share this view. If so, he can write to the Minister and he will receive a detailed reply; but he knows, from his previous experience, that the Minister is likely merely to repeat that the matter has been fully considered and that no change can be made. The Member may prefer therefore to address a question in the House to the Minister of Films and so ensure publicity for his criticisms.

The principal Ministers of most departments sit in the Commons and may have a junior Minister to answer in the Lords. Questions can be asked in either House, but the number asked in the Lords is a trickle compared with that in the Commons. Any M.P. may put three questions a day. One or two M.P.s make the most of their opportunity and fire a large number of questions in the course of a session, but most members are content with an occasional question. A check made recently showed that one question per member about once every two weeks was the average.

As any action of a Government department may be the subject of challenge, departments maintain elaborate records in the hope that they will be able to answer anything that can cross the mind of even the most imaginative Members. But of course it is a losing battle. There is always some point on which the department has not kept records or on which its records are incomplete. If it has been caught out once, the likelihood is that the department will maintain records on that particular point for ever after, though the information will perhaps never again be required.

Questions for oral answer in the Commons are printed on the Order Paper with a star in front of them—some of these questions for 10 November, 1964, are reproduced in Appendix VI. On Mondays to Thursdays inclusive throughout the session one hour, less the time taken for a few items which do not require more than ten minutes, is allowed for Question Time, but, since more questions are put down than can be answered orally within the fifty minutes or so, Ministers take it in turn to head the list. After they have been at the top of the rota they drop to the bottom, and the House thus has the opportunity to obtain oral answers from all Ministers at some time or another. On Tuesday, 10 November, 1964, the order was Treasury, Post Office, Housing and Local Government, Commonwealth Relations, Power, Overseas Development, Technology. On the following Monday the list read Post Office, Housing and Local Government, and so on, and ended with Treasury. Six weeks later Technology had taken the lead and the Treasury had climbed back to second place. So it started all over again. Some departments are obviously more of a target than others, but every Minister must take his turn at the wicket.

Although it is not his scheduled day for answering questions, a Minister may be asked to give an explanation on a matter of great urgency on any day of the week. The circumstances must be exceptional before this is agreed, for the House attaches great importance to keeping to the normal rota. The Prime Minister never heads the list. On Tuesday and Thursday of each week he answers questions after other Ministers at exactly 3.15 p.m. In the fifty minutes available for oral answers about fifty questions may be dealt with, the remainder being given written replies. The number of written answers varies considerably from day to day: it is sometimes under twenty, and it may exceed a hundred.

Questions are placed on the Order Paper of the Commons on the basis of first come, first served. The Member for Rexall may have his Question as the second among the oral Questions addressed to the Minister of Films on the day on which that Minister is second in the batting order, and it may therefore appear as No. 10. If so, Rexall's M.P. is certain to receive an oral reply—it would not suit him if, because his question was not reached, the reply appeared among the written answers in Hansard—and he will be able to put at least one supplementary to the Minister. Though Members dislike Supplementary Estimates from Government departments, they are very fond of supplementary questions. Much, however, depends on the Member's ability; if he is skilful and can arouse the interest of the House, the Member will be encouraged to fire extra Questions. If he is maladroit or seems to be labouring a point, he will probably have no chance for more than a single supplementary. If there are a number of important Questions later on the Order Paper, the House may be anxious to reach them and show itself unsympathetic to Members who cause a hold-up. No Minister will escape easily if he appears to be withholding information, but some Ministers are treated much more lightly than others.

The drafting of a Parliamentary Question is an art. A Member will want to draw up his question in such a way that it calls for a clear statement and does not enable the Minister to go off at a tangent, but the Member may hold back something to use as a supplementary. The M.P. for Rexall may have been advised, for example, that the cost of converting the old theatre would be only half the cost of erecting a new cinema; but he will perhaps confine his Question on the Order Paper to a simple inquiry whether the Minister is aware of the deep concern in Rexall at his decision not to convert the music-hall and whether he is prepared to reconsider the use of these premises.

Government departments watch the Order Paper carefully, and as soon as a Question is put down the officials start collecting information for a draft reply. They may have only forty-eight hours in which to obtain material for their Minister's answer, and if that time is insufficient, perhaps because the Question involves reference to regional offices or consultation with a number of other departments, the Member may be asked to postpone his Question. Or the Minister may reply to the Question that he is obtaining the information and will write to the hon. member, though if a Minister gives this reply too often the House will begin to think his department is in need of gingering up. Departments do their utmost to have a full reply ready by the date for which a Question has been put down. The section of the office which deals with Parliamentary Questions is organized to work very speedily and its requests to other sections must be given immediate attention.

The Question about the Rexall cinema will be cut from the Order Paper and enclosed by the Ministry of Films in a bright red cover; on the outside will be written the name of the Member, the party to which he belongs, and the constituency he represents, the nature of the Question, the date on which the reply is to be given, and whether it is starred or unstarred. The file will be passed from hand to hand within the office and each official who handles it will mark on the outside the time when the file left him, so that any delay may be tracked down. All Civil Servants are taught to read Parliamentary Questions carefully. This is less obvious than it sounds, for few people do in fact read with care, and, unless the wording of a Question is studied, it is sometimes easy to conclude that it means something different from what it says. The most common trap is, of course, for an official who knows the details of a case to think he can tell what the Member really wants to find out, though that may not be what has been asked. The Civil Servant's job is to draft an answer to the point put by the questioner. It is not his business to try to read the Member's mind, though he may advise his Minister what the questioner probably wants to know.

The reply to the Member for Rexall is simple enough. An Assistant Secretary in the Ministry may in the first place draft a reply to the effect that the Minister is not aware of any deep concern, that the matter was fully examined before the decision was reached, and that the Minister is not prepared to reopen it. But in that form the answer might prove to be dangerous. Since the Question is No. 10 and the Minister is second, the officials must prepare for supplementaries. They are aware that many people dislike the site proposed for the cinema, and can guess that the M.P. has had a flood of letters of protest. The Minister cannot be left open to the gibe that, since the member has received so many letters which object to the decision, the Ministry of Films must be out of touch with local opinion if it does not know of the dissatisfaction with the scheme. The department believes that most people in Rexall are either indifferent or favourable and it will not concede that the site is unpopular. But the answer will be redrafted so that the Minister states that he is aware that in this, as in all such schemes, there is some division of opinion, etc.

What the supplementary or supplementaries will be the department cannot know exactly; but the officials will have a shrewd idea of the field likely to be covered by them, and will provide the Minister with information on which he can answer any queries that seem probable. Officials become highly expert in drafting replies and in providing succinct notes which enable Ministers to dispose effectively of supplementaries. Ministers themselves are, however, the best judges of how a question should be tackled in the House. They know the members and they can take the feeling of the Chamber. The answer which would be acceptable one month might raise a storm the next. While the official may suggest the witty quip, the Minister will perhaps meet with disaster if he brings it out in the wrong circumstances or even in the wrong tone of voice.

When a Minister is scheduled to answer Questions, an official of his department will be in attendance in the Official Box, just in case further information is wanted at the last minute or something arises during Question Time which calls for immediate action. The member who has put down a Question does not repeat it. He rises in his place when his Question is the next on the Order Paper to be answered. A Minister may have a large number of Questions addressed to him on the same day. He will be provided with notes covering far more than the actual Questions, and much of the material will never be used. Points which officials feel sure will be raised are quite likely to pass unnoticed, and all the time taken up in preparing a masterly summary is wasted. But even the most experienced Minister and his staff are bound to be caught out sometimes. A Minister will be lucky if he can get through all his Questions without having to admit that he must make further inquiries about some aspect of a case, or sheltering behind a claim that the Member has strayed away from the scope of the original query and that it is unreasonable to expect a reply without notice.

The House will not expect the Minister of Films to do more than indicate that the decision taken about Rexall must stand and refer to the facts. If the Member for Rexall feels strongly enough about it, or if for some other reason he wants to pursue the matter, he will express his dissatisfaction in some such words as: "In view of the Minister's unsatisfactory replies, I beg to give notice that I shall seek to raise this question on the adjournment." On each sitting day thirty minutes are allowed for the adjournment debate after the close of other business. A member who wishes to take this opportunity to draw attention to some matter he considers to be important asks the permission of the Speaker to do so, but the rules are strict and many subjects suggested for an adjournment debate are rejected. The Member for Rexall will have to put his points very carefully if he is to be permitted to make the new cinema the subject of an adjournment debate. He will submit to the Speaker the matters he proposes to ventilate; if the Speaker consents to the application, the Minister of Films will be told of the ground to be covered, and thus come prepared with his defence.

The cinema owners of Rexall will perhaps ask for an interview with the local M.P. If he has made up his mind that a cinema in Rexall is desirable, he will explain when he sees them that he is not prepared to oppose the project. His protest will be against the erection of a new building instead of the use of the old theatre and he will contend that at least the theatre site should be used. Even if the Ministry of Films agreed to reverse their decision about the site, however, the cinema owners would not necessarily be any better off, so they will go on to the next point. The owners will point out that they will suffer some financial loss by the competition, and that they are helpless in the matter. No matter how well they run their cinemas, some people will always prefer a new place. It is true that the population of Rexall is increasing, but even so the proprietors feel certain that their attendances will be reduced and their profits most adversely affected. They will urge the M.P. to protest that it is wrong that a Government department should come along and interfere with their livelihood without paying compensation. If the Government wishes to put up a new cinema as a matter of policy—a cinema which in their view is unnecessary and which no commercial company would contemplate—the Ministry of Films should pay compensation on a basis agreed by an independent arbitrator. The owners declare that it is manifestly unfair that the Minister should decide whether any compensation is payable and, if so, the amount: everybody knows, the proprietors add, that Government departments are very miserly in their dealings with the public. The cinema owners will perhaps also explain that they are perturbed about the supply of films for exhibition. The Ministry produces a number of films of a kind which the Rexall cinemas have often used in the past and which they may want to show in future. When the Government cinema at Rexall is in operation the Ministry might withdraw the films from the other houses in the town. The M.P. for Rexall will be asked to seek an assurance that Ministry films will not be the monopoly of the Ministry cinema.

The Member will no doubt consult others about the aspects to be examined. His inquiries will possibly indicate that the question of compensation to existing cinema owners in districts where the Government has erected cinemas is one which has been debated on other occasions, but not during the current session. The Minister of Films has always refused to agree to independent arbitration, but the M.P. may decide to raise the point once more. On the question of giving the existing cinemas the opportunity to show the Ministry's films, the M.P. will perhaps seek further information.

He knows that he will not be permitted to range over the whole of the activities of the Ministry of Films in the adjournment debate, and he may decide to concentrate on the irresponsible refusal to convert the old theatre or to use its site, and the question of arbitration on the amount of compensation to cinema owners. The M.P. for Rexall need not raise in the debate the point about the distribution of Ministry films. The department will give him an assurance that all cinemas will be treated equally, except when there are special circumstances which make it necessary to reserve certain films for the Ministry's own cinemas.

Officials will prepare a full brief for the Minister on the criticisms to be raised by the M.P. for Rexall during the debate. The Minister will be reminded of the reasons for not converting the old theatre and for choosing a different site for the new cinema. On the question of independent arbitration, the officials will point out that the Act leaves the amount of compensation to be fixed by him with the consent of the Treasury. It has never been the policy to go to arbitration in such matters, and the officials will refer to the difficulties which might arise. When the fictitious Bill was before Parliament, the Government considered compulsory arbitration and decided against it. The Minister will be advised to say in his speech that any case put forward for compensation by the cinema owners of Rexall will receive careful examination but that the amount must be a matter for Ministerial decision.

On the day of the debate departmental officials will again sit in the Official Box. Although the ground to be covered has been announced in advance, there is always the possibility of some new argument or a last-minute surprise, and the officials must be ready to prime their Minister, if he needs any additional arguments. The Rexall M.P.'s speech will perhaps start with a violent protest against the erection of a new cinema instead of converting the old theatre. This, he will assert, is just one more example of the gross extravagance which stalks the corridors of Whitehall and which is particularly evident throughout the Ministry of Films. Even if he admits that conversion would not be entirely satisfactory, he will point out that he is convinced reasonable amenities could be made available by using the old theatre. The Ministry is aiming at quite unreasonably high standards. He would not object so much to the construction of a brand-new cinema if funds were unlimited, but the amount of money made available for cinemas must in the present condition of the country be kept within bounds. By converting the old theatre half the money would be saved, and the department could then provide a second cinema somewhere else. Surely it is better that two towns should each have a cinema than that public money should be wasted to erect a luxurious building in Rexall.

Apart from this, the M.P. feels that in the present acute shortage of housing it is a scandal that the Ministry of Films should use up man-power on the erection of such a building. His succeeding point is that, even if the Ministry cannot be convinced that the old theatre should be converted, the new building should be on the site of that theatre. This view is, he will gently say, fully supported by the local council and by others who know much more about the position than a London department. He will appeal to the Minister not to be hide-bound and to accept good advice even at this late date. The Member may proceed to the question of compensation to the cinema owners of Rexall, who are faced with heavy losses because a Government department has entered into competition with them.

This is all more or less as the Minister had expected. He will describe how carefully the conversion of the theatre was considered and point out that the cost of conversion would not be quite so low as the member suggested unless the work were to be carried out in a very unsatisfactory fashion. Maintenance of the theatre after conversion would be a very heavy item, and in the Minister's view the erection of an entirely new cinema, which will be larger but not splendiferous, is justified from an economic point of view. The site chosen is the most convenient for the majority of probable patrons when one keeps in mind coming developments, and particularly the extension of the Research establishment. The Minister will refuse to agree that an outside and independent arbitrator should decide on compensation. He will promise that any claims which the cinema proprietors can substantiate will be most sympathetically examined, and so on.

Where a mistake has been made or new factors are presented, the policy will have to be considered; but it is relatively rare for a Government department's decision to be challenged successfully in an adjournment debate. No vote is taken after such a debate and so there is no question of the defeat of the Government on a motion, but the Commons makes its opinion known by other means.

Before a departmental decision is reached a number of officials will have looked at the matter from every angle and will, where appropriate, have consulted outside experts as well as Government specialists. All decisions are made in the sure knowledge that they will come under the scrutiny of Parliament if public dissatisfaction is expressed. The Minister who sticks to a departmental policy despite criticism in Parliament is not necessarily obstinate or under the influence of thick-headed or arrogant officials. It is indeed a weakness if a department turns somersaults and reverses its decisions under attack. The Minister and his officials have either failed to collect all the facts or have been guilty of faulty judgement. And, of course, both of these things happen. When they happen too often Parliament does not applaud the willingness to confess to errors. It rightly demands that changes be made in the department.

Chapter Sixteen

CONDITIONS OF SERVICE (1)

THE Civil Service has always employed a large number of its staff on an unestablished basis. Whereas the established staff are for all practical purposes guaranteed employment for the whole of their working life, the unestablished employees may have their services terminated on a week's or month's notice. Fifty years ago, out of a non-industrial staff of about 200,000, some 60,000 were unestablished. Few men and women were given establishment during the Second World War, and the majority of the staff at the end of hostilities was on a temporary basis. In 1949 the unestablished staff represented 45 per cent, and by the spring of 1964 the unestablished employees had been reduced to 155,000, or about one in five of the total non-industrial complement.

The man or woman who enters the Civil Service in youth is given establishment almost automatically if he can satisfy the requirements of the Civil Service Commissioners, either by examination or otherwise, and is engaged on non-industrial work. Those who gravitate to State employment later sometimes find it difficult to obtain the advantages of establishment, even though they may spend most of their life in a Government department. Comedians spin their jokes about the men and women who apply for a temporary job in the Civil Service and linger there for twenty years on end.

Between the established and unestablished staff, one of the main differences is that the latter receive no pension. It is a most important distinction. In the past the pension scheme has been one of the greatest attractions of the Civil Service, and it is still valuable. For a century the State has granted superannuation terms to the whole of its established staff. Before the end of the eighteenth century some officials obtained a pension on retirement, either by mulcting their successor in office or by drawing on a special fund set up by their department, under arrangements which for the most part had no legislative authority. The Parliamentary inquiries of the late eighteenth and early nineteenth centuries expressed their amazement at some of the pension schemes which they found in operation. One committee drew attention to the fact that certain offices retained the proceeds of the sale of old stores and used this income to pay pensions to their staff.

Parliament granted retirement allowances in 1810 to some officials, and extended the scheme widely in 1834, at the time when sinecures were finally suppressed; but it was not until 1857 that all Civil Servants who obtained a certificate of qualification from the Civil Service Commissioners had the benefit of pension. The Superannuation Act of 1857 governed the provisions of Civil Service pensions for many years and gave surprisingly generous terms. On retirement an official could receive as much as two-thirds of the salary he had earned during his last year of employment, and if for any reason, other than dereliction of duty, he had to retire earlier than he normal age he could still claim pension on the same terms.

Pensions were on a contributory basis for some years, and Civil Servants had to surrender 15 per cent of their salary towards them. The agitation of the staff against such deductions led to a change in the law, and superannuation is now non-contributory in the Civil Service. Few things have been more dear to the heart of the Civil Servant than his pension. The staff have campaigned vigorously for improvements and have always rallied some M.P.'s to their support. Officials contended that a man should be given a lump-sum payment in addition to his pension, and, at the beginning of the century, staff associations produced figures to demonstrate that few Civil Servants lived for very long to enjoy their retirement—in these days of longevity the statistics would now show a very different picture. As a result of pressure skilfully directed by the staff over a number of years, the Government consented in 1909 to a revision of the superannuation benefits to provide for a lump-sum payment on retirement. As a *quid pro quo* the staff had to agree that the maximum pension should be reduced from two-thirds to one-half of the salary earned prior to reaching the retiring age of sixty. This provision for a gratuity applied only to male staff at first, but some twenty-five years later it was extended to all employees.

Instead of basing the pension award on the salary for the final year of a man's service, the plan is now to calculate it on the average of the salary for the last three years. At the present time the Civil Servant is granted, for each year he has served in an established capacity,[1] a pension of one-eightieth of the average of the salary earned during the final three years of his service, and, in addition, he receives a lump-sum payment amounting to three-eightieths for each year served. If a man's earnings have been £950, £1,000, and £1,050 in his last three working years, his pension and gratuity will

[1] Temporary service is also taken into account, in whole or in part.

be based on £1,000. Should he have served for forty years, he will receive forty-eightieths of the amount as pension and one-hundred-and-twenty-eightieths as gratuity, so that he has a pension of £500 per annum and an immediate cash payment of £1,500.[1] If his services have not extended over so long a period, his pension and gratuity are reduced by one-eightieth and three-eightieths respectively for each year short of the forty. The lump-sum payment is tax free.

The maximum pension and gratuity which the Civil Servant can receive at the age of sixty are calculated on a service of forty years, but if a Civil Servant continues beyond that age he can earn further pension benefits and a larger gratuity. It is Government policy to encourage men to remain at work after sixty.

Officials talk about their pension rights, but they have no legal entitlement to pension, which is given at the discretion of the Treasury; in fact, pensions are invariably paid on the normal scale unless a Civil Servant has been guilty of some grave offence. When salaries are under discussion, the value of the pension is always considered as a factor and is often referred to as "deferred pay". In the past, the official who retired of his own free will before sixty lost all pension benefits as well as the gratuity he had earned. The Tomlin Commission proposed that the pension should be placed on a contributory basis, and if this plan had been adopted, officials who left the Civil Service earlier than the normal retiring age would have been more favourably placed, since their contributions would have been repayable. The Government, however, decided against the proposal and, though it has been revived on several occasions since 1931, no such change has been favoured either by the Treasury or by the staff.

The staff has always complained that it was unjust that a Civil Servant who retired voluntarily under the age of sixty should be deprived of pension. Five years ago it was agreed that an official who wished to retire between the ages of fifty and fifty-nine could do so without sacrificing his superannuation benefits; he would not draw a pension at once, but when he reached the normal retiring age of sixty he could claim a pension based on his actual years of service. This concession has not wholly satisfied the staff associations, some of which press that an official should be permitted to retire at his own discretion and receive forthwith the pension he has earned. Were such an option offered, it is difficult to estimate how many Civil Servants would seek careers outside the Civil Service. Probably

---

[1] The figures have been taken merely as an easily worked example. The average pension and gratuity are higher.

not many more than do so at the present time. Men and women usually either leave the Service during the first two or three years of their employment, when the pension they have earned is immaterial; or else, having got through their first few years in Government employment more or less successfully, officials tend to hold fast to their jobs till sixty or more. A Civil Servant who has served in a department or departments for as long as ten years is likely to fall in love with *paperasserie* and the sequestered life: he cannot conceive of a satisfactory existence without his files and he shudders at the thought of measuring himself against the harsh competitive world.

It had long been considered a weakness that the Government could not pension off members of its staff who, without being grossly inefficient, were unable to pull their weight in an organization. Power to do so could be obtained only by amendments to the Superannuation Acts, and proposals that the State should be able to pension off men and women between the age of fifty and sixty met with much opposition. Civil Servants who had entered Government service had done so in the assurance that they would be given lifelong employment unless mentally or physically afflicted or guilty of misdemeanour. It seemed a revolutionary suggestion, a complete break with the tradition of a hundred years, that those who had worked loyally and to the best of their ability should have their services terminated before they reached the normal retiring age of sixty.

The arrangement has, however, been introduced. The innovation was made first in the Foreign Service, which felt it necessary to obtain from Parliament the authority to get rid of members of its staff who in middle age were considered to lack the ability to undertake the more responsible work and were blocking the way for younger and more capable men. Sanction was sought to terminate "the careers of men who, though they may have been excellent subordinates, are unsuited to fill the highest posts". Their treatment was to be generous: "It will be necessary to grant to such men, who will have given many of the best years of their lives to the public service, pensions sufficient to keep them from poverty, and to mark the fact that no disgrace is implied by their retirement." It was argued that, unless the Foreign Secretary had power to pension off such officials, he might be pressed to create jobs for them, an argument which recalls the objection made to examinations open to all: once permit everyone to compete for Civil Service posts, and candidates who had scored well, though not well enough, might have to be found places by unnecessary expansion of the bureaucracy. Parliament accepted the principle of special pensions for officials who were retired for the good of the Foreign Service, and passed the Foreign Service Act, 1943. The number of officials in the Senior Branch of the Foreign Service who have been compulsorily retired under these special arrangements has averaged about half a dozen a year out of a staff of some 700.

Members of the home staff may also be retired after fifty in the interests of efficiency and receive the pension they have earned; unlike those in the Foreign Service, however, they do not qualify for any addition. The authority was granted by Parliament in the Superannuation Act of 1949. (The Superannuation Acts were amended in 1964, but only on points of detail). Out of a staff of over 500,000 established non-industrial Civil Servants in the Home Service, 100 were pensioned off in 1964 under this Act on certification that their retirement was in the interests of the Service. The power is used very sparingly. A Minister referred a few years ago to the reluctance of departments to pension off officials under sixty. "Theoretically," he wrote, "it is now possible to retire an officer, with a pension, at any time after the age of fifty. On one occasion I tried to do this. I roused against myself all the camaraderie of the Civil Service and every obstacle was put in my way. Eventually a compromise solution was evolved."

The Civil Service is no longer a refuge for sickly youths, and the medical examination is very strict for new entrants; but, when illness does afflict an official, he is relieved of economic worries to a very considerable degree. He is paid his full salary for six months and half his salary for a similar period, if his incapacity lasts so long. Only where medical opinion is wholly satisfied that he is unlikely to be able to work again will the established Civil Servant be discharged, and he will receive a pension or a lump-sum payment. Should he die while in service, his widow will be paid a year's salary, or an official may contribute $1\frac{1}{4}$ per cent of his earnings throughout his career and so ensure a pension for his wife should he predecease her.

Long holidays have always been a feature of the Service. An inquiry of the late eighteenth century pointed out that some public offices discovered reasons why they should close for as many as fifty-three weekdays a year at a time when other places might close for only three or four. Government departments planned annual leave on a liberal scale: the higher grades are entitled to six weeks a year, and after a certain period of service eight weeks, while other grades received three, four, or six weeks with full pay. Those Civil Servants who would have been entitled to eight weeks' holiday were, however, cut to six weeks at the beginning of the Second World War, and further reductions made in 1955.

Hours of duty have also been favourable. A few Government offices in the nineteenth century might open for as little as three or four hours a day; most public offices worked no more than six hours. Sir Charles Trevelyan explained to a Parliamentary Committee in 1848 that, though the Treasury hours of attendance were from ten till four, "it is considered to be sufficient if everybody is present at half past ten". The six-hour day remained the rule in many Government departments until the beginning of this century; but by the beginning of the First World War the majority of Government offices worked either a seven or a seven-and-a-half-hour day, with a half day on Saturdays. On the outbreak of the Second World War an eight-hour day was introduced throughout practically the whole of the Service.

It was the intention that Civil Servants should have restored to them their pre-war seven-hour day but this has not been done. Nor is Whitehall so generously treated with holidays as in pre-war days. The Priestley Commission recommended considerable reductions: clerical officers start with sixteen and receive nineteen days holiday after ten years in the Service, those up to senior executive officer start at nineteen days and, as their length of service grows, are entitled to a maximum of thirty-two days. Above this grade, to assistant secretary level, the leave is twenty-six days during the first ten years and then thirty-two days. The highest ranks have thirty-two days, however short their service may be. The happy times when the middle grades could expect six weeks and the top grades eight weeks' holiday have gone.

Civil Servants, however, still have more holidays than most employees, but Whitehall no longer offers the same advantages as a generation ago. Some sections of outside industry and commerce can now offer security of tenure and working conditions at least as good as in Government departments. Large numbers of recruits come forward, but the flow is less than in former days and competition for posts is not so keen.

It was once a ground of criticism that the Civil Service attracted applicants who were too good for the duties which they were asked to perform. In times especially of widespread unemployment candidates presented themselves for posts which were well below their capacity. A committee which investigated recruitment at the end of the First World War referred to the "unnecessarily good material for many of the duties imposed" on the Second Division (now the executive class), and a later Commission commented that three-quarters of the successful candidates in a competition intended for those with elementary education had been educated at secondary or private schools. This was obviously wasteful of talent.

Some commentators feared that the same kind of situation might arise when the Civil Service Commissioners invited university graduates to compete for posts in the executive class. The practice until recent years was for junior executive officers to come mostly from the grammar schools and for the universities to provide only the members of the administrative class. Doubt was expressed whether the arrangements for attracting graduates as executive entrants were justified. The main objection was that such a scheme restricted the opportunities of school-leavers, but the argument was also put forward that graduates who entered the executive class would be employed on work of a kind which did not make full use of their abilities and that this might give rise to a discontented element within the Service. It is premature to make any judgement on the innovation until more experience has been gained of the employment of university men and women in a class hitherto reserved for those of a lower educational level.

Even for the best candidates, promotion cannot, unless in exceptional circumstances, be very much accelerated. It is not earned by length of service to the extent that it was in Trevelyan's day, but seniority still counts for a very great deal. Except in the highest ranks, only those who have served for a number of years in one grade will even be eligible for consideration for advancement to the next grade. Officials must therefore wait until they are "within the range of promotion" before they have any possibility of climbing the ladder.

A witness before the Playfair Commission said, "Anyone who has known the public service knows the extreme difficulty of promoting a man in the lower ranks over the head of a man who has been a long time in the office, simply that he may do better work; it is the most difficult thing in the world to do; the whole feeling of the office is against it." Vast changes have taken place in Whitehall since this comment was made, but not very much in this respect.

Everybody concerned with selection of candidates for promotion will agree that the interests of the Service must come first, but, having said so, they are likely to differ on what are the best interests. A man who has worked loyally and to the best of his ability for a long number of years deserves to be given credit for his faithful service. The junior official may be more able, but nevertheless it is perhaps fairer to choose the senior who is not quite so competent. If men of long service feel aggrieved by the choice made for promotion, the work of the office is likely to suffer, though the man chosen for advancement may be the best candidate. Officials who are passed over tend to be regarded by their colleagues as unlucky rather than as undeserving of promotion, whatever the circumstances. It is always the safest course to promote on the basis of length of service, unless in very obvious cases of incompetence. Nobody can then complain that promotion has been affected by favouritism.

So long, therefore, as a man does his work reasonably well, promotion will probably come to him in his turn. Some men will perform the higher duties rather better than others, and to a number of officials promotion may well mean a strain on their capacity until they have mastered the intricacies of the new job; but the theory is that, except for the top grades, there will be relatively little difference in the long run.

Chapter Seventeen

CONDITIONS OF SERVICE (2)

THE training of Civil Servants was looked upon as relatively unimportant until quite recently. The Civil Service had its mysteries, of course, and they were a matter for pride; but they could, it was felt, only be learned by individual study within a department, and it seemed heresy to suggest otherwise. If a man was doing his work well enough, it was senseless to move him to another job unless for some very good reason. Should the interests of the department require a switch to be made, instructions were issued for the change and the staff took over the new duties without any troublesome preliminaries. The theory was that, all administration being essentially the same, any Civil Servant could do the job of any other Civil Servant of the same grade, picking up such expert knowledge as he needed while actually on the work. Nothing had been done to arouse the interest of the staff in the wider field of administration or to build up morale, and the Service frowned on such fripperies. Men and women often became soured through having to pass many years engaged on dull and monotonous jobs, but that was not an uncommon fate outside as well as inside the Service. By and large, Government departments were probably no worse in this respect than private enterprise. They were certainly no better in the view of those competent to judge. Departments clung to practices which, while perhaps justifiable when their work consisted principally of regulatory functions, were inappropriate when the State undertook large social measures.

As a result of severe criticism, a Committee on the Training of Civil Servants was appointed in 1944.[1] It proposed that "there should be a routine of training for all new entrants under a responsible officer. A document setting out the traditions and aims of the Service, and a booklet giving the history and functions of the Department and a guide to office procedure, should be given to each entrant.... There is need to develop resistance to the danger of the Civil Servant being mechanized by the machine," the Committee observed. "Large numbers of people have inevitably to spend most of their working lives upon tasks of a routine character." It recommended that courses of planned instruction should be given in departments

---

[1] Cmd. 6525 (1944).

under a special officer, with a separate branch of the Treasury to exercise general supervision where necessary. The Committee solemnly advised departments against allocating accounts work to "a person not at home with figures". The practice had apparently been to send the man who did not add or multiply well to take over a job in a figure section. There he would either conquer his deficiency or others would help him out or push him out.

As a result of the Committee's recommendations, the Treasury set up a Training and Education Branch which has been considerably expanded in recent years. Each department has its arrangements for training new entrants and some attempt is made to assess a man's aptitude before posting him. A few departments have always required their staff to have special training: the auditors in the Comptroller and Auditor-General's Department take accountancy courses; staff in the Inland Revenue Department dealing with estate duty study law, and officials of the Board of Trade who are engaged in bankruptcy work have to acquire special knowledge for their work. The intricacies of income tax are such that the Inland Revenue Department runs courses for some of its executive staff, lasting for over a year.

Men are not now allowed to remain on the same jobs for very long periods, unless quite exceptionally. Indeed, the pendulum may have swung to the other extreme, for there is some justification for the complaint that a Civil Servant is shunted to another branch just as soon as he begins to appreciate what he is supposed to be doing. In some departments a sort of general post takes place every two or three years. Inevitably, work is dislocated as experienced officials are moved around. Nor are men and women so transferred always happy about having to learn new jobs when they are comfortably settled on some duty they thoroughly understand, and which does not call for much effort.

The emphasis is naturally on the training of the newcomers to the administrative class from the universities. The Assistant Principal grade is intended to be a cadet grade. "In their first years," state the Civil Service Commissioners, "Assistant Principals will be mainly occupied in learning their jobs, being brought into touch from the outset with the policy questions of their Department. Much of their work will be on paper, and will consist of the writing of letters and memoranda, and generally 'devilling' for their seniors. But they will also have plenty of opportunities for personal contracts, both with colleagues in their own and other Departments (e.g. when acting as secretaries at inter-departmental conferences) and with members of the public. They will be given every opportunity to put forward their own constructive proposals for action and will be encouraged to take responsibility for decisions as soon as they have proved themselves fit for it. Assistant Principals also fill a number of the posts of private secretary to Ministers and senior Civil Servants, and those who occupy such posts are right at the hub of the Government machine." The Treasury arranges for a short course of lectures to newly appointed Assistant Principals, but otherwise they train on the job—"the Aristotelian view of training, that one only becomes an expert Civil Servant by being a Civil Servant". It was felt, however, that there was need for more formal training of administrative recruits after they had spent some time in a department, and in 1963 the Government set up the Centre for Administrative Studies where Assistant Principals in their third year of service have a seven weeks' course and those employed in economic departments receive a further seven weeks' tuition. The Centre is an experiment and is probably only the first step. Twenty years ago the Committee on the Training of Civil Servants which examined the question of an administrative college decided against it as a Government venture, but the suggestion has often been repeated since then and in 1964 another group of inquirers recommended that consideration should again be given to the establishment of a college where Civil Servants could be given specialized training in administration, as is done in a number of other European countries, particularly France and Germany. The Labour Government decided not to proceed with any such scheme for the present but the project is likely to be pressed in future.

Complaint is often made that the Civil Service has far too few people with a scientific background in the administrative grades. The tendency has in the past been to appoint men and women and women with arts degrees—the cult of the amateur has flourished for generations in Whitehall. The Civil Service now tries to attract some men with a science degree to enter the administrative class, but it has not been very successful. Such men prefer to seek careers in industry or to enter the Government service as scientists.

Those who have taken up scientific posts in the Civil Service have rarely been appointed later to jobs in the administrative class. Young scientists with a few years experience in the Service are now being encouraged to transfer to the general administrative class, but it is a process which has not gone very far. The arts men still hold the predominant number of places in the administrative grade, and only a trickle of men with science degrees enter as Assistant Principals.

Even the Treasury, which has largely the choice of candidates, is ill-equipped with officials who have had a scientific education. The Treasury does not take entrants to the administrative class until they had had some experience. After they have served two or three years in an office, Assistant Principals who are looked upon as particularly promising are, subject to their department's consent, offered transfer to the Treasury. This method of staffing the Treasury is intended to ensure that the premier department has a flow of candidates who have proved their worth as practical administrators so far as that can be done within so short a period. A department in which a good young Assistant Principal has shown his mettle may be reluctant to lose his services, but most departments like to plant in the Treasury someone who has a knowledge of their problems, however rudimentary that knowledge may be, and will perhaps serve as a friend at court. This does not always prove to be so. Staff transferred to the Treasury often carry away a poor impression of the department in which they have started their career and seem to find it hard to believe that their old office can be trusted to do anything sensibly.

The arrangements by which the Treasury picks its administrative staff from other departments is of recent origin. They were introduced to meet the criticism that Treasury officials had no chance to gain experience of operational work at first hand. The plan has its disadvantages. It may denude the departments of their best men, and it may have the effect of packing the Treasury with recruits who have been chosen merely because they fit neatly into the existing Treasury pattern.

Promotion from Assistant Principal to Principal is more or less automatic after a few years, and Principals receive advancement to Assistant Secretary almost as a matter of course. The next step, to Under-Secretary, calls for merit as well as a certain amount of luck if it is to be obtained before the age of about forty. It is, of course, always helpful to be posted to a department which is expanding, since this brings new posts in its train.

The whole of the staff of a department is under the Minister's control, and he is responsible for every promotion within it. The lesser appointments will not be submitted for his approval, though they will be made in his name. He may, however, take an interest in promotions from Principal to Assistant Secretary, but he will usually be content to accept the advice of his senior official advisers. He is likely to have a keener interest in promotions to Under-Secretary, for the choice will generally lie between the Assistant Secretaries of the department, most of whom the Minister will have met and of whose ability he will have formed his own opinion. His is the deciding voice in such promotions, but if he were to play favourites and make appointments which the office believed to be prejudiced, the staff would protest.

Occasionally a department will have no suitable men to promote to such posts as Under-Secretary, and then the Treasury may be asked to suggest a candidate from elsewhere. Or the Treasury may ask a department to reserve a senior post for a transferee whose job has come to an end. Also, where the number of higher posts which fall vacant in an office is exceptional, perhaps because of extensions of work, the incidence of retirements, and so on, the Treasury may propose that some of the posts should be allocated to nominees from other departments where promotion prospects are under average. Such arrangements can be made only if goodwill exists on the part of the receiving department. The highest official posts—Deputy Secretary and Permanent Secretary—are filled on the recommendation of the Joint Permanent Secretary of the Treasury. In his capacity as Head of the Civil Service, he puts the name of his nominee to the Minister of the department where a vacancy arises for such a post and, if and when he has obtained the Minister's agreement, he submits the recommendation to the Prime Minister.

In a debate in the Lords some years ago on the position of the Head of the Civil Service, the then Lord Chancellor said: "The supreme head of all the Services of the Crown is the Sovereign. The Ministerial head of His Majesty's Civil Service is the Prime Minister and the First Lord of the Treasury. The principal officer of the Service is the Permanent Secretary to the Treasury; that title was introduced in 1867, and the post has since carried with it the official headship of the Service. . . . No formal instrument recording the fact appears to have been issued. . . . The function of the holder of this post is to direct, subject to Ministerial authority, the work of the Treasury, including that part of the Treasury's work which is concerned with the general supervision of the Civil Service, and the central oversight of the official machinery of Government; his duties in this regard include that of advising the Prime Minister and First Lord, after consultation with any other Minister concerned, on appointments to certain senior posts in the Service which require the Prime Minister's approval, namely, the Permanent Heads of Departments, their

Deputies, Principal Finance Officers, and Principal Establishment Officers. . . ." In the Commons it was explained by the Chancellor of the Exchequer that the file leading up to the decision of 1867 had been lost.

The arrangement whereby the Permanent Secretary of the Treasury makes recommendations has often been attacked as concentrating in the hands of a single man a very great deal of power over the careers of senior officials. There is always the risk that merit alone may not be the criterion.

It is, of course, possible for a Minister to reject a candidate. If he had made up his mind that a particular man is the best for the job, he could go on turning down all other candidates put up by the Treasury. In the end, he might succeed in convincing the Permanent Secretary of the Treasury that the ministerial nominee is preferable to any others. Or it might be that the Permanent Secretary would be forced to report to the Prime Minister that agreement could not be reached with the departmental Minister. It is suggested cynically that disagreements do not often occur because strong Ministers who are interested enough to stand out for a candidate get their own way.

Lord Attlee, who served as the Minister in several departments, Deputy Prime Minister, and Premier, and had exceptional experience of the promotion system in operation, made the following comment: "Every Minister naturally wants to get hold of the ablest Civil Servant for the headship of his department. If he is a junior departmental Minister he should look any gift horse presented to him by the Permanent Secretary to the Treasury very narrowly. He would be wise to consult his colleague under whom the postulant has served. He may, of course, be a brilliant and rising young man, but, quite likely, he is a failure who is being passed on to the less experienced pending his welcome retirement."

Vacancies in the higher ranks do not occur very frequently, and a Minister may be in charge of a department for the whole of the four or five years of a Government's term of office without any change in the holders of the posts of Permanent Secretary or Deputy Secretary. When he takes control, he will find the senior staff are already in post. Difficulties rarely arise between new Ministers and their senior staff, though clashes have occurred in the past and it would be too much to expect that they will not occur now and again in the future. It is, however, practically unknown for the Minister to suggest that his senior staff are out of sympathy with the political programme. The loyalty of the officials is to the party in power.

The Government appointed a Committee in 1948 to consider the restrictions on the political activities of Civil Servants,[1] which were governed by rules made some twenty years before. While most industrial employees were permitted to take part in national and local politics, non-industrial Civil Servants were "expected to maintain at all times a reserve in political activities and not to put themselves forward prominently on one side or the other". The Masterman Committee reported the view of some staff representatives that

> Civil Servants, because of their experience of the administrative machine, were particularly well qualified for service in Parliament, and it was both inconsistent with the natural rights of the Civil Servant as a citizen and harmful to the public interest, if he were not allowed to offer himself for this other form of public service and to serve the community for the time being in another capacity, without being expected to sacrifice his career, security of employment and pension rights.

The Committee recommended that officials should be debarred from standing for Parliament or from taking part otherwise in political work only if they were members of certain grades who came into contact with the public and exercised, or might be supposed to exercise, authority. Of the total staff of the industrial and non-industrial Civil Service, it felt that more than two-thirds should be completely free and should be allowed to stand for Parliament. The Committee firmly rejected the proposal that there should be any further relaxation in the higher grades.

> The general tenor of the evidence from senior officials was to the effect that, whilst they were not antagonistic to all change, they were strongly opposed to take any risk of creating a political Service [the Committee reported].... They believed that the overriding consideration must be to maintain both the existing reputation of the Service for political neutrality and public confidence in its freedom from all possibility of bias.... If Civil Servants were allowed to engage in politics, to stand for Parliament, to return to the Service after sitting as M.P.s, and thus to declare their adherence to one party or the other, the public's belief in their impartiality and Ministers' confidence in their ability to give equally loyal service to whichever party was in power would be rapidly destroyed, with disastrous results to the country. No countervailing advantages would be derived from such a development, and the small loss of freedom which Civil Servants voluntarily accepted upon entering the Service was insignificant in comparison with the vital importance of preserving so great an asset as a non-political Civil Service.

Staff associations felt this report to be an outrage when it was first issued. The staff side of the National Whitley Council told the

[1] P.P. 1948-9, V. 12.

Press it was "shocked that such proposals should be put forward in 1949. It is still more shocked that the Government has announced acceptance of this Report without without any prior discussion with the National Staff Side." When the report was debated in the Commons, the view of the Civil Service staff associations received a very great deal of support. Members were contemptuous of the idea that Civil Servants could not be trusted to use their common sense and must be preserved from contact with politics. "Throughout the report," said a member, "there is an idea—implicit but nevertheless a very definite idea—that public confidence in the Civil Service could quite easily be undermined, that it is poised precariously on a razor's edge so to speak, and in this I think the committee completely misunderstands the public attitude of mind towards our Civil Service." Another comment was: "I believe the people of this country have a very soundly based and fully justified faith in the impartiality of their Civil Service, and it is a faith which is not based on a woolly notion that Civil Servants have no political views, but which is founded on the knowledge that its members are a responsible, intelligent body of people whose discretion can be relied upon." Although the Government had announced its intention of putting the recommendations of the Report into effect, so serious was the criticism in the Commons and so very well organized the protests of the staff that it rescinded its decision. The Government decided that there should be discussions with the staff associations through the machinery of the National Whitley Council, and that Council set up a joint committee to consider the proposals. Its report was published in 1953,[1] and the present rules governing the political activities of Civil Servants are largely based on its advice. Of the employees in State service, more than half, including the industrial staff and most of the minor grades of the non-industrial staff, are not politically restricted; clerical staff, typists and some minor technical staff, representing 20 per cent, may, with their department's approval, take part in all political activities, except Parliamentary candidature; and the executive and higher staff while not allowed to intervene in national political activities, are permitted to participate in local political activities unless there is departmental objection.

Few officials do in fact take any prominent part in national politics —one or two are extremist enough to declare that they will not even exercise their right to vote. Civil Servants are very conscious that the Service must be neutral and that Ministers and others must never

[1] Cmd. 8783 (1953).

have reason to doubt that the employees of the State serve every Government with the same loyalty and skill. Officials would be gutless if they did not have their reservations about some of the things that politicians do or want to do, but they realize that they would fail dismally in their duty if they permitted their personal views to affect the quality of the service they offer. If officials as a class have a tendency, it is to resist anything in the nature of an extreme course in any direction: when the Conservatives are in power, the officials may incline towards the Left, but very, very gently; when the administration is Labour, the officials may incline towards the Right, but so slightly that only other Civil Servants can detect any movement at all.

There are, of course, Civil Servants who are violent political partisans, but they are not found among the higher ranks. "The characteristic which has long been recognized in the British administrator and extolled as a special virtue is his impartiality, and, in his public capacity, a mind untinged by political prepossession," said the Masterman Committee. "Differing in type and mental attitude from the politician or the party-man, the Civil Servant conceives it his duty to advise on the facts before him. He does not advocate a system of political doctrines. Even if his personal sympathies attract him towards a political party, he does not express his sympathies in public. There is, however, more involved than the mere repression of party views. The administrative Civil Servant voluntarily enters a profession in which his service to the public will take a non-political form. It will consist in the wise and accurate estimation of the reasons for and against a particular course of action, formulated not for the purpose of influencing the public mind, but for the benefit of those who have actually to take decisions. The deliberate choice of a profession in which he knows that his service to the public will take this form gives a bent to the mind. It is very unlikely that a Civil Servant formed by years of training and the exercise of administrative functions would hold clear-cut views in the sense of being a consistent supporter of the entire programme of one party, even if on the whole his sympathies lay with it."

This still remains true. A Minister appointed to take charge of a department on a change of Government may feel that what has been done under his predecessor is stupid and illogical and shortsighted, but he must not expect his officials to join in a chorus of agreement. Civil Servants do not venture to pass opinions on any political régime in public, either before or after an election. The official is warned "not to indulge in political or party controversy, lest be so doing he should appear no longer the disinterested adviser of Ministers or able to execute their policy. He is bound to maintain proper reticence in discussing public affairs, more particularly those with which his own department is concerned."

When Labour assumed office in 1964, some people suggested that senior officials would be lukewarm to the economic and other reforms to which the new Government was committed. This is an old cry. On the accession of Labour to power in 1945, it was claimed that top Civil Servants might not be anxious to implement social plans. Ministers who served in the 1945–51 administrations testified that such suspicions were quite groundless and agreed that the departments had never failed to assist to the utmost in the execution of reforms.

Considerable doubts were raised, however, whether the Labour Government elected in 1964 would be able to rely on the Civil Service as it stood. Much discussion took place about the French system where a Minister brings with him into his department a number of people on whose judgement he knows from experience he can depend and who act as a kind of office *cabinet*. When questioned about introducing such a procedure in this country, the Labour Prime Minister said he did not favour the arrangement here. When he served as President of the Board of Trade in the Government which met with defeat in 1951, he explained, he had tried the experiment of appointing a few people "with the right kind of political approach". His experience was, he went on, that he would have done far better to rely on the Civil Servants already in the department.

Nevertheless, since Labour came into power, it has taken the unusual course of creating a number of posts for economists, scientists, and industrialists from outside industry and the universities, men who have in the past been associated with socialist programmes or are regarded as being in tune with Labour's ideals and aspirations. It was only to be expected that such a step should give rise to much comment and that the question of patronage should be raised and the undesirability of choosing officials because of their political leanings. There were complaints that the Government might be tending to adopt something like the American spoils system, where a number of officials are appointed by each new administration and leave when another of a different political complexion comes into power.

In making the special appointments the Labour Government made it clear that it had received the fullest co-operation from the Civil Service. The new posts are not in general administrative. No Civil Servant has lost his job or been demoted. The same men as before still remain at the apex of the official hierarchy.

Some of those brought in to take up the new posts earned far higher incomes than are paid in the Civil Service. A number of them had their salaries supplemented by their former employers, others agreed to make a financial sacrifice in order to serve the country.

This situation has led to the contention that the Government should pay its top staff more generously and so attract better men to make a career in the service of the State. The scale of remuneration of senior Civil Servants is never easy to determine. While the lower and middle grades have the right to submit their claims to the Civil Service Arbitration Tribunal, if agreement on pay cannot be reached otherwise, higher officials cannot do so. Nor is this unreasonable, for the holders of such posts are the men who represent the Government side in arbitration. If the salaries of their own grade were under consideration, they would have a foot in both camps. However dispassionate they might strive to be, some doubt would exist whether they were really impartial.

A Committee on Higher Civil Service Remuneration considers what increases, if any, should be made to the salaries of grades above Assistant Secretary. "None of our witnesses have argued that Civil Service salaries should be related to the highest individual salaries that can be attained in the most highly competitive professional and commercial posts," stated the committee. "The Civil Service is and will remain a service in which dazzling rewards are inappropriate."

The four chief posts in the Civil Service carry a salary of about £9,000 per annum; thirty Permanent Secretaries of departments receive over £8,000; another 250 earn around £5,000; and more than 750 have a maximum of £4,000. All of them can look forward to a non-contributory pension of half their salary on retirement at sixty, and the men at the very top are almost invariably knighted or awarded a higher honour.

Chapter Eighteen

PUBLIC ACCOUNTS COMMITTEE

THE final stage in the history of a grant of money by Parliament for the use of a Government department is the examination by the Public Accounts Committee of fifteen M.P.s under the chairmanship of a member of the party in opposition.

As mentioned earlier, the estimates of expenditure of all departments for the year 1962–3 had to be sent to the Treasury before the end of 1961. The first instalment of money comes by authority of the Vote on Account agreed before the last day of March, and, also before that date, Parliament passes the Consolidated Fund (No. 1) Act; the remainder of the money is voted before the start of the summer recess and, usually before the end of July, both Houses have given their approval to the Consolidated Fund (Appropriation) Act.

In 1962–3, the Ministry of Films had put forward two supplementary estimates, the first in July 1962 and the second in February 1963, via the Treasury on each occasion. On 31 March, 1963, all departments closed their accounts for the 1962–3 financial year and by October 1963 the accounts had been audited. The examination of the accounts before the Public Accounts Committee for the year beginning on 1 April, 1962, was not finished until June 1964.

Each Government office prepares a quite simple account of its transactions: a departmental Appropriation Account is designed to show primarily how the expenditure and revenue compare with the estimates agreed by Parliament. The Account brings out clearly whether the expenditure has been greater or less than the amount originally estimated, not only in total but sub-head by sub-head. Where a sub-head has been exceeded the authority of the Treasury should have been obtained for "virement". If this has not been done, the Public Accounts Committee will want to be informed of the reason. Where one or more Supplementary Estimates have been approved, this is brought out in the Account. Any variations between the amount voted and the amount spent, or between the estimated and the actual revenue, are the subject of brief notes. The first part of the Appropriation Account of the mythical Ministry of Films is shown, for the year 1962–3, in Appendix VII for comparison with the estimate of the department for that year in Appendix V.

At the same time as the form of the estimates was revised in 1962–3, the Appropriation Account was recast and simplified. Among other things the arrangements for recording any exceptional payments were modified. Until then, the departments included in their Appropriation Accounts a special sub-head for "Losses and Compensation". No provision was made in the original estimates for such expenditure—obviously a department could not guess what amount would be needed for these purposes—but when the need arose during the year a Losses and Compensation Sub-head was added. It was recognized that every department was almost certain to have to meet expenditure of this kind, nevertheless the fiction was maintained that losses were something extraordinary, and until a couple of years ago the Treasury had to give its sanction before the new sub-head was opened. And real difficulty arose if a department was unable to find the money for its losses by making savings elsewhere in its Parliamentary vote.

Any excess on a vote is likely to cause trouble. Unless quite exceptionally, an excess does not arise from the amount required to be paid out in Losses and Compensation, but from unforeseen payments which have had to be made so late in the financial year that no opportunity was available to present a Supplementary Estimate. In the past, the Public Accounts Committee has been fiercely critical of departments which have exceeded their votes. The Committee has also become very much concerned about the huge amounts which remain in most votes at the end of the financial year, suggesting that departments draw up their estimates so that a generous margin is always left in order to guard against any of the ordinary risks of exceeding the total amount.

The Appropriation Account of every department is certified and audited by the Comptroller and Auditor-General. He has a staff of 600 under his control, most of whom are outposted to the departments. They examine all payments and report on those which appear to call for inquiry. If a department's reply to their questions is not satisfactory or if, even so, the matter is of importance, the Comptroller and Auditor-General refers the point to the Public Accounts Committee. The audit by the Auditor-General's staff is much more detailed than that of a commercial auditor and covers a much wider ground. The Auditor-General not only wants to be satisfied that the money has been used for the purpose for which it was voted, he must be convinced that the financial arrangements for the control of expenditure are properly made and are strictly observed by everyone concerned, that the methods of placing contracts provide for the best bargain to be obtained for the State, and that there has been no apparent lack of foresight in embarking on any scheme; if a department pays too much for some goods, or if it fails to collect money from debtors, or if it does not in every way protect the public purse, then the Public Accounts Committee will be informed. The audit is in effect an administrative audit as well as a financial one.

Every year the Government publishes the Appropriation Accounts of the departments in several volumes, each with a preface by the Comptroller and Auditor-General, which consists of a report to Parliament. The Public Accounts Committee must consider all the Accounts, and without their approval none may be passed unless on the express authority of Parliament; even when they have agreed an Account the authority of Parliament may still be necessary, though it is usually formal once the P.A.C. has given its sanction. A verbatim report of the proceedings of the P.A.C. is published as a Blue Book each session, a volume running into some 600 pages of small print.

Complaint is sometimes made in the United States of the system under which Congress calls numerous officials from the same department to answer questions. "Congressional enquiries have the right to question officials of the Government," said a critic recently, "but matters of policy should be stated by responsible officials and not in bits and pieces by an adjutant here, a camp commandant there, or a clerk somewhere else." The exact opposite is the complaint sometimes heard in Britain, for the P.A.C. acknowledges only one official in a department—the Accounting Officer. He may bring with him other officials to the P.A.C., but he must ask the Committee's permission before they can answer questions and, whatever they may say, the responsibility rests with him. The P.A.C. is, of course, well aware that the head of a large department cannot know all the details of the work, but, as Accounting Officer, the onus rests on him and he is expected to make himself knowledgeable. Throughout the year matters on which it seems possible that the P.A.C. will ask questions are carefully recorded in the department, and the Accounting Officer is provided by his staff with a "brief". In a large office it may run into 200 or more typewritten pages and it will roam over the whole range of departmental activities. The Accounting Officer may have a few days away from the office to study it, for nobody at the head of a department likes to appear before the P.A.C. and confess that he cannot answer questions on the work of the office of which he is in final charge under his Minister.

Since many of the services of a department will have been

specifically approved by the Treasury, the P.A.C. calls representatives of the Treasury at the same time as the Accounting Officer. The Committee cannot criticize a department for pursuing policies which have been imposed on it by the Government, but it can and does criticize the manner in which the policies have been executed. In the course of a century, the P.A.C. has examined most of the principles relating to the conduct of Government financial business and given decisions on points that have been, or might have been, in doubt within the Treasury or other departments. These are collected in the Epitome of the Reports from the Committee of Public Accounts, one volume covering from 1857 to 1937,[1] and a second from 1938 to 1950.[2]

The Accounting Officer is specifically put in charge of the funds of his department, but he is the servant of the Minister, and he must therefore obey the instructions of his political chief. If the Minister asks for a payment to be made which his Accounting Officer considers lies outside the scope of the Parliamentary Vote or is otherwise objectionable, his duty is to put his opinion in writing. Should the Minister overrule him and repeat his written orders, the Accounting Officer is bound to make the payment; but he then reports the facts to the Treasury and the Comptroller and Auditor-General and, through these channels, the dispute comes to the notice of the P.A.C. The Accounting Officer is thus relieved of liability, but in no other circumstances can he evade responsibility. Where expenditure has been incurred which the C. and A.G. is unwilling to pass, the P.A.C. is advised. Unlike the Auditor-General of the United States, who has authority to require officials to reimburse the Government if unauthorized payments are made, the C. and A.G. cannot disallow expenditure, but that right may be exercised by the Public Accounts Committee.

The Committee normally meets for two or three hours on each Tuesday and Thursday during Parliamentary sessions. Most witnesses undergo only a short examination, but a number of departmental accounts is very thoroughly inspected. The Committee probes deeply into any matter which it feels calls for explanation, and an Accounting Officer may be summoned before the P.A.C. more than once in the course of a session. Every member is entitled to put as many questions as he likes to witnesses, who may be shot at from all sides. A Treasury witness told the P.A.C. at one meeting that the preparation of legislation in respect of part of another department's activities was under consideration, and in the following year the

[1] H.C. 154 (1938).   [2] H.C. 155 (1952).

Chairman asked: "Have you got on with that?" "We have not made much progress with it," the Treasury witness replied. "We have been considering it. We considered it during the course of last summer. . . . The position is now very much as it was then. I ought to say that there is no question whatsoever of our not fulfilling the undertaking which we have given to introduce legislation at the first convenient opportunity, but we cannot say that the first convenient opportunity has arrived." "Who is considering it—Treasury officials?" "Treasury officials in consultation with the Department. . . ." "It is being actively considered. Is that right?" "Yes." A second member put in: "I suppose the next stage is that it will be in course of being considered. When will it be promoted?" "It is being considered now." A third member asked, "Have the Treasury in mind what figure it must get to before they get to the stage of considering it?" And so on.

Though it does not publish the evidence until nearly the close of a Parliamentary session, the P.A.C. usually issues three or four reports in the course of a year. These reports used to be sent to the Treasury which answered for the departments as a whole, but it has now been agreed that each Ministry should make its own reply to the P.A.C.'s observations. Very often changes are made as a result of the criticisms of some procedure or action. But not always, for a department does not invariably agree with the P.A.C., nor can the Committee's wishes be met in some instances, either because of the practical difficulties or for some other reason. The P.A.C. is sometimes not easily convinced that the obstacles which the department foresees at times are really quite insurmountable.

The following example gives an indication of the P.A.C.'s procedure. Large sums are handed over yearly to the University Grants Committee, which distributes them on behalf of the Government to individual universities. In the 1950–1 session the P.A.C. questioned two representatives of the Treasury on the control of this expenditure. It was explained that the Chancellor of the Exchequer appointed the members of the University Grants Committee and that committee put forward applications to the Treasury for the funds required; but that the Treasury made no detailed examination of the University Grants Committee's proposals. "I think only in very exceptional cases would the departmental Treasury disturb the balance of the recommendations put up by the University Grants Committee as a whole," a Treasury witness explained to the P.A.C. "If I might say so, I am sure that the inquiries made by the University Grants

Committee are extremely thorough, very careful and painstaking, and carried out with a full sense of responsibility." The Comptroller and Auditor-General said that he did not "audit in any way the accounts of the universities or the use of the moneys paid out of those grants." The P.A.C. inquired whether a Treasury departmental official served on the University Grants Committee and was informed in the negative, a Treasury witness pointing out: "I do not think we feel that it would be helpful. . . . I am convinced that this Committee as a whole, collectively and individually, has a very high sense of its responsibility not only for University education but financially, and they feel themselves under a great obligation only to put forward recommendations which they believe are economical and fully justified." The Chairman asked, "Would you say . . . that at no period since the war has the University Grants Committee put forward to you any but what they consider the most economical suggestions of the minima that they ought to spend?" and, on being told by the same witness, "Yes, I think, broadly speaking, that is true," the Chairman remarked. "What put the question into my mouth, if I may just elaborate it, is the statement you made that you are fairly sure that these gentlemen do never put forward anything but the bare minimum of their requirements. That is outside my power of belief in regard to any body of enthusiasts. Anybody who is an enthusiast about something nearly always puts up a figure and thinks, 'We will try this.' " And so on.

In the following year a Treasury witness was accompanied to the P.A.C. by a representative of the University Grants Committee, and members of the P.A.C. pursued the question of the control of the money. The representative of the Grants Committee explained that individual universities sent their proposals for buildings to the Grants Committee, which had a sub-committee to examine them and which also forwarded them to the Ministry of Works so that the experts of that department could consider them. This sounded foolproof, but a member of the P.A.C. asked bluntly: "What control have you over the moneys? If these universities have made applications and you have made grants to them, do you retain any real control over the way in which the money is spent?" "Not in any formal sense," was the reply. "Of course, we know, as the accounts are rendered, how it has been spent, but it is part of the system that the universities are autonomous, and although they do pay regard to the known wishes of the [University Grants] Committee there is no formal control." In answer to a further question, he added: "It has been the policy of the Government all along that the universities should be left to manage their own affairs."

After this examination in 1952 the P.A.C. reported: "Expenditure by the universities out of the grants made to them is not accounted for to the Comptroller and Auditor-General. The audited accounts of the universities are furnished to the University Grants Committee, by whom they are checked to ensure that the correct amounts have been brought to account and that the accounts are in the form prescribed to enable the Committee to present uniform annual returns of income and expenditure to Parliament. . . . In view of the steep increase in this expenditure previous Committees of Public Accounts, while not wishing to suggest that university expenditure should be subjected to detailed Treasury control, have considered that Parliament is entitled to some assurance that these large grants are administered with due regard to economy." The P.A.C. also referred to non-recurrent grants and were of opinion "that the present system of controlling these grants . . . is less than Parliament is entitled or accustomed to receive where such appreciable amounts of voted money are involved" and that "the records should be open to examination by the Comptroller and Auditor-General".

But this failed to move the Treasury, which replied to the P.A.C.: "My Lords find difficulty in accepting the Committee's recommendation that the Comptroller and Auditor-General should have the right to inspect the books and accounts of universities so far as these relate to money advanced by means of non-recurrent grants for capital development. Such an inspection could have two objects: first, to ensure that the grant was duly appropriated to meet the expenditure towards which the grant was made, and secondly, to bring to light any lack of economy in the expenditure itself. So far as the first object is concerned, it is difficult to see what purpose the Comptroller and Auditor-General's inspection could serve which is not already served by the existing audit of University accounts. As regards the second object, the question whether due economy has been exercised in the design and equipment of buildings for academic purposes inevitably raises questions of academic policy, and for this reason my Lords have hitherto taken the view that Their own control over the amounts of non-recurrent as well as of recurrent grants should be exercised on broad lines, and that questions of detail should be left to the University Grants Committee. . . . For these reasons, My Lords . . . would be reluctant to accept the Committee's recommendations on this point."

The P.A.C. summoned the representatives of the Treasury and of the University Grants Committee once more in 1953. "Why does the Treasury resist the suggestion . . . that the Comptroller and Auditor-General should be able to look at these accounts?" the witnesses were asked; and they again took their stand on the importance of giving "substantial help to the universities without in any way impairing their academic independence". The report made by the P.A.C. after this examination did not mince words: "On the question whether the system of financial control is adequate and whether, for example, the University Grants Committee are able to exercise proper control, Your Committee take the view that these are matters which concern Parliament, and on the information available to them they are not at present able to give Parliament an unqualified assurance that there is no irregularity or abuse and that the grants have been spent on the purposes for which they were voted and with due regard to the elimination of waste and extravagance. Such assurance in their opinion can best be given through the Comptroller and Auditor-General, whose approach to these matters is different from that of the professional auditor. . . . Your Committee . . . recommend that in future the books and accounts of the universities that relate to their expenditure of grants for non-recurrent purposes should be open to inspection by the Comptroller and Auditor-General." And, lest there should be any doubt about their views, the P.A.C. added that "they remain unconvinced by Treasury arguments that the independence of the universities would thereby be prejudiced".

To these comments the Treasury apparently felt it must make some concession, and it replied: "My Lords have considered with great care the renewed recommendation of the Committee that the books and accounts of the Universities that relate to their expenditure of grants for non-recurrent purposes should be open to inspection by the Comptroller and Auditor-General. They are most anxious to satisfy the desire of the Committee for full information. . . . The relationship between the Universities on the one hand, and Parliament and Her Majesty's Government on the other hand, is, of course, a very special one. . . . The need for a much larger output from the Universities . . . has made Universities far more dependent on State help than before the war. It has been the constant aim of successive Governments to make sure that this help is available under conditions which ensure prudent administration while at the same time safeguarding the autonomy of the Universities. . . . It has been the essence of the relationship between the Universities and Her Majesty's

Government that Their Lordships have sought to avoid any detailed control of the activities of the Universities. Neither they nor the University Grants Committee on Their behalf have ever claimed the right to examine the Universities' books. Their Lordships cannot avoid the conclusion that, were the Comptroller and Auditor-General given the right to inspect the Universities' books, the results would be that Their Lordships would before long find Themselves compelled to expand Their intervention in University matters and to enlarge Their own control in a way which would certainly change, and They believe would be prejudicial to, the present harmonious relationship between the Universities and the University Grants Committee." Then came the suggestion that some action might after all be possible to meet the demand of the P.A.C. "My Lords have again considered whether there is any way in which They can satisfy the purposes which the Committee have in mind without throwing the books of the Universities open to the inspection of the Comptroller and Auditor-General," the Treasury minute continued. "... My Lords are considering whether the assurance which the Public Accounts Committee require about this expenditure could not be provided by some other means—as, for example, the appointment by the University Grants Committee of one or more suitable persons who would report to that Committee on the question whether any, and if so what, changes are necessary to secure that Universities' methods of contracting, and of recording and controlling expenditure are reasonably designed, and properly applied, to ensure effective safeguards against waste, extravagance, or other abuse. My Lords envisage that such a report would be made available to the Public Accounts Committee, together with a note of any action taken or proposed to be taken upon it." Shortly afterwards the Chancellor of the Exchequer announced that the University Grants Committee had appointed a committee to report to it on the question "whether, and if so what, changes are necessary to secure that the universities' methods of contracting, and of recording and controlling expenditure from non-current grants, are reasonably designed, and properly applied, to ensure effective safeguards against waste, extravagance, or other abuse".

An inquiry set up under the chairmanship of Sir George Gater examined the expenditure of non-recurrent grants, principally for buildings but also for furniture and equipment. No one, of course, suggested that a new university building should be constructed in the cheapest possible style, but the investigators wanted to be sure that proper business arrangements were adopted. In their report, published in 1957,[1] they made proposals for tightening up the system of tendering and controlling the work of construction, and in general the Universities accepted the recommendations. The Universities also undertook to furnish information to the Treasury so that a register of commitments and payments could be maintained. These records were to be available to the Comptroller and Auditor-General.

The Public Accounts Committee agreed to these revised arrangements for an experimental period of three years. At the end of the period, the P.A.C. again examined the Treasury about the universities' expenditure. The Treasury witness explained that a further inspection had been made in 1960 by an independent investigator—Sir Arthur Rucker—whose report on "Methods Used by Universities of Contracting and of Recording and Controlling Expenditure"[2] confirmed that the recommendations made by Sir George Gater were being carried out.

The Comptroller and Auditor-General was still not allowed to audit the accounts of the universities. He was, however, entitled not only to examine the records of commitments and payments but also to see the certificates issued by the universities' own auditors which confirmed that grants made by the Exchequer had been applied to the proper purposes for which they were provided. In addition, the C. and A.G. could seek any further information he thought necessary.

The Public Accounts Committee, having listened to this evidence about the experience gained in the period during which the new scheme had been in operation, and after receiving a firm assurance that where overspending had occurred this was not due to faulty execution or control on the part of the universities, accepted that the arrangement should continue.

Thus, after a wordy conflict lasting ten years, a compromise had been reached. The Public Accounts Committee had not gained all it had asked, since the C. and A.G. was still denied any right to audit the universities' accounts. But, under the pressure of the Committee, a better measure of control had been introduced in the expenditure of the grants to ensure that "the greatest possible economy is exercised". The scale of the grants has increased and the total for universities, colleges, etc., has grown in ten years from some £28,000,000 to £130,000,000 in 1964–5. Responsibility for the expenditure now rests with the Ministry of Education to which it has been transferred from the Treasury.

[1] Cmnd. 9.   [2] Cmnd. 1235.

In agreeing to content itself with the revised arrangements, the Public Accounts Committee had a final word. The C. and A.G., it pronounced, should exercise continual vigilance and report any developments which he thinks merits consideration.

The University Grants Committee is in a very special position, and because of this received a degree of latitude in its expenditure rarely countenanced by the Public Accounts Committee. Government departments have no choice about the nature of the audit or by whom it should be undertaken.

Every year his submissions to the Public Accounts Committee focuses attention on weaknesses. The knowledge that errors may be exposed and that the Permanent Secretary of a department will be personally examined before the P.A.C. exercises a powerful influence on officials in the departments. Blunders are not eliminated—everyone who reads the newspapers learns of serious miscalculations and of gross carelessness; but the staff of auditors, constantly on watch for laxity or irresponsibility, ensures publicity for grave failures which otherwise might be buried deep in the departmental archives.

Chapter Nineteen

MINISTERIAL RESPONSIBILITY

THE politician appointed to the charge of a department is unlikely to be a professional in its work. If he is a doctor, he will not usually be made Minister of Health; or, should his training be as an architect or engineer, it is improbable that he will be put in control of the Ministry of Public Building and Works. As a rule Parliament prefers that the political head of a Government department should be a non-specialist and the Civil Service also tends to suspect the Minister who possesses technical qualifications in the field covered by his department. Most M.P.s when on the back benches or in Opposition will have made some study of one or more of such subjects as health, education, information services, the colonies, or finance and will know something of the related departmental problems. There are few successful politicians who have not learned how to absorb information quickly or who lack shrewd judgement of men and affairs.

Civil Servants in the chief posts of a department likewise rarely have technical qualifications. Scientists hold high rank in the Ministry of Defence and medical men are among the principal officers of the Ministry of Health, but the permanent head of an office is not a technician. He is an administrator, with the responsibility of weighing up the facts put before him and applying a skilled intelligence in finding a solution to a problem or in deciding the course of action which is desirable and feasible.

The theory has been that the prospective administrator should come into the Service and learn how to make use of specialists, bringing to bear a clear mind on problems which may range over a vast variety of subjects. The old joke in Whitehall is that four experts will produce four different opinions and that only the administrators' impartial assessment can produce the right solution. Civil Servants refer to administration as an art, and are proud of their ability to absorb information on complex subjects. A Minister also needs the same facility to some extent, but he will not attempt to do the work of his officials. He cannot hope to control a Government department as the chairman or the managing director might run a company. Other things apart, the politician lacks the time to do so. He must keep in touch with his constituency and speak at political and other functions; and a large part of every day will be taken up with his Parliamentary duties while the House is in session. As a Minister, he will be allotted a room in the House to which he can retire when his presence is not required in the Chamber itself or in a committee. A stream of visitors will, however, leave him little opportunity to study official files or deal with other departmental business when the House is sitting. Only in the mornings will he be able to devote much time to the work of his office.

Much importance is attached to the choice of the Minister's departmental private secretary, who is usually an official employed by the office. He need not be a member of the department, nor is he necessarily a Civil Servant. A few Ministers have preferred to bring with them a private secretary from outside the Service in whom they have confidence and who is accustomed to their methods of working. By far the greater number, however, agree that the advantage lies in choosing their private secretary from the staff of their new department. The private secretary to a Minister is usually a Principal, occasionally an Assistant Secretary. The man appointed receives an allowance of several hundreds a year in addition to his yearly salary, and the position also has the attraction of great prestige; its holder performs highly interesting and varied work and the post is a stepping-stone to promotion. Most officials who reach the very senior ranks of the Civil Service have in their younger years served as a private secretary to a Minister.

The choice of a Principal to act as a Minister's private secretary is usually made from among men who have had several years of experience in the department and are regarded as likely to climb to authoritative positions at a later stage in their career. They are the bright young men of the office with a good university degree who have already won a reputation for outstanding work and who possess an extensive knowledge of the operations of the department. The Minister will make his own selection from the two or three candidates who are recommended by the Permanent Secretary as having the right departmental background and other qualifications. The post is a key one and a wise choice will ease a Minister's path.

The departmental private secretary is not to be confused with the Parliamentary Secretary or the Parliamentary Private Secretary. Unlike them, he is not political but a member of the Civil Service complement. He must know the senior officials and be well acquainted with the work of the department, and in particular have the "feel" of the administration. The Private Secretary will organize the Minister's personal secretariat, known as the "Private Office", to which among other staff an Assistant Principal may be attached to gain experience.

Though his rank may be that of Principal, the Private Secretary will exercise a considerable amount of authority. A request from him will be almost the same as a Ministerial demand. He will be able to indicate how the Minister is likely to react to proposals and to advise on the best method of approach; will know where his chief can be found at any time; and will arrange most of the interviews and be present at them, making notes to ensure that there can be no misunderstanding of the Minister's decisions. The Private Secretary will live in his master's pocket; he will accompany him to the House and to some social functions, and he will gain an insight into the larger world. The day will come, however, when the young man must return to humdrum departmental duties and lose his mantle of magnificence; in most instances this knowledge will keep power from going to his head, but he will have to tread very warily if he is to remain on good terms with his colleagues, who will in any case blame the Private Secretary for the Minister's foibles.

Official policy is no part of the responsibility of the Private Secretary. Like all other officials in a department he is subject to the control of the Permanent Secretary and it is the latter who has the final departmental authority under the Minister. No Private Secretary would remain in his post for very long if he clashed with the senior officials.

Whether or not a Minister is a member of the Cabinet, he will receive copies of all Cabinet papers and these will be dealt with in the Private Office. Until 1916, Cabinet decisions were not formally recorded, but the secretariat which now services the Cabinet is an indispensable feature of the administration. The Cabinet Secretariat circulates memoranda, agenda, and minutes; collects information required by Ministers; and acts as a co-ordinating agency for the Government. Every Minister has the privilege of submitting papers to the Cabinet, and such papers are usually drafted on his behalf by departmental officials. The Civil Servant is warned that a Cabinet paper should not exceed a single sheet since otherwise overburdened Ministers will not read it, but every official soon learns that Ministers will complain if a proposal is not made absolutely clear when it reaches them. Many matters cannot be described adequately in the space of a single sheet, and while therefore the note circulated to the Cabinet may be short, it is often accompanied by explanatory appendices which may be very long.

Before proposals are decided by the Cabinet, they have usually been examined by a Cabinet Committee. Some of the Committees are permanent—e.g. the Defence Committee—but many of them are set up to consider a particular problem and, after reporting to the full Cabinet, are disbanded. The Committees may consist wholly of Ministers or they may be composed partly of Ministers and partly of departmental officials, with a secretary from the staff of the Cabinet Secretariat. The number of Cabinet Committees at any one time is known only to Ministers and the Secretariat, but there are always several in which the Permanent Secretary of a major department is likely to be involved directly. Where his Minister is a member of a Committee on which no departmental officials serve, the Permanent Secretary will be consulted on the different lines of action suggested, and will be kept closely in touch with the proceedings at all stages.

Civil Servants are not summoned to Cabinet unless on the very rarest of occasions. Where an issue is submitted to the Cabinet on which agreement has not been reached in committee, the decision may be difficult to forecast, for some schemes are no doubt approved largely because they are strongly pressed by a Minister who occupies a key post or who has a very high personal standing with his colleagues. A Minister may carry great weight with the Cabinet at one time and the same Minister's influence may wane at another. Having briefed their political chief and perhaps inspired him with great enthusiasm over some method of solving a question, officials can only sit back with as much patience as they can muster and await the result, knowing that it may depend on something quite extraneous.

Committees abound within the Civil Service. There are committees confined to one department, committees with representatives of a number of offices engaged on related work, committees in which all the departments take part and which therefore speak for the Service as a whole. Some are permanent, others are dissolved after considering a single issue; a number are able to report within a few weeks, others may labour for years before reaching conclusions; meetings may be held daily where the matter is urgent, or a committee may meet only once a quarter. Much committee work must be done by the senior officials, and, as their number is relatively small, the same men and women often face each other across a conference table. But this does not necessarily mean that the views of the members can be foreseen. The representatives are not there to express personal opinions; they may be the spokesmen for their Ministers or they may put forward the views of the departmental specialists.

The influence which a Minister can exert on an office naturally varies according to the departmental functions, his own ability, and the amount of time he is able to give to the work. He has the indisputable right to decide everything within a department, but clearly he cannot do so since, even had he the knowledge, he would be overwhelmed with the volume. Yet he retains the responsibility, though he sees little of the work. When his department does a good job, the Minister will receive the credit; when blunders are made, Parliament will blame the Minister. Civil Servants are anonymous; they cannot ask a Member to speak up on their behalf in Parliament, nor are they permitted to express their personal views to the Press. Few even of the highest-placed Civil Servants are known to the public by name.

Although a Minister must leave most of the day-to-day decisions to his staff, his influence on how the Department should be run is obviously very great. He can make his wishes clearly known and lay down the broad policy which he expects to see followed. A brief experience of a new Minister enables the senior officials to judge how their political head will look upon different aspects of the work and to gauge what cases he would want to have referred to him for personal attention. Once a ruling has been given on a particular point, it will represent the policy of the department and no one will depart from it without the permission of the Minister. A single decision may affect numerous cases, and Ministerial directions given on even a few points may exercise great influence throughout the whole of a department.

The Permanent Secretary will probably see the Minister at least once a day and keep him informed orally of developments over a wide field of departmental activities. A number of cases will be left for the Minister to study, either because he has expressed a wish to see them or because, in the opinion of the Permanent Secretary, they raise points which it is necessary or desirable that the Minister should decide. A great mass of correspondence will come to the Private Office every day, but the Private Secretary will send most of the letters to the divisions of the department for reply, and the Minister need never be troubled to look at them. Where letters are from M.P.s or other public men, the answer will normally be signed by the Minister or the Parliamentary Secretary. The replies will be drafted by Civil Servants, but they may need to be reworded before dispatch, for officials tend to be somewhat stilted in their style. A letter from a Government department quoted in a legal action started off: "I am directed ... to say that they [the Board] have ascertained that the statutory requirements in regard to the reconsideration of your

daughter's case consequent upon her attaining the age of 21. . . ."
Letters which begin "Sir" and end "I am, Sir, Your obedient
Servant" are less common than a few years ago, but a certain stiffness
and prolixity still lingers on in letters emanating from Government
departments. The Civil Servant is unhappy with a direct statement,
and he prefers to qualify; others may say that "the car killed the
chicken", but the official will prefer the version that "the car inflicted
a fatal injury on the alleged chicken". The official clings to the well-
worn phrase which, if not elegant, has the merit of having stood the
test of time, and he avoids straightforward phrases in favour of something more high-sounding. Officials are aware that what they write
may be examined word for word by lawyers or accountants on the
lookout for some loophole, and that their letters may be the subject of
comment in newspapers.

Gobbledegook flourishes in Government departments and a little
pomposity creeps into much departmental correspondence. Many
attempts have been made to encourage officials to adopt an easier
and friendlier style. But all professions cling to their own brand of
jargon and the Civil Service is no less fond than others of its own way
of expressing itself. "Officialese" comes to exert a strange fascination
over those who have once learned to use it, and indeed there is often
no complete cure for the malady.

A problem in all departments is that of deciding how much to refer
to a Minister. If a large number of cases are submitted, the political
head may not be able to study the papers properly and may give
decisions which show that he has not appreciated the problem; on
the other hand, if the officials send only what they consider to be the
most vital matters, the Minister may feel that he is being kept in the
dark. What is a vast load to a politician not very competent at paper
work will be tackled readily by a quick reader with an orderly mind
and the gift of concentration. The experienced Minister will have
acquired the knack of picking out what is important in official files
and of giving his directions clearly.

A Minister is responsible for the actions of his officials, but this
does not mean that Civil Servants can do what they like and that their
political chief is bound to support them through thick or thin, or that
their mistakes will go unpunished. A few years ago the then Prime
Minister summed up the position to the House of Commons when
criticism was made that an official had dispatched an important
cablegram to a foreign country without the authority of his political
chief: "The principles governing ministerial responsibility and its

exercise are well known. A Minister is, of course, supposed to know the general course of policy pursued by his department in any particular direction, and he naturally could have cause to complain if he had not been informed of a course of action which departed from the general course he was pursuing. But you cannot say nothing is to be done that the Minister does not see. He is responsible, however, for everything that goes on and making sure nothing goes on which he does not like." Some M.P.s were not satisfied with the explanation, and soon afterwards the Home Secretary made a more detailed statement to Parliament, as follows:

There has been considerable anxiety . . . as to how far the principle of Ministerial responsibility goes. We all recognize that we must have that principle in existence and that Ministers must be responsible for the acts of civil servants. Without it, it would be impossible to have a Civil Service which would be able to serve Ministries and Governments of different political faiths and persuasions with the same zeal and honesty which we have always found. . . .

There has been criticism that the principle operates so as to oblige Ministers to extend total protection to their officials and to endorse their acts, and to cause the position that civil servants cannot be called to account and are effectively responsible to no one. That is a position which I believe is quite wrong. . . . It is quite untrue that well-justified criticism of the actions of civil servants cannot be made on a suitable occasion. The position of the civil servant is that he is wholly and directly responsible to his Minister. . . . In the case where there is an explicit order by a Minister, a Minister must protect the civil servant who has carried out his order. Equally, where the civil servant acts properly in accordance with the policy laid down by the Minister, the Minister must protect and defend him. . . . Where an official makes a mistake or causes some delay, but not on an important issue of policy and not where a claim to individual rights is seriously involved, the Minister acknowledges the mistake and he accepts the responsibility, although he is not personally involved. . . . But, when one comes to the fourth category, where action has been taken by a civil servant of which the Minister disapproves and has no prior knowledge, and the conduct of the official is reprehensible, then there is no obligation on the part of the Minister to endorse what he believes to be wrong, or to defend what are clearly shown to be errors of his officers. The Minister is not bound to approve of action of which he did not know, or of which he disapproves. But, of course, he remains constitutionally responsible to Parliament for the fact that something has gone wrong, and he alone can tell Parliament what has occurred and render an account of his stewardship. . . .

Many of the cases submitted to the political head go to him only because his formal approval is required under statute; such cases can be disposed of without delay. Other cases need no more than a quick glance at a single document to arrive at a ruling. For those which call for detailed study, all the information will be brought together in summary form to facilitate the Minister's consideration; if he decides to look through the departmental files, which may run to a dozen or more in a single case, he will find cross-references which have been made so that relevant documents can be picked out among the mass of material. When he reads such files, the Minister will realize that administrators as well as technical specialists frequently disagree. Where different lines of action are favoured by different officials, they explain their reasons fully, and, while the minuting is always polite, any weakness in an argument is ruthlessly exposed.

When a case is laid on the desk of a Minister for a policy decision, the officials will have presented the complete picture to the best of their ability. If the Minister makes a decision which the Permanent Secretary feels to be mistaken, he is entitled to put forward the departmental opinion once more to the Minister. Officials are not supreme, and Civil Servants do not go about muttering to themselves, "Ministers come and Ministers go but the departments are here for ever" if they disagree with a decision which has been given. The Minister represents the will of the people and, holding office of the Sovereign, he is entitled to and receives the greatest respect from all officials. This does not mean that they go about in fear and trembling and are afraid to open their mouths. Once the Minister has reached his decision, however, the officials will support it through thick and thin. They will produce arguments to prove that the action taken was masterly and provide convincing briefs which prove that any criticism is either the result of lack of knowledge on the part of the Opposition or is just sheer perversity .

A newly appointed Minister of Films will want to be told about the main activities of the department, though he will have some idea of the Ministry's work from public references. After discussing the principal duties with the Permanent Secretary and the Deputy Secretary, he may see each of the dozen chief officials one by one and hear from them a description of their work. The Minister may ask about the procedure for acquiring a new cinema: how is the area chosen, who decides the size of the cinema to be erected, on what basis is the increase in the number of cinema-goers calculated for the present and in future years. If the Ministry's policy has been to use its funds in providing a few large cinemas rather than a greater number of small ones, the Minister may question whether this is the correct course and ask for a note about it. He is likely to be staggered by the detailed survey which he receives. Whatever else he may think he will be under no illusion about the industriousness of his advisers. The memorandum will perhaps point out that there have been several examinations of the subject and that each year the Advisory Council considers the policy again and reports whether it recommends any change; an explanation will be given of the economics of large and small theatres; the Minister will have his attention drawn to the limit set to the total deficit in the operation of Government cinemas. A summary may be attached of the points made in the debate when the Bill on the subject went through both Houses, extracts of speeches may be copied, and so on.

It would not be unexpected that the Minister should feel that he ought to see the scripts of films, for films are a subject to which everyone considers he has something to contribute. The Private Office will submit the scripts to him, each with a synopsis of the plot so that he need not waste his time in reading anything else unless he wishes. He may feel that references to some aspect of life crop up too often in the films. If he instructs changes to be made, no one will deny his right to alter anything; but he is likely to find that the references are quite deliberate, not the result of carelessness. A memorandum will reach the Minister, perhaps explaining that other departments have asked for the inclusion of certain material, it may be to assist recruitment for some Government service or to draw the attention of the public to some matter of importance which might otherwise be overlooked. Probably a committee has considered the content or perhaps the film exhibitors have expressed preferences.

If a new Minister makes changes in a department's policy in such matters, he will not do so because he feels his officials have been irresponsible in their decisions. He may believe his Civil Servants are lacking in drive and initiative and are quite unintelligent, but he will see that they have never acted without what seemed to them the best of reasons and after a close inspection of all the facts. The Minister may be satisfied that the officials are following the wrong policy, but the officials will try hard to demonstrate that it is a well-considered policy. Indeed, the Civil Servants spend so much time in examining all sides of a question that the Minister may wonder how they ever manage to reach any decision at all, and if indeed the examination is not in many cases incommensurate with the importance of the matter under discussion. A Minister who asks about the hours worked in his department may receive an analysis of the attendance records of every section over a period of a month, together with a graph showing the incidence of overtime grade by grade. "I ask a casual question," said one Minister, "and weeks later, after I have forgotten all about it, back comes a great big bulging file with all the unnecessary answers."

A new Minister will alter some things in his department. Obviously, a Labour administration will change some of the decisions of a Conservative Government, and *vice versa*. But, while different regulations may be approved and new policies introduced, the vast majority of officials do the same kind of work, though the approach may vary from time to time. A Minister has the power to reverse any departmental policy, and, subject to the Treasury and the Cabinet and in some matters Parliament, he can do what he likes. A change in policy does not necessarily involve legislation, nor does the introduction of additional services always require the presentation of a Bill. The provision of expenditure in a departmental estimate will by itself enable some measures to be instituted, though new services cannot normally be financed from the funds under the Vote on Account.

Other services will be impossible to start up without legislation. The Law Officers of the Crown will advise whether existing powers are adequate to cover any proposal that may be under consideration, or whether further legislation must be sought. The pressure on Parliament is heavy and the time available for new measures is very limited, since there are certain enactments which take up a large part of each session. After time has been earmarked for the Finance Bill, the departmental estimates, the Appropriation Bills, and the legislation which the Government has forecast in the Queen's Speech, few days remain for the less important Bills. All Ministers have their own measures, great or small, which they would like to see on the statute book or which their departments have convinced them ought to be included. The queue is always long and is sometimes clamourous.

The legislative process is cumbersome and the steering of a Bill through Parliament is likely to place a heavy burden on the most capable Minister and the most experienced departmental staff. If the Treasury Solicitor advises that a service which a department wishes to initiate requires specific Parliamentary authority, the Minister must expect to undertake a great deal of work which is quite personal. Others will have their part to play, but a large part of the burden will rest on him, however anxious his officials will be to carry all they can. It is undesirable to take an actual measure to describe the various stages, and so many subjects are covered by existing enactments that it is perhaps better to follow the course of an imaginary measure. A fantastic scheme has been chosen so that by no possibility could a reference to any department be suspected.

In the mythical Ministry of Films it may be taken for granted that numerous complaints will be received to the effect that the department is doing nothing to find stars for British productions. It will be pointed out that large sums in dollars are being spent on American films, and that this is due to the fact that the British film industry lacks sufficient stars. The Ministry of Films ought, it is claimed, to seek out talent in the young and thus ensure a flow of native stars for the future. The department may not disagree with the view, but it will be perplexed about the right way to tackle a job which has defeated many others. So the Minister will perhaps begin by appointing a committee to recommend how children should be selected for training in films. The terms of reference must be clearly drawn up so that the committee will not be tempted to wander into pleasant byways or impinge on the work of others, but at the same time it must be granted sufficiently wide powers to cover the whole field. Complications of all kinds will present themselves as the inquiry proceeds. If the committee recommends that the choice of the children to be trained should be made by the schools, the Ministry of Education will immediately become involved.

That Ministry will probably feel that the schools have so heavy a programme that they cannot be expected to do more, but they may find that pressure to introduce the scheme is so great that all such objections must be overruled. The Ministry of Education will have to consult the local educational authorities; it may be decided that the school-teachers should pick out suitable children in the first place and that the candidates should be medically examined. But not by the school doctors—that is a job for the ordinary medical practitioner. So the Ministry of Health will be brought in. It will be early recognized that, whatever the artistic ability of a child, film stars must have other qualifications for success. Perhaps therefore it will be necessary to set up panels to decide whether the children selected at the first stage are lacking in some obvious ingredient for fame. Such panels should be composed of those with experience in films, and the question must be examined whether they are to consist of full-time members or whether film actors and actresses will give their part-time services, preferably without cost to the Exchequer. Another committee will consider the composition of such panels and also the question of appeal against the decision of the selectors. For it can be taken for granted that disgruntled parents will protest because their children have been rejected. There is certain to be some official who suggests that the Ministry should produce sets of photographs for the guidance of selection panels, and another who will emphasize the need for common standards in recommendations, so that a series of forms will be needed. A statistical branch will have to keep careful records to ensure that not too many children of one sex are chosen that the age-grouping is in accordance with the industry's requirements, and that each country has its quota, since Scotland and Wales will be on the alert to see that their candidates are not at a disadvantage.

More than a year may pass before the department has received the reports from the different committees and is able to formulate its policy. Once the decision has been taken by the Minister to introduce legislation, assuming that the Law Officers have advised that the existing powers are inadequate, the Legislation Committee will need to give an indication whether time can be found for a Bill. If so, the department will seek the authority of the Treasury to approach the Parliamentary Counsel's office for assistance, and a counsel will be allocated to work on the Bill. The Ministry will have drawn up a memorandum stating the powers which it wishes to obtain, and this document, which may be very lengthy, will be passed to the Parliamentary draftsman. He will prepare a first draft of the Bill for discussion between himself, the Ministry of Films, and the other departments concerned. The drafting is likely to be a lengthy job. The legal mind will see all sorts of perplexities, while the department will be anxious not merely that it should have adequate powers but that there should be no loopholes. Draft will follow draft, and a complicated measure may be revised in print a dozen times or more before it is agreed to cover all the points and is accepted by everyone as the best that can be expected.

Having obtained the consent of the Legislation Committee of the Cabinet to the introduction of his Bill, the time will come when the Minister of Films will be able to give notice to Parliament. Bills can be introduced in either House, but since the Minister of Films is a Member of the Commons he may decide that the Bill is better discussed first in that chamber. The First Reading is a formality and merely consists of reading the title of the Bill. A single sheet is laid on the table, with the description on one side and on the other the names of the sponsors—the Minister of Films and a number of other Members.

Before the Second Reading takes place the complete text will be available to the House, and M.P.s will have ample time to study it; the interval between the printing of the Bill and the debate will be several weeks. The Minister will want to have publicity for his measure, but he will not be able to release copies to the Press until Members have had an opportunity to see the Bill. Once prints are available to Members, the Bill is no longer secret, and the Minister will be anxious that the newspapers should know of his proposals direct rather than that they should make their own interpretations. If copies are available at 11 a.m. the department will perhaps arrange for a Press conference at a few minutes past the hour. One of the Ministry officials will be hovering round the Vote Office to obtain copies for distribution to the newspaper correspondents as Big Ben strikes eleven.

A Press conference may be taken by a senior department official, but Ministers usually prefer to explain their new Bills to the Press personally. The Minister of Films will be accompanied to the Press conference by the Permanent Secretary or another high official and will also have his publicity officers beside him. The Civil Servants will know the Bill intimately and be able to give the Minister any information he needs in order to reply to questions from the newspaper correspondents, but at this stage the queries of the newspapermen will not be difficult to answer. Only later, when they have had time to examine the clauses of the Bill, will the serious criticism arise.

The Bill will be printed with every fifth line numbered and with the financial clauses in italics.[1] At some time—usually about the same time as the Second Reading—the financial resolutions will be put to the Commons, for any money matters must be moved specially. The real battle will begin with the Second Reading. Almost all Bills are difficult to understand, and it is the practice to attach a memorandum to a Bill in which the department explains the purpose of the measure; if there are financial clauses, the Treasury may attach a separate memorandum or the Treasury and the department may collaborate in a single explanatory and financial memorandum. But even this may not help to make the measure understood. In the debate on a new Bill an M.P. stated: "The only thing in this Bill that I have been able to understand . . . is the sentence which says ' "the Minister" means the Minister of Housing and Local Government.' There is no getting away from that." He protested that "it is not enough for leading counsel and highly paid civil servants to produce incomprehensible nonsense", and said that a correspondent had

---

[1] A specimen page of a Bill appears in Appendix VIII.

written to him that a distinguished barrister not only could not understand the Bill, "but he could not understand the Explanatory Memorandum". Exchanges of this kind are the stock-in-trade of any
Opposition, but it is perhaps of interest to quote a paragraph from the
Financial and Explanatory Memorandum which was intended to
describe clearly the intentions of this measure: "Parts I and V of the
Bill, which provide for payments (of principal and interest) in respect
of past events and transactions," reads the Memorandum, "require
those payments to be made to holders of claims on the fund (or in
some cases persons deriving title to land from holders of claims)
subject to the limitation that the principal amount of a payment is
not to exceed the amount of the relevant claim. Claims which are
not affected by payments of past events and transactions, and the
remaining amounts of claims which are so affected, undergo a complete change of character before those provisions of the Bill which
look to the future take effect. They cease to be disposable assets, and
they enure for the benefit, not of holders of the claims or of the interests
in land on the basis of which the claims are made, but of all persons
having interests in that land. Land to which claims or remnants of
claims have become attached in this way is described in the Bill as
having 'an unexpended balance of established development value';
and it is this balance (with the addition of a supplement representing
interest) which forms the upper limit for payments for loss of development value under Parts II and III of the Bill, which provide for
compensation in respect of planning restrictions imposed and land
acquired compulsorily after the Bill comes into force."

The Ministry of Films does not face the problem of explaining a
measure of this complicated kind. Its Bill is a minor measure which
is easy enough to follow, but nevertheless no one in the Commons
will expect it to pass without a great deal of comment, for the Opposition will always have criticisms of any Government Bill, unless it is
an agreed measure or of a purely formal kind. At the Second Reading
the Minister will deal with the need for the legislation and describe
what the measure is intended to accomplish. He will normally be
followed by a speaker from the Front Bench of the Opposition. In
the course of the debate the Bill will probably be called unnecessary,
misconceived, or plain silly, and perhaps all three; it may be condemned as lacking in imagination, which is a safe comment to make
on any Bill; and if some Members declare that it goes too far, others
will be sure to protest that it merely scratches at the surface of the
problem. The Government and Opposition will take it in turn to

speak on the measure, and a Government Minister, perhaps the Parliamentary Secretary of the department, will wind up the debate. The division which follows will be won by the Government, since it holds the majority and its Whips will have summoned supporters to the House in sufficient force.

Next comes the Committee stage. The whole House may sit as a committee to consider a Bill, but, unless it is a piece of legislation of major importance, or special reasons exist why it should be taken on the floor of the House, the Bill will be sent to one of the standing committees. There are six such committees. One deals with legislation which the Speaker has certified relates exclusively to Scotland: this committee consists of the seventy-one Scottish Members plus between ten and fifteen other Members. Members drawn from all parties compose the other committees, with a majority selected from Government supporters. Apart from the Scottish committee, the allocation is made largely according to the state of business in the different committees.

The Minister will have to be ready to defend every line of his Bill in committee, and a vote will be taken on each clause. Officials of the department will sit beside their chief to advise him on points that are brought up. Some amendments are certain to be accepted by the Minister, for a Bill is never so perfectly drafted that improvements cannot be made, and few Bills are capable of being drawn up with so much foresight that a committee of Parliament cannot convince a Minister that some clause is obscure or misleading or will fail in its purpose unless altered. Although large numbers of amendments are made in a Bill, most of them are of a quite minor kind. The department itself may produce many amendments as a result partly of afterthoughts. When 400 were put down on behalf of the Government, a spokesman explained that most of them were drafting and consequential.

The Civil Servants may have their moments of panic as the new Bill is examined by a committee of the Commons. Suggestions for a variation which looks innocuous enough may be put forward, but the officials will realize that it is likely to involve a major revision of of the scheme and lead to all sorts of administrative difficulties. Their advice to their political chief will have to be given tactfully but at the same time firmly. It is better that the Minister should risk a little unpopularity in committee rather than that the measure should be attacked by the Press and public and prove unworkable because some new and contradictory provision has slipped in by way of amendment.

The Commons Committee reports to the full House. This report stage may be a lengthy business or the House may agree the amendments at once. At the Third Reading the principles of the Bill will again be debated and there is likely to be another division, the result of which will be received with loud cheers by the Government supporters when their victory is announced. The measure will then be referred to the Lords. Here it will go through the same process of First and Second Reading, Committee stage, and Third Reading. A peer who supports the Government will be put in charge of the Bill and the departmental officials may find their task even more difficult in the Upper House. The Minister of Films will know his own Bill in some detail and be eager to have it accepted, but the peer in charge of the measure while it is in the Lords may not have been concerned with it at all in its drafting stage and will probably need very detailed briefing on every point.

With the Lords' amendments, the Bill will be returned to the House of Commons, and, if the amendments are accepted, it need only await the royal assent to become an Act of Parliament. Under the new Act, the Minister will perhaps be authorized to introduce the scheme on an "appointed day" which he can choose within several months of the time the measure is placed on the statute book. It may prove possible to bring the plans into operation within a few weeks, but unexpected snags have a way of turning up in all new measures, and the department is very likely to require the whole of the period to complete its arrangements and allow for running in the machinery.

The example chosen is, of course, deliberately absurd. All legislation, however, whether it be an unimportant routine measure or a social reform of far-reaching effect, must pass through these Parliamentary stages. Even a quite simple Bill involves a vast amount of labour within one or more departments, and a complex measure may absorb the full-time services of dozens of officials for months on end.

Chapter Twenty

SERVICE STANDARDS

"IT is suggested," said a Committee on the Training of Civil Servants, some years ago, "that civil servants tend to form a class apart from the rest of the community and are apt to forget that John Citizen is a composite of innumerable John Smiths. Nothing could be more disastrous than that the Civil Service and the public should think of themselves as in two separate compartments. . . . The civil servant must never forget that he is the servant, not the master of the community, and that official competence need not, and should not, involve loss of the human touch."

That the Civil Servant should feel himself to be set apart is, however, almost inevitable. As soon as his formal education is completed, he is put into a strait-jacket, and forced to realize that the whole of his working life will be spent in an atmosphere far removed from the rough and tumble of the business world. He is likely to be engaged in duties of a kind that have no parallel elsewhere in this country. He is told that his position "clearly imposes upon him restrictions in matters of commerce and business from which the ordinary citizen is free", and that he may not, if he occupies a responsible post, join with others in any political movement. Nor may he write letters to the Press on political matters or otherwise align himself with any particular policy. As soon as he reports for duty, he is required to sign a declaration on the subject of the Official Secrets Act, 1911 and 1920. Most probably he will not see any information which would be of the slightest value to anyone, and he is unlikely to give his undertaking a thought until, at the end of his employment in Government service some forty years later, one of the signed copies of the declaration is returned to him, bearing the boyish signature which he hardly recognizes as his own.

Nor is it enough for him to avoid offending against the provisions of the Official Secrets Act. The State requires the exercise of the greatest discretion from its employees. A Board of Inquiry held to consider allegations of gambling in foreign currencies by a few Civil Servants pointed out:

> The first duty of a civil servant is to give his undivided allegiance to the State at all times and on all occasions when the State has a claim upon his services. With his private activities the State is in general not concerned,

so long as his conduct is not such as to bring discredit upon the Service of which he is a member. But to say that he is not to subordinate his duty to his private interests nor to make use of his official position to further those interests, is to say no more than that he must behave with common honesty. The Service exacts from itself a higher standard, because it recognizes that the State is entitled to demand that its servants shall not only be honest in fact, but beyond the reach of suspicion of dishonesty. . . . Practical rules for the guidance of social conduct depend almost as much upon the instinct and perception of the individual as upon cast-iron formulas; and the surest guide will, we hope, always be found in the nice and jealous honour of civil servants themselves. The public expects from them a standard of integrity not only inflexible but fastidious, and has not been disappointed in the past. We are confident that we are expressing the view of the Service when we say that the public have a right to expect that standard, and that it is the duty of the Service to see that the expectation is fulfilled.

These and other extracts from the report will be brought to the attention of every new entrant. His conditioning has begun.

Though he cannot know more than a fraction of the work covered even by his own department, if it is a large one, the official soon learns that nothing can happen in any branch of the Government service which will not reflect on him. What one Civil Servant does is considered to be what every other Civil Servant would do if he had the opportunity, criminal acts excluded. All officials are supposed to think alike; sometimes, they are referred to as looking alike. An audience will not be puzzled by a reference to a man as being a civil service type; however unjustly, they will probably think of someone lacking in drive and imagination, very prim and proper, and a slave to rules and regulations and perhaps inclined to arrogance. The representation of an official in a play on the stage or on television or in a film is rarely complimentary, and he is often portrayed as a figure of fun and held up to be a jack-in-office with exaggerated ideas of his own importance. The methods adopted by the departments are regarded as over-complicated and time-wasting. Every official is bound to have to suffer quips about intolerable red tape and hear stories of how three bureaucrats just managed to cope with the work of one man.

However absurd such comments may be, repetition has its effect. When evidence was taken about the difficulty of finding recruits for certain professional posts in Government service, several witnesses suggested that this was due to some extent "not to conditions of employment but to popular prejudice against the Civil Service". Candidates for these particular positions, however, were mostly men of over twenty-five years of age who would be more likely to be put off than young candidates who enter Government employment as soon as they leave school.

Most officials become accustomed to be viewed with a certain measure of suspicion. Some are worried by the constant and niggling criticism and their sense of grievance may reflect itself in their attitude. Civil Servants who come into day-to-day contact with the public in, for example, a department's inquiry office, are often thought to be less helpful to applicants than the employees of private firms. Though something has been done to train Civil Servants who occupy such jobs, the feeling exists that they are too aloof and tend to be uninterested. One explanation for the difference may be that the staff of commercial companies realize the connection between orders and the prosperity of the business for which they work and realize that they may suffer in the long run if potential customers are dissatisfied. Civil Servants—"whose salaries", as one commentator remarked bitingly, "fall like manna from heaven and who never have to sully their thoughts with base considerations of profit and loss"— arc in a quite different position. A job of some kind always exists for the official, or, if a position cannot be found for him, he will be entitled to his pension. Where his office is engaged in a trading operation, it is usually on a monopoly basis, and, whether the service is good or bad, people must make use of it or go without. Whatever happens, the department will not go bankrupt, with the consequences that would follow if a commercial company proved unable to pay its way.

All investigations into recruitment to the Civil Service have recognized the danger that, in a Service which selects its staff at an early age, some candidates may be unsuitable for official work, and the need for a proper system of probation has been strongly urged. The rules of the Service provide for every entrant to undergo a period of probation before he receives confirmation of his appointment to the permanent staff; but some doubt has been expressed whether the system has in fact been successful in weeding out the men and women who, though they pass examinations with credit, are unfitted for employment in a Government department. "The probation served by every recruit should, in our view, be more of a reality than at present," said the Committee on Training in 1944. "If a probationer shows during his training that he is unsuited to the work assigned to him, an effort should be made to reallocate him to duties which fit him better. Even in such arrangements there may still be misfits who during their probation and early training show no aptitude for Civil Service work, and in these cases we think that, in their own as much as in the national interest, they should leave the Service." The same view is faithfully repeated again and again.

Civil Servants who have the duty of reporting on candidates undergoing probation may, however, well hesitate to put in an adverse report on a recruit who is doing his or her best. Rejection is to some extent regarded as a criticism of those who have made the original selection. Moreover, the reporting officer knows that if he rejects a new entrant who is in consequence put under notice of discharge a staff association will be likely to appeal against the decision, and it is not always easy to state convincingly what makes a recruit unfitted for departmental work. Unless a candidate is wilfully causing trouble, or is obviously incompetent, or is clearly determined to dodge work, the chances are that, faced with giving his views on a probationer of whose capabilities he does not think highly, the reporting officer will suggest that the newcomer should be tried out on another duty. The period of probation may be as long as two or three years. Before a probationer has been tried out on several jobs, a year or more may have elapsed. With each month that passes, it becomes more difficult to turn a man or woman out of the Service. Those in whose hands rests the final decision will remember that, if the Civil Service gets the reputation of rejecting candidates during probation, the flow of recruits may be reduced.

While it is taken for granted that some men or women may prove unsuitable in one commercial office or another when tried out, employers tend to look with grave suspicion on anyone who has been discharged from the Civil Service during probation. Everyone is well aware that the Service is very tolerant to those who have once been recruited, and so prospective employers are likely to conclude that a probationer unable to scrape through in a Government department must really have serious defects. A man must, it is argued, be utterly shocking in his work or his behaviour if, with the many thousands of different kinds of jobs on offer, he cannot be found a niche in the public service. The probationer who is rejected is therefore handicapped if he has to seek employment outside the Civil Service.

Senior Civil Servants who are asked to pronounce on a probationer's qualifications are no doubt acquainted with this attitude, and it may be another of the reasons why they hesitate to turn down anyone during probation. The departments are never anxious to reveal the proportions of successes to failures. It was stated some time ago, however, that the number of those who failed probation in the executive class was about one in 500 and in the clerical class one in 900. No direct entrant over a period of several years recently to the administrative class of the Foreign Service, or anyone recruited as an Assistant Principal to the Home administrative service under Method II, has failed to have his appointment confirmed to the permanent Civil Service.

The chances that a new recruit will be rejected during his probation are thus very slight indeed, and once he has passed that milestone in his career, he is virtually irremovable. An ex-Minister, writing of his experience, stated: "One of the very first things my Permanent Secretary thought fit to teach me was, 'Whatever you think of me or any other Civil Servant here, you cannot sack us'. . . . I was amazed to find that in fact a Minister had no individual control over his staff from the newest joined junior clerk or typist right up to the top." The official was having his little joke. A former Home Secretary explained the constitutional position to the House of Commons. A Civil Servant, he said, "holds his office 'at pleasure' and can be dismissed at any time by the Minister; and that power is none the less real because it is seldom used. The only exception relates to a small number of senior posts, like permanent secretary, deputy secretary, and principal financial officer, where, since 1920, it has been necessary for the Minister to consult the Prime Minister, as he does on appointment."

In practice, it is almost unknown for a man or woman to be discharged after establishment in the Civil Service unless with the concurrence of other Civil Servants, and officials cling together. The more the Service is denigrated, the more officials will present a united front to their critics and cover up the bad bargains. Dismissal is a disgrace reserved for the dishonest or corrupt.

It is conceded that the official must have protection against the whims of Ministers. Civil Servants have always taken pride in the freedom to express their views frankly on matters referred to them, in the full assurance that they will not imperil their present position or destroy their future prospects by presenting the facts as they see them and submitting their honest opinion. This is a privilege necessary in all grades of the Service, but especially in the most senior ranks who report direct to political chiefs. When new schemes are under consideration, or some alteration is proposed in a current programme, the Civil Servant may at times feel impelled to favour a course of action which he knows or suspects will be contrary to his

Minister's wishes. Unless the officials had the independence which arises from the knowledge that they will not be discharged or demoted, except for flagrant misconduct, the danger would be that men and women within the departments would be deterred from advising their chiefs to the best of their ability and the Civil Service would undergo changes which could prove disastrous. The most popular Civil Servant would be the one who could be relied upon to tender counsel which the Government in power wanted to hear, and we might produce a race of officials afraid to speak their minds.

The posts where influence is exercised are those of Assistant Secretary and above—about 1,200 men and women, most of whom are attached to Whitehall headquarters offices. By the time they have climbed to the first of the higher ranks, such officials will be in their middle thirties or older.

Some are disillusioned and cynical—such an element is to be found in every profession; others are over-eager to reform the world according to their own ideas and have a touching faith that miracles can be accomplished by means of Statutory Instruments. Most officials learn to guard against too great an enthusiasm. It is not for them to believe passionately in some course of action rather than another. If they are asked to recommend how such and such a problem may be solved, or some scheme carried out, they give advice to the best of their knowledge, but only the stupid imagine that their judgement cannot be mistaken. The officials' job is to assemble all the relevant information and to weigh up the probable consequences of this step or that so far as can be foreseen. A departmental recommendation may be wrong but no effort will have been spared to provide as complete and balanced an appreciation of the situation as the combined wisdom of the department can produce. The appraisal will not be affected by political considerations, for the Civil Service is uncommitted in its ideology.

An official may often have the impression that some of those who come into his office regard him only as an obstacle to be surmounted by almost any legitimate means. The businessman may be seeking permission to bring supplies into the country or send articles out of it, or he may wish to have something prohibited, or be asking the aid of a Government department to get some course approved which will be of material benefit to himself though not so acceptable to others. The Civil Servant in a trade department, for example, will not as a rule find his callers concerned with the public interest. One day an administrative or executive officer may hear strong appeals from producers that imports of certain goods should be restricted forth-with; next afternoon he will perhaps listen to a deputation of retailers who declare persuasively that the country ought to open its ports wide to exactly the same things. Both groups may even purport to be acting on behalf of the consumer and refer to fair play for the housewife and so on. The Civil Servant will be told, if he is ever silly enough to inquire, that the ordinary business would quickly end up in the bankruptcy court if it attempted to follow the principles which control the work of a Government department.

The conception is in many instances quite different. The Government has the duty of deciding what services should be maintained or expanded and whether new activities should be introduced or old ones suppressed or modified. Profit and loss in financial terms often cannot be the main consideration. The Civil Servants do not decide policy, though they may influence it. The decisions on major matters rest with the politicians. Officials quickly learn that no Government is ever likely to be quite consistent and that what has been rejected one month as undesirable may be welcomed as admirable not very long afterwards.

Soon after Labour assumed office in 1964 it set up four additional departments, and made a number of changes in the distribution of work among the departments and then announced that it "had carried through the biggest reorganization of the machinery of government that has been carried out in peacetime in the past century". One immediate result was that some Civil Servants received unexpected and very welcome promotion in the newly created Ministries and other were switched in their existing grades from one office to another. For many of the staff who were transferred, the changes made very little difference: they continued to do exactly the same work, in the same places, and under the same conditions, and merely came under Department A instead of Department B. Responsibility for shipping, for instance, which had been with the Board of Trade and in a previous reshuffle went over to the Ministry of Transport, was switched back again under the umbrella of its former master. No one imagines, however, that the officials at ports who examine shipping on behalf of the Government underwent any alteration in their duties as a result of this kind of general post. The Stationery Office would need to print new notepaper and forms and the Ministry of Public Building and Works provide new notice-boards showing "Board of Trade" instead of "Ministry of Transport".

At the time of this so-called revolution in the administrative machine, many criticisms of Whitehall were widely ventilated. Every Government tends to decry the performance of its predecessors, and the Labour Government expressed its views forcibly that it had inherited a sick economy and was faced with the immense task of reinvigorating neglected industries. The public decided that in these circumstances the Civil Service must have been guilty of grave failures under the previous administration. There was much talk about the poor advice, bad judgement and lack of enterprise on the part of the departments. The truth or otherwise of such charges must remain obscure, since the advice given by the departments to politicians is not published, and the public cannot know whether the departments' recommendations were accepted or rejected. The papers of one Cabinet are not disclosed to the next, and the official files are not open to inspection for many years later. The officials are denied the right to put forward their defence to the criticisms since Civil Servants cannot engage in what is a political battle.

The departments were pilloried, not only for incompetence in questions of economic, scientific, and defence policy but also for laxity in organization. The departmental machinery was said to be inadequate and the directing staff to have lost dynamism. Whitehall was represented as over-complacent, wasteful in man-power and money, slow-moving and backward in the use of modern techniques.

It is not, of course, only after an election that these criticisms are made. Hardly a year passes in which the Civil Service is not described as unbusinesslike, and the view is expressed that only ignorance or laziness prevents the adoption of better methods of handling official work. Except to a limited degree, however, comparisons of Government offices with commercial firms are impracticable. The conditions under which Government departments perform their functions are necessarily different. The objects to be achieved are of another kind, and in particular the pace and method of working in Whitehall are largely dominated by the fact that ministers are answerable to Parliament. No Government office can have the same freedom of action or take the same risks as a commercial enterprise. Though a company will have to satisfy the shareholders, its operations are not subjected to constant scrutiny and its transactions will not be under fire every time even a relatively trivial error is exposed. A succession of investigators have for generations considered the problem—some, indeed, have begun their examination with the avowed intention of finding a means of speeding up the work—but all of them have agreed that the lessons of commercial practice are rarely applicable.

The departments are always under the microscope. The auditors who report to the Public Accounts Committee each session watch how public monies are disbursed; the Estimates Committee investigates some branches of Whitehall every year; *ad hoc* committees are set up from time to time to delve into this activity or that; M.P.s ask questions by the hundred and Ministers have to be prepared to answer in Parliament or in writing for every decision made by officials.

In such circumstances it is not surprising that the departments maintain a series of checks and counterchecks and keep elaborate records. The official may grow over-timorous as he thinks of the consequences if he fails to follow the prescribed drill slavishly and he clings to "red tape" as the only safe course. Exaggerated respect for precedent and the fear of breaking new ground are likely always to be present.

There is sometimes justification for the complaint that reforms in Government offices take place much too slowly. Inaction arises in part from the lack of time to consider what might be done to make improvements. Contrary to general belief, the higher officials are overloaded: planning and readjustment of the procedure takes second place to the problem of coping with the day-to-day flow. Moreover, nearly all Civil Servants come straight from school or university and have no experience of any other kind of organization. By the time a man has reached a position where he has authority to make changes, he is conditioned to the system. Its merits have been dinned into him from the first morning he walked into his department and he has absorbed the doctrine that any interference with the complex administrative machine may be a perilous venture.

The view exists in some quarters that if any alterations are needed one of the Parliamentary Committees will suggest what ought to be done. It is more prudent after all to wait until such a Committee inspects some section of the work. Either the Committee will be content that all is well, in which case things can remain as before and the department will be able to rebut any criticisms by pointing out that the procedures have been examined; or, if the Committee recommends changes, the officials can throw themselves wholeheartedly and energetically into the task of carrying out the proposals. If anything should go wrong, Whitehall can shelter behind the Committee. It is striking how many obvious modifications have been adopted only after some committee or another has taken the initiative and the responsibility. All committees compliment the Civil Service on its performance, but equally all of them always find some fault or another.

The idea that the Civil Service is far behind in mechanization is, however, largely unfounded. It was a pioneer in Organization and Methods and has its groups of officials specifically to investigate blocks of work or examine new techniques. But the departments have been reluctant to make much use of outside advisers. Commercial companies also have their O. and M. teams but nevertheless recognize the value of calling in widely experienced management consultants at times. The Civil Service does not believe in introducing such experts, even where there is no security angle. Whitehall must open its doors to Parliamentary Committees but it guards the citadel against others. It likes to feel self-contained and depend on its own people, brought up in the atmosphere of the departments and properly respectful to Civil Service tradition.

The scheme is being tried of bringing into the departments a number of men from industry to take up middle-grade official posts on a temporary basis; and at the same time Civil Servants are being encouraged to accept jobs outside the Service for short periods and so extend their experience. So far, such exchanges have been on a very small scale. If the scheme is expanded, the result may be salutary. The seconded officials are likely to look at the system with a new vision when they return to Whitehall, and newcomers imported from industry may be struck with the futility of some departmental processes which escape the attention of those who have grown up with them and have never known any other way of tackling the work. Five-year contracts may become more common and be of great benefit to the departments since appointees will be less prejudiced, not so nervous about their future career, or so anxious to conform in everything.

No organization employing 700,000 people and offering them a lifelong career can ever hope to be free of those who are foolish or obstinate or conceited in the approach to their work. The Civil Service is accused of being over-lenient to slackness in its ranks, and there is some truth in the view that the inefficient are sheltered behind the formidable wall of official solidarity. It is very simple for Civil Servants to delude themselves that everything with which they are concerned is not far from perfection and that everyone who dares to criticize is either ignorant of the complexity of the administrative machine or is merely a mischief-maker.

In the past the British Civil Service was the admiration of other nations which were glad to take it as their model and learn from its example. It has never failed to maintain the high virtues of honesty and integrity and loyalty, but the charge has been increasingly made in recent years that the departments have rested too long on their past achievements and have shown a lack of urgency in facing the technological and scientific revolution. At any time of economic upheaval, the public makes little distinction between the responsibility of the politician and of the official.

Whitehall has its blemishes, as has every institution, but they are neither so numerous or so serious as is often claimed. The great departments of State command the devoted labours of many brilliant men and women, and the Civil Service is still among the best in the world as an executive machine.

Appendix One

ANNUAL SALARIES OF THE MAIN CIVIL SERVICE GRADES AT 1 JANUARY, 1965

HOME ADMINISTRATIVE CLASS

Permanent Secretary (or Permanent Under-Secretary)	£8,285
Deputy Secretary (or Deputy Under-Secretary)	£5,885
Under Secretary (or Assistant Under-Secretary)	£4,785
Assistant Secretary	£3,385–£4,385
Principal	£2,259–£3,087
Assistant Principal	£965–£1,606

EXECUTIVE CLASS

Principal Executive Officer	£3,885
Chief Executive Officer	£2,569–£2,983
Senior Executive Officer	£1,995–£2,414
Higher Executive Officer	£1,606–£1,896
Executive Officer	£614–£1,483

CLERICAL AND CLERICAL ASSISTANT CLASSES

Higher Clerical Officer	£1,246–£1,483
Clerical Officer	£399–£1,038
Clerical Assistant	£326–£810

DIPLOMATIC SERVICE

Grade 1 Ambassador		£8,285
2 Ambassador		£5,885
3 Ambassador		£4,785
4 Administrative £3,385–£4,385	Executive £3,560	
5 Administrative £2,259–£3,087	Executive £2,569–£2,983	
6 Executive		£1,995–£2,414
7 Administrative £1,770–£2,167	Executive £1,606–£1,896	
8 Administrative		£965–£1,606
9 Executive		£614–£1,483
10 Clerical		£399–£1,038

SCIENTIFIC CLASS

Chief Scientific Officer	£8,285
Deputy Chief Scientific Officer	£4,510–£4,785
Senior Principal Scientific Officer	£3,385–£3,885
Principal Scientific Officer	£2,259–£3,087
Scientific Officer	£965–£1,606

MEDICAL

Principal Medical Officer	£4,635
Senior Medical Officer	£4,385
Medical Officer	£2,269–£3,780

INFORMATION OFFICER CLASS

Chief Information Officer A	£3,385–£4,385
Chief Information Officer B	£3,124–£3,385
Principal Information Officer	£2,569–£2,983
Senior Information Officer	£1,606–£1,896

ARCHITECTS, ENGINEERS, SURVEYORS, ETC.

Superintending Grade	£3,385–£3,885
Senior Grade	£2,380–£2,725
Main Grade	£1,691–£2,237
Recruitment Grade	£850–£1,663

Appendix Two

PLAN OF ORGANIZATION OF THE IMAGINARY MINISTRY OF FILMS

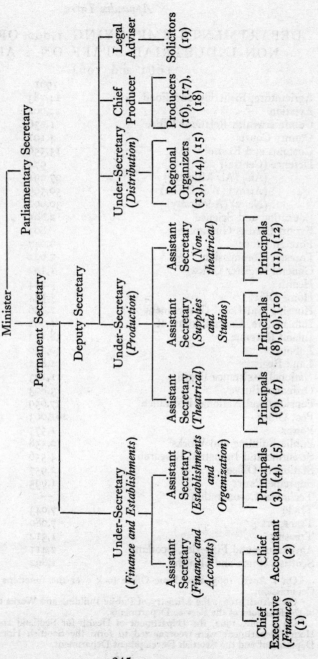

DEPARTMENTS EMPLOYING 1,000 OR MORE NON-INDUSTRIAL STAFF ON 1 APRIL, 1961 and 1964

	1961	1964
Agriculture, Fisheries, and Food	14,783	14,682
Aviation	22,602	24,257
Commonwealth Relations Office	1,236	1,729
County Courts	4,101	5,132
Customs and Excise	15,556	15,805
Defence (Central)	974	2,134
(Air) (Air Ministry)	27,991	26,488
(Army) (War Office)	50,599	48,374
(Navy) (Admiralty)	30,692	32,035
Education and Science	2,805	3,333
Export Credits Guarantee	803	1,055
Foreign Office	6,047	7,725
Forestry Commission	2,622	2,756
General Register Office	1,102	1,179
Health	5,224	5,118
Home Office[1]	3,594	14,925
Housing and Local Government	2,806	3,107
Information, Central Office of	1,092	1,380
Inland Revenue	58,152	58,007
Labour	20,150	21,291
Land Registry	1,841	2,451
National Assistance Board	11,173	13,161
Ordnance Survey	3,803	3,918
Pensions and National Insurance	37,659	39,215
Post Office	261,003	275,601
Power	1,575	1,599
Public Building and Works[2]	10,558	20,313
Scientific and Industrial Research	4,556	5,260
Stationery Office	2,957	2,946
Supreme Court	1,695	1,807
Technical Co-operation	—	1,564
Trade	7,043	7,727
Transport	7,080	7,623
Treasury	1,312	1,470
Agriculture and Fisheries, Scotland	2,411	2,592
Scottish Home and Health[3]	1,892	2,884

[1] On 1 April, 1963, the Home Office took over the functions of the Prison Commission.

[2] On 1 April, 1963, the Ministry of Public Building and Works took over some of the functions of the Service Departments.

[3] On 1 June, 1962, the Department of Health for Scotland and the Scottish Home Department were reorganized to form the Scottish Home and Health Department and the Scottish Development Department.

COMMISSION AS AN OFFICER OF HER MAJESTY'S DIPLOMATIC SERVICE

Elizabeth the Second, by the Grace of God of the United Kingdom of Great Britain and Northern Ireland and of Her other Realms and Territories Queen, Head of the Commonwealth, Defender of the Faith, Etc., Etc., Etc. To all and singular to whom these Presents shall come, Greeting!

Whereas it appears to us expedient to nominate some Person of approved Industry, Fidelity and Knowledge to perform the functions of an Officer of Our Diplomatic Service at any of Our Diplomatic, Consular or other similar Establishments abroad or in either the Department of Our Principal Secretary of State for Foreign Affairs or the Department of Our Principal Secretary of State for Commonwealth Relations or elsewhere as in the judgment of either of Our said Principal Secretaries of State the exigencies of Our Service may require; Know Ye, therefore, that We have constituted and appointed, as We do by these Presents constitute and appoint, Our Trusty and Well-beloved

to be an Officer of Our Diplomatic Service at any of Our Diplomatic, Consular or other similar Establishments abroad or in either the Department of Our Principal Secretary of State for Foreign Affairs or the Department of Our Principal Secretary of State for Commonwealth Relations or elsewhere as aforesaid: Giving and Granting to him in that character all Power and Authority to do and execute all necessary Writings, Memorials and Instruments as also to assist Our Ambassador, High Commissioner or Minister at the place where he may be appointed to reside or either of Our said Principal Secretaries of State or such other person as may be appropriate in all things which may belong to the duties of an Officer of Our Diplomatic Service as aforesaid. And We therefore request all those whom it may concern, to receive and acknowledge Our said Trusty and Well-beloved

as such Officer of Our Diplomatic Service aforesaid and freely to communicate with him upon the things that may appertain to the Affairs of Our Embassy, High Commission or Legation at the place where he may be appointed to reside or to those of Our Diplomatic Service at large.

Given at Our Court of St. James's

the

day of   in the

Year of Our Lord One thousand Nine hundred and

in the   Year of Our

Reign

By Her Majesty's Command.

(Countersigned)

Appendix Five

ESTIMATE OF THE MINISTRY OF FILMS

I. ESTIMATE of the amount required for the year ending 31 March, 1963, for the salaries and expenses of the Ministry of Films including a grant-in-aid.

One million one hundred thousand pounds (1,100,000)

II. Sub-heads under which this Vote will be accounted for by the Ministry of Films.

1961–2		1962–3
£		£
550,000	A. Salaries, etc.	670,000
38,000	B. Travelling and Incidental Expenses	38,000
200,000	C. Purchase of Rights	160,000
934,000	D. Film Production	944,000
690,000	E. Film Distribution	646,000
1,320,000	F. Film Exhibition	1,334,500
	G. Institute for Film Research and Development in Sound Recording (Grant in Aid)	
3,000		2,500
5,000	H. Souvenirs	5,000
3,740,000	Gross Total	3,800,000
	Deduct	
2,750,000	z. Appropriations in Aid	2,700,000
£990,000	NET TOTAL	£1,100,000

INCREASE £110,000

Additional expenditure in connection with the Service is estimated as follows:

1961–2		1962–3
£		£
1,000	1. Maintenance, Furniture, Light, etc. (Class IX, 1 and 2)	1,000
3,000	2. Rental Values and Rates (Class IX, 13)	4,000
2,000	3. Stationery and Printing (Class IX, 14)	2,000
2,000	4. Central Office of Information (Class IX, 15)	3,000
2,000	5. Miscellaneous	2,000
£10,000	TOTAL	£12,000

Appendix Six

EXTRACTS FROM VOTES AND PROCEEDINGS OF THE COMMONS

QUESTIONS FOR ORAL ANSWER—*continued*
Questions to the Prime Minister will begin at 3.15 p.m.

✻Q 1 **Mr W. W. Hamilton** (West Fife): To ask the Prime Minister, whether he will authorise experimental closed circuit televising of the proceedings of the House of Commons as a possible prelude to full national coverage.

✻Q 2 **Mr W. W. Hamilton** (West Fife): To ask the Prime Minister, whether he will initiate immediate all-party talks on the problem of electoral reform.

✻Q 3 **Mr Simon Wingfield Digby** (West Dorset): To ask the Prime Minister, what changes he has authorised in the relationship between the Secretary of State for Defence and the Ministers of Defence for Army, Navy and Air, respectively; and what other changes are being made in the organisation of the Ministry of Defence.

✻Q 4 **Mr Simon Wingfield Digby** (West Dorset): To ask the Prime Minister, by what authority responsibility for the Forestry Commission has been transferred from the Minister of Agriculture personally, as laid down in the Forestry Act 1945, to the Minister of Land and Natural Resources.

✻Q 5 **Mr Hector Hughes** (Aberdeen, North): To ask the Prime Minister, if he will invite the heads of the Russian and Chinese Governments to a representative international conference in Britain to discuss international disarmament and peace.

✻Q 6 **Mr Hector Hughes** (Aberdeen, North): To ask the Prime Minister, if he is aware that the Prime Minister of China has invited President Johnson of the United States of America to take part in a world summit conference to abolish nuclear weapons; if he has received a similar invitation; and what action he proposes to take.

✻Q 7 **Sir Ian Orr-Ewing** (Hendon, North): To ask the Prime Minister, what arrangements he is making for questions concerning the Minister of Technology to be answered in this House.

✻Q 8 **Mr Anthony Royle** (Richmond, Surrey): To ask the Prime Minister, which department has responsibility for answering questions dealing with aircraft noise.

✻Q 9 **Mr Charles Fletcher-Cooke** (Darwen): To ask the Prime Minister, if he will set up a committee of inquiry into the origins of the recent strike at Hardy Spicer Ltd.; whether he will give its members power to send for papers and persons; and if he will make a statement.

✻Q10 **Mr John Hay** (Henley): To ask the Prime Minister, what action he will take to ascertain the facts in trade disputes during the recent General Election alleged to have political motivation.

✻Q11 **Sir Herbert Butcher** (Holland with Boston): To ask the Prime Minister, if he will now publish the report on the remuneration of Ministers and Members of Parliament.

✻Q12 **Sir Myer Galpern** (Glasgow, Shettleston): To ask the Prime Minister, if he will appoint a junior Minister to concentrate on Glasgow housing.

✻Q13 **Lieutenant-Colonel Sir Walter Bromley-Davenport** (Knutsford): To ask the Prime Minister, if he will set up an inquiry into strikes, both official and unofficial, which took place at the time of the General Election; what form the inquiry will take; and what are to be its terms of reference.

✻Q14 **Dame Irene Ward** (Tynemouth): To ask the Prime Minister, what are the regulations regarding the employment in the Civil Service of persons who by birth are nationals of a foreign state; and to what extent it is the practice to allow them access to secret and classified papers.

APPROPRIATION ACCOUNT OF THE MINISTRY OF FILMS

ACCOUNT of the sum expended, in the year ended 31 March, 1963, compared with the sum granted, for the salaries and expenses of the Ministry of Films, including a grant-in-aid.

| Service | Grant | Expenditure | Expenditure compared with Grant | |
			Less	More
	£	£	£	£
A. Salaries, etc.	670,000	662,479	7,521	—
B. Travelling and Incidental Expenses	38,000	42,930	—	4,930
C. Purchase of Rights Original £160,000 Supplementary £70,000	230,000	222,633	7,367	—
D. Film Production Original £944,000 Less Supplementary £49,500	894,500	880,173	14,327	—
E. Film Distribution	646,000	646,000	—	—
F. Film Exhibition Original £1,334,500 Less Supplementary £2,000	1,332,500	1,311,171	21,329	—
R. Institute for Research and Development Original £2,500 Supplementary £2,500	5,000	5,000	—	—
G. Souvenirs	5,000	14,806	—	9,806
Gross Total Original £3,800,000 Supplementary £21,000	3,821,000	50,544		14,736
		Surplus: £35,808		
Deduct:				
Z. Appropriations in Aid Original £2,700,000 Supplementary £20,000	Estimated 2,720,000	Realized 2,718,000 Deficiency £1,320		
NET TOTAL	£1,101,000	£1,064,685 Net surplus £34,488		

Actual surplus to be surrendered: £34,487 17s. 8d.

PAGE FROM PARLIAMENTARY BILL
National Health Service Act 1946 (Amendment)   **1**

A

B I L L

T O

Amend the National Health Service Act 1946 with   **A.D. 1965**
regard to the provision of domestic help by local
authorities.

BE IT ENACTED by the Queen's most Excellent Majesty, by and
with the advice and consent of the Lords Spiritual and
Temporal, and Commons, in this present Parliament
assembled, and by the authority of the same, as follows:—

5 **1.** In section 29(2) of the National Health Service Act 1946, Amendment of
there shall be inserted at the end the words—   1946 Act.
                                                1946 c. 81.

" Provided that in the case of persons receiving a weekly
        allowance from the National Assistance Board no
        charge shall be made."

10 **2.** *There shall be defrayed out of moneys provided by Parliament* Expenses.
any increase attributable to the provisions of this Act in the sums
payable under any other Act.

3.—(1) This Act may be cited as the National Health Service Short title,
Act 1946 (Amendment) Act, and this Act and the National citation and
15 Health Service Acts 1946 to 1961 may be cited together as the extent.
National Health Service Acts 1946 to 1965.

(2) This Act shall not extend to Scotland or Northern Ireland

[Bill 66]   43/1

SHORT BIBLIOGRAPHY

(1) OFFICIAL PUBLICATIONS

Committee on Fees and Emoluments of Public Offices (1837)
Committee on Miscellaneous Services Expenditure (1848)
Organization of the Permanent Civil Service (Northcote–Trevelyan Report) (1854)
Papers relating to the Reorganization of the Civil Service (1854)
Committee on Nomination and Selecting Candidates (1860)
Civil Service Inquiry Commission (Playfair Commission) (1887)
Commission on Civil Establishments (Ridley Commission) (1889)
Commission on the Civil Service (MacDonnell Commission) (1910)
Machinery of Government Committee (1918)
Committee on Problems of Recruitment to the Civil Service (Gladstone Committee) (1918)
National Whitley Council: Reorganization Report (1920)
Commission on the Civil Service (Tomlin Commission) (1931)
Committee on Ministers' Powers (1932)
Diplomatic Service Reform (1943)
Committee on Recruitment to Established Positions in the Civil Service (1944)
Committee on the Training of Civil Servants (1944)
Committee on the Scientific Civil Service (1945)
Higher Civil Service Remuneration (Chorley Committee) (1949)
Committee on Political Activities of Civil Servants (1948)
Committee on Information Services (Drogheda Report) (1954)
Commission on the Civil Service (Priestley Report) (1957)

(2) OTHER PUBLICATIONS

Sir Herbert Brittain: *The British Budgetary System* (1959)
W. J. Brown: *The Civil Service, Retrospect and Future* (1943)
Brian Chapman: *The Profession of Government* (1959)
E. N. Chester, ed.: *The Organization of the British Central Government* (1957)
E. W. Cohen: *The Growth of the British Civil Service, 1780–1939* (1941)
Sir James Crombie: *H.M. Customs and Excise* (1962)
T. A. Critchley: *The Civil Service Today* (1951)
H. E. Dale: *The Higher Civil Service* (1941)
Frank Dunhill: *The Civil Service* (1956)
C. S. Emden: *The Civil Servant in the Law and the Constitution* (1937)
Sir Harold Emmerson: *Ministry of Works* (1956)
H. Finer: *The British Civil Service* (1945)
E. N. Gladden: *Civil Service: Its Problems and Future* (1945)
E. N. Gladden: *The Essentials of Public Administration* (1958)
H. R. G. Greaves: *Civil Service in the Changing State* (1947)
Sir Godfrey Ince: *Ministry of Labour and National Service* (1958)
Sir Charles Jeffries: *Colonial Office* (1956)
Sir Gilmour Jenkins: *Ministry of Transport and Civil Aviation* (1958)

E. Martindale: *Women Servants of the State, 1870–1938* (1938)
Sir Harry Melville: *Department of Scientific and Industrial Research* (1958)
Sir David Milne: *Scottish Office and other Scottish Departments* (1962)
Bosworth Monck: *How the Civil Service Works* (1952)
R. Moses: *Civil Service of Great Britain* (1914)
H. E. Mustoe: *Law and Organization of the British Civil Service* (1932)
W. A. Robson: *British Civil Servant* (1937)
K. C. Wheare: *Government by Committee* (1955)
Sir John Winnifrith: *Ministry of Agriculture and Fisheries* (1900)

A number of Government departments publish reports on their work annually or every few years (e.g. the Ministry of Pensions and National Insurance, the General Post Office, the Mint, and the Forestry Commission). Much valuable information is to be found in *Public Administration*, the journal of the Royal Institute of Public Administration, and reports on developments affecting all sections of the staff are published in the *Whitley Bulletin*. The principal staff journals are *Civil Service Opinion*, *Red Tape*, and the *Post*.

Index

INDEX